DATE DUE

Freedom and Limit

A Dialogue between Literature and Christian Doctrine

Paul S. Fiddes

*Principal, Regents Park College,
University of Oxford*

MERCER UNIVERSITY PRESS

1979   1999

TWENTY YEARS OF PUBLISHING EXCELLENCE

ISBN 0-86554-649-5
MUP/P192

© 1999 Mercer University Press
6316 Peake Road
Macon, Georgia 31210-3960
All rights reserved
Paperback edition.

Hardback edition first published by St. Martin's Press 1991.

∞The paper used in this publication meets the minimum
requirements of American National Standard for Information
Sciences—Permanence of Paper for Printed Library
Materials, ANSI Z39.48-1984.

For Francis Warner
poet, scholar, friend

Contents

General Editor's Preface

In a series of books concerned with literature and religion, *Freedom and Limit* focuses more specifically on the relation between literature and Christian theology. Each of the five authors dealt with in detail are studied in terms of a dialogue between doctrine and the creative imagination, between the movement *from* mystery and the movement *to* mystery.

Paul Fiddes suggests that perspectives gained from doctrine can assist the critical reading of literature, while conversely novels, plays and poems can help theologians to make doctrinal statements. Indeed, at the heart of the study is a questioning about the very 'shape' of the Christian story. Is it best portrayed as a 'u-shaped curve' from Paradise, down through the Fall, and back up to restoration and glory? The author argues rather that a 'line of tension', a movement forward under the opposing pressures of freedom and limit, a shape which emerges from the conversation between literature and doctrine, is more true to the biblical narrative, and better expresses human fallenness and redemption from it.

Iris Murdoch, one of the writers to whom attention is given in this study, has suggested that 'the story is almost as fundamental a human concept as the thing, and however much novelists may try, for reasons of fashion and art, to stop telling stories, the story is likely to break out again in a new form'. Paul Fiddes stresses no less strongly the power of the story and the poetry of imaginative literature, finding that they offer to us both the reassurance of order and the possibility of something new. His critical appreciation of literature is maintained in careful dialogue with an equally profound understanding of the nature and role of theology, Christian doctrine and its continuities.

At once radical and conservative, in the best sense of each word, this book offers insights into major Christian theologians and theological movements of the twentieth century, while sustaining a discussion with literary figures from Shakespeare to Umberto Eco and William Golding, and with writers both Christian and non-Christian. It is a remarkable achievement.

David Jasper

Part I
Foundations

1

Imagination and Revelation

INTRODUCTION: THE QUEST

'Of the making of many books there is no end, and much study is a weariness of the flesh': so runs the complaint of a professional writer, or scribe, in Ancient Israel.[1] The frustration of Koheleth ('The Speaker'), whose words are recorded in the Old Testament book which bears his name, actually stems from the nature of the world as he finds it to be; the writer is wearied by his subject. Koheleth observes the endless succession of events in the natural and human world, which baffle the eye by their multiplicity and yet at the same time tire it with their repetition. There is 'nothing new under the sun', and yet the old affairs still escape even the wise man's control. So the complexity of what we experience in the world has a double effect: the eye is weary, but is still not satisfied.

> All streams run to the sea,
> but the sea is not full;
> to the place where the streams flow,
> there they flow again.
> All things are full of weariness;
> a man cannot utter it;
> the eye is not satisfied with seeing,
> nor the ear filled with hearing.
> (Koh. 1:7–8)

In human life, Koheleth observes, 'for everything there is a season, and a time for every matter under heaven', whether it is to weep or laugh, to keep silence or to speak. But he adds that human beings are engaged in a vain 'business', since we can never find out what the right time might be:

3

God has made everything beautiful in its time. . . . yet man cannot find out what God has done from the beginning to the end. (Koh. 3:11)

Such laments have a special poignance, because of the craft of the one who utters them. The 'wise men' of Ancient Israel, of whom Koheleth is a late representative, were a major provider of the skills of reading and writing that were needed in the royal court, the Temple and the diplomatic service. The scribes cultivated the art of 'steering' their way through the decisions of life by observing the regular patterns in nature and human experience, classifying similar things, and taking note of cause and effect. They treasured the results of their observations in lists, proverbs, parables and riddles. The pupil scribe copied out these wise sayings by rote and thereby acquired not only literacy but also a certain approach to life, a confidence that experience could be mastered with the help of these guidelines won from hard observation. But as the wisdom movement developed, an awareness grew that the vast scope and complexity of the world defeated human control, until such as Koheleth and the author of the book of Job ask in some despair:

> But where shall wisdom be found?
> And where is the place of understanding?
> Man does not know the way to it,
> and it is not found in the land of the living.
> The deep says, 'It is not in me',
> and the sea says, 'It is not with me'.
> (Job 28:12–14)

While these scribes do not give the same place to the covenant relationship between the God of Israel and his people as do the prophets and priests, they still admit that 'God understands the way to wisdom' (Job 28:23). They had in fact from their early days believed that God alone is supremely wise, and this conviction, as time passes, provides them with an answer to the problem of the mystery of the world. They finally come much closer, as we shall see, to the other religious traditions of Israel which laid stress upon God's *revelation* of his purpose for life in the oracles of the prophets and the teaching of the priests.[2] But Koheleth and his colleagues have certainly identified some features of the world which present a problem to be answered: the world appears elusive in its complexity, and yet also staled by habit. How then shall we live with meaning and purpose within such a world? How shall we write about it? As Proust observes several thousand years later, 'Habit weakens every impression.'[3]

Now, stories and poems are doing nothing less than grappling with the same double problem of reality. They offer a new world to our imagination in two ways – consoling us with the assurance of order in an everyday world that appears random and chaotic, and promising something new in a world that appears dulled by routine. In the first place, the story in a novel or play creates a world that has shape in the midst of our formless and fragmented life. The events of a story are fixed and immutable in their own universe; however absurd or tragic the action has been, we can return to it again and again, revisiting it and being sure to find a complete world. As Frank Kermode points out, the story arouses the sense of an ending, where the chronicle of life seems to be an endless chain of mere successiveness.[4] Tragic dramas reflect the threats of death and loss that come to us daily, but with the difference that here they bear the meaning of being part of a whole story where in life they may seem random and haphazard. Hamlet on the point of death can command his friend to go on living in 'this harsh world. . . . to tell my story',[5] and Othello requests of the officers who witness his suicide that:

> When you shall these unlucky deeds relate,
> Speak of them as they are; nothing extenuate,
> Nor set down aught in malice; then must you speak
> Of one that lov'd not wisely, but too well.[6]

Othello may be self-deceived in his summary of his story, but at least he has one. Form consoles, and so we ask also of a novel that the world within it should be consistent in its own terms, not that it should be the world we are familiar with. The worlds of roadside inns in Fielding, of minor country houses in Jane Austen, of the homes of middle-class intelligentsia in Iris Murdoch are all neater than in real life – but this is what comforts us at the same time as awakening us to something new. The story with its 'once upon a time' offers us the hope of ever-open beginnings in a world where nothing seems new under the sun. It invites us to immerse ourselves into lives other than our own, to extend our range of consciousness; we feel as does a rather ordinary lady in one of Virginia Woolf's novels, who takes part in a village pageant and exclaims: 'You've made me feel I could have played. . . . . Cleopatra!'[7]

The ways that stories have an effect upon us are also character-istic of the poetic image. Metaphors, similes and symbols have their place in the narration of a novel, but are the very essence of poetry with its compression of meaning. Stories offer the promise of new creation, both with the consolations of form and the challenge of novelty, and the poetic image has a similar impact; by comparing one thing with another, it shows both an underlying unity between things in the world, and also puts them together in new ways. The poet asks, in effect, 'Have you noticed that this is like that?', and this both brings something new out of a verbal sign and unifies it with others. This is supported by rhythm which uses time to give a sense of form and structure, and by correspondences in sound as well as in meaning, using such devices as rhyme or assonance. For example, in a sonnet describing his sense of desola-tion, Shakespeare uses an image of trees in winter:

> That time of year thou mayst in me behold
> When yellow leaves, or none, or few do hang
> Upon those boughs which shake against the cold,
> Bare ruined choirs, where late the sweet birds sang.
>
> (Sonnet 73)

Bringing together the poet's feeling of loss of creativity ('where late the sweet birds sang') with the cycle of nature as the wood moves from Autumn into Winter offers some elegiac consolation, unify-ing a human experience with natural life. At the same time the reader is awoken to new correspondences – not only between trees and poet as places of song, but between the trees and the branchy pillars of monastic choirs, fallen into ruin with their dissolution in the reign of Henry VIII. By bringing two verbal signs together in an image, new levels of meaning are given to both. Between the objects compared there is room for vibrations of undertones and overtones; something altogether new happens which cannot be paraphrased in prose.

The emphasis upon form or novelty in a metaphor can certainly vary. Sometimes the use of metaphor lays more stress upon the giving of form to the world than an awakening to new insight; this is the case, for example, in many of the similes in the wisdom literature of the Old Testament. I have already mentioned that the scribe notices correspondences between things in order to detect regularities and so predict successful action in the future. These nuggets of experience can be caught in proverbs that have metaphor at their heart: 'The beginning of strife is like the letting out of water' (Prov. 17:14), 'The dread wrath of a king is like the growling of a lion' (Prov.20:2), 'A wife's quarrelling is like a continual dripping of rain' (Prov. 27:15).

On other occasions, however, the use of metaphor can lay stress upon a new and unusual insight. Elsewhere in biblical literature, we find that the prophets can use image in a surprising and even shocking way. Hosea presents God as comparing himself to a moth and dry rot in the house of Judah (Hosea 5:12), and Jeremiah accuses God of being like a brook that has dried up (Jer.15:18).[8] In the lyrical poetry of the Song of Songs, the wooer describes the hair of his beloved as being like a flock of goats moving down the slopes of a mountain, and her beauty as 'terrible as an army with banners' (6:5,3). Unexpected imagery like this seems to dissolve the world as we know it, to disintegrate the familiar in preparation for a new order. The Metaphysical Poets of the seventeenth century often use such 'radical imagery',[9] choosing a vehicle for the metaphor which seems to have no obvious emotive associations with the object to which it is linked; Donne, for instance, uses scientific and geometrical imagery for human experiences, comparing lovers to twin legs of a compass, love to experiments in alchemy and the body to a map.[10] In our time T.S. Eliot inherits these devices, his use of them in 'Prufrock' leading to a protest by C.S. Lewis:

> For twenty years I've stared my level best
> To see if evening – any evening – would suggest
> A patient etherized upon a table;
> In vain. I simply wasn't able.[11]

But all use of image will contain, to some degree, both ingredients of a new world – the dislocating and the unifying, the novel and the formal. Imagination, as Coleridge perceived, is a vitality which 'dissolves, diffuses, dissipates, in order to re-create'.[12]

MYSTERY AND THE LITERARY IMAGINATION

The quest for a new world in literature would be mere escapism if we did not feel that the text was reaching out beyond itself to something of 'ultimate concern' to us. It would be mere fantasy if we did not sense that it was pointing to a mysterious reality which can only be hinted at. In fact we find that novels, plays and poems do transcend themselves towards Mystery, and we are alerted to this by the way that they are themselves self-conscious about their search.

Stories often show their awareness of the quest by taking as their theme the telling of a story. For example, the narrator may show his characters discovering that a particular story has the power to give shape to their own lives. In Patrick White's novel, *Voss*, an explorer faces his death at the hands of natives who have captured him in the Australian desert, and finds that the ancient story of the cross of Christ provides a form for what would otherwise be a mere collection of accidents. An ancient story and image, which he had previously discarded as an irrelevance and a weakness in the business of taming a continent, now enables him to make something of his death:

> He himself, he realized, had always been most abominably frightened, even at the height of his divine power, a frail God upon a rickety throne. . . . Of this too, mortally frightened, of the arms or sticks reaching down from the eternal tree, and tears of blood, and candle-wax. Of the great legend becoming truth.[13]

It is not that the 'great legend' gives him some kind of message by which he can find a moral in his suffering. It gives him a pattern by which he can find *himself* in what would otherwise be a meaningless end to his journey. This story, like all stories, promises order in the chaos of experience. The Southern Cross in the night sky, the stars like nails, the spear which the natives thrust into the sides of the horses, his own flowing blood, are things to which he can relate with the help of this story. But *the Story itself*, his ultimate concern, can only be hinted at by bringing the ancient story together with his own.

Another way that the narrator or playwright may make story a self-conscious theme and show the work to be in quest of the Story is by setting one story inside another, as in Shakespeare's *A*

Midsummer Night's Dream. Towards the end of the play the manual labourers present their 'lamentable comedy' to an audience of nobility gathered on the stage, of whose own earlier tragi-comic antics in the woods we have ourselves been the audience. Chaucer's Canterbury pilgrims tell their tales, but in their very journey make up another level of tale into which Chaucer inserts himself (or a version of himself) as a fellow-pilgrim. The effect of such devices is to make us feel that the stories have not really come to an end; they are self-enclosed and complete artefacts, but are still open to resolution somewhere. 'It seems to me/That yet we sleep, we dream'.[14] The barrier between art and reality has been broken down, and we are also faced with the realisation that we too, the audience, are in search of a story. At the conclusion of *The Tempest*, Shakespeare has Prospero come forward to take his farewell of the audience, but he does not doff his disguise as an actor would conventionally do in order to invite applause; he asks us to assist his journey back to Milan by our prayers. With a shock we find that the story is still going on, and that we are part of it.

A little before the end of this play, Prospero had made the elegiac pronouncement that 'Our revels now are ended.' In multiple levels of meaning, this 'ending' applies to the short magical entertainment Prospero has just presented within the play, to the reign of Prospero on his island, to the whole play of *The Tempest* itself, to the death which the audience constantly faces, and beyond this to the end of the world.

> . . . . like the baseless fabric of this vision,
> The cloud-capped towers, the gorgeous palaces,
> The solemn temples, the great globe itself,
> Yea, all which it inherit, shall dissolve,
> And, like this insubstantial pageant faded,
> Leave not a wrack behind. We are such stuff
> As dreams are made on; and our little life
> Is rounded with a sleep.[15]

The dream which is surrounded by a sleep, like an island surrounded by the sea, is the dream within the play, the dream of the play itself, and the dream of life. So we, the audience, are made aware that we are characters in a story, and the play has set us on the quest to find the mystery at the heart of the dream.

If metaphor and symbol transcend themselves towards mystery

within the setting of novel and drama, this is even more true in the form of poetry. A poem, containing a multiplicity of images, is characterised by compression of meaning. It hides meaning in order to find it again with increase, so that 'Philosophy is clarification, but art is mystification' (Iris Murdoch).[16] By bringing two verbal signs together in a metaphor, new levels of meaning are given to both; between the two objects being compared (usually called tenor and vehicle)[17] there is room for a vibration of undertones and overtones. In their juxtaposition or 'interaction ',[18] many relationships are evoked that need not be, or cannot be, expressed. As Paul Ricoeur puts it, a metaphor both affirms and denies, saying 'this is and is not'.[19] So the poet deliberately 'hides' his meaning through the use of image, but at the same time he knows that he cannot control the expansion of meaning that takes place when he does so. He cannot plan or catch all the echoes. The wisdom writers of Ancient Israel, as we have seen, use image in a straightforward way for the analysis of experience, but they also freely admit that the implications of some comparisons elude them. For instance, they note that the following four kinds of movement have a similarity, so that each is a metaphor of the other, but in the end they escape being categorised:

> Three things are too wonderful for me;
> Four I do not understand:
> The way of an eagle in the sky,
> The way of a serpent on the rock,
> The way of a ship on the high seas,
> And the way of a man with a maiden.
> (Prov. 30:18–19)

The possibility for multiple levels of meaning, and for an orientation towards Mystery, increases as we move along a spectrum from the explicit metaphor (or simile) to the implicit one. At the extreme explicit end of the scale is allegory, a kind of extended simile where two levels of meaning run parallel with each other; in Bunyan's *The Pilgrim's Progress*, for example, the meaning of each stage of the journey from the City of Destruction to the Gates of Heaven can be unpacked into some stage of the Calvinist–Puritan experience of salvation. At the extreme implicit end of the scale of imagery is symbol, a kind of compressed metaphor. The wood, for example, into which the lovers stray in *A Midsummer Night's*

Dream, or the wood in which Dante loses his way in the *Purgatorio*, have associations beyond their literal meaning; but the tenor of the comparison is not clearly in view in the way that it is with the Valley of the Shadow of Death in Bunyan's dream.

In poetry, drama and novel, the imagination thus reaches out towards mystery, towards a reality that is our final concern but which eludes empirical investigation and bursts rational concepts. The power of making pictures in the human mind ('imagination'), transcends itself towards something Other than the world which lies open to scientific discovery. Of course, this phenomenon of the imagination, and the nature of the Other reality, can be interpreted in rather different ways. For instance, in distinguishing between various functions of the imagination in his *Critique of Judgement*, the philosopher Kant identifies the sense of the 'sublime'. At one level, he suggests, our image-making faculty (imagination) simply assists our understanding in its task of making sense of objects around us in the world.[20] Beyond this, it enables us to know these objects with aesthetic judgement, making 'its own laws' and so finding purpose and beauty within them;[21] but beyond even this, the imagination can give us a sense of the sublime, where we are launched from a beautiful object in the world into an experience that we can only hint at with the use of images. Because we feel a loss of all limits, we lose touch with the object altogether and are immediately aware only of our own feelings.[22] For Kant, then, the intuition of 'another Reality' can only really be said to be a depth in our own feelings. The human reason certainly throws up ideas of realities which transcend the world of sense impressions, and such ideas include a universal purpose behind all things, God as the giver of this purpose and the eternal destiny of our personalities. But these *noumena* cannot actually be known, as the human mind (in Kant's view) has no categories to know anything except objects in the phenomenal world.

In thinking about the mystery to which the imagination reaches out, some then will follow a Kantian line in understanding it to be an elusive dimension in our own feelings, pointing to some depth of human values. Others will want to give the mystery a greater objectivity of its own, over against human experience. That is, they will want to retain a 'metaphysics', and will argue in support that there are other modes of knowing than observation and deduction relying on the evidence of the senses alone. In our century, Heidegger has spoken of a 'primordial thinking' which links us to

Being Itself, a Depth in existence which transcends our own merely finite beings.[23] Still others will want to give that Depth of Being the personal name of God, following the acclamation by Gerard Manley Hopkins:

> Ground of being, and granite of it: past all
>   Grasp God, throned behind
> Death with a sovereignty that heeds but hides, bodes but
>   abides. . . .[24]

MYSTERY AND CHRISTIAN DOCTRINE

The aim of this present study is not directly to argue for the rightness of the view of the Mystery which Hopkins affirms on behalf of all Christian believers. Rather, I am enquiring how someone who *does* take such a view might relate imaginative literature to the doctrinal statements which he makes. For while a movement *towards* mystery is characteristic of novels, poetry and drama, quite the opposite might seem at first sight to be true of Christian belief. In literature, stories and images are used playfully and experimentally to hint at a kind of reality which the reason cannot properly comprehend. But a faith based on events of revelation asserts that the Final Mystery has actually disclosed Himself to us, and human images and stories take their place in witnessing (however imperfectly) to this encounter with a self-revealing God. The initial movement is not from the world to mystery, but from mystery to the world. As the theologian Karl Barth expresses it, 'revelation seizes the language'.[25]

As soon as we have stated this difference of movement, we must of course hasten to qualify it. Holy scripture (as we have seen in the examples quoted so far) is itself a piece of literature containing narrative, poetry and drama with all the openness to multiple meaning that these have. The character of scripture should, indeed, lead us to realise that the primary forms of talk about God are metaphor and story, and that they invite an assent of faith which is like the imaginative assent we give to these forms in literature. After all, only a kind of speech which resists being trapped in a single, fixed meaning can begin to express the mystery of the Kingdom of God which we are invited to enter rather than analyse. The Jesus of Mark's Gospel refers to his parables as a deliberate piece of mystification, like a poet hiding his meaning in density of image: 'For those outside everything is in parables so that they may indeed see but not perceive, and may indeed hear but not understand . . .'.[26] Nevertheless, the belief that there has been a movement *from* Mystery to us, that God *comes* continually to his world and has finally come without reserve into time and history ('incarnation'), does mean that religious belief will be more than the 'suspension of disbelief' given to literary texts. It makes a difference that the basic movement is *from* being confronted by the reality of God *to* verbal expression, that in short (as Eberhard Jüngel puts it) 'God comes into language.'[27]

Belief in this movement will prompt a desire to find and state some 'truths' about the mystery at the heart of life. As Newman observed, what begins as 'an impression on the imagination' becomes 'a system or creed in the reason'.[28] John Coulson comments that unless imaginative faith (or 'real assent') *does* grow into the certainty of holding some beliefs, it will evaporate into a mere emotive feeling and cease to endure.[29] So there is always a momentum within belief, to infer concepts from images, to impose limits upon the boundless energy of symbol, and to attempt a summing up of the accidents and loose ends of stories in one unified Story.

The predicament of the wise men of Ancient Israel, with which we began this study, makes this direction of movement clear. In response to the despair of Koheleth at being unable to gain control over an elusive world, a later scribe adds a postscript to the book summarising the conclusion to which the wisdom movement eventually came:

> The end of the matter; all has been heard. Fear God, and keep his commandments; for this is the whole duty of man.
>
> (Koh. 12:13)

In face of the bewildering expanse of the world and the impossibility of finding patterns of meaning within it, Judaic faith begins from the *Torah*, the collection of writings in which the community believes that God's purpose for the nation is revealed. This is the true Wisdom which interprets the world, and Judaism comes to identify it with the figure of Wisdom that played and rejoiced before God as his first-born when he created the heavens and the earth (Prov. 8:22–31). Later, Christian faith found the centre of divine revelation to be no longer in a law code but in a person, Jesus Christ, and giving him the same title of Wisdom it affirmed

that the world could only be understood through the story of his
death and resurrection:

> He is the image of the invisible God, the first-born of all creation;
> for in him all things were created, in heaven and on earth. . . .
> He is before all things, and in him all things hold together. . . .
> For in him all the fulness of God was pleased to dwell, and
> through him to reconcile to himself all things, whether in earth
> or in heaven, making peace by the blood of his cross.
>
> (Col. 1:15–20)

Earlier in the faith of the Old Testament, before the establishing of
the written *Torah* as the centre of revelation, the prophets believed
that the Word of the Lord which came to them gave order to the
chaos of life, and opened up new possibilities. The puzzling
disaster of their exile in Babylon could be explained, for example,
as the chastening hand of God, who was now offering them a new
Exodus. So Isaiah of Babylon writes a poem which is at the same
time an oracle in which God himself claims to interpret the past
and promise the future:

> Let all the nations gather together,
> and let the peoples assemble.
> Who among them can declare this,
> And show us the former things? . . .
> Thus says the Lord,
> Who makes a way in the sea,
> a path in the mighty waters. . . .
> 'Behold, I am doing a new thing;
> now it springs forth, do you not perceive it?
> I will make a way in the wilderness
> and rivers in the desert.'
>
> (Isa.43:9–19)

As a poet, Isaiah of Babylon presents a succession of images
which, as they accumulate, hint at order and newness in a way
that cannot be translated into proposition. The hearer's imagination moves between the waters of Sheol/death (v. 2), the waters of
chaos which God overcame in creation (v. 16), the waters of the Red
Sea divided at the Exodus (v. 17), and oases in the desert (v. 20). As
Coleridge remarks, a poet 'hovers between images'[30] so that the

mind never settles into one and reduces the meaning. But in tension with this flow of images, the prophet claims a word of revelation which directly promises order and a new world: God will 'break down all the bars' of their captivity in Babylon (v. 14). Thus the promise of the prophet, like the canon of Torah and the life and death of one person (Christ), is a way of 'delimiting' or 'foreclosing' the meaning of symbols and stories.

In practical terms, then, a belief in divine revelation as a movement from mystery to the world will elicit attempts to *state* the mystery, to tell *the* Story, and so to clarify the language of faith. The theologian continues this process of creating a coherent and consistent system of thought, putting into concepts (doctrine) the wholeness of reality that imagination and faith are feeling after. Theology, in the wider sense of God-talk, will thus show a tension within itself between two kinds of speech which are both response to revelation – symbol and story on the one hand, and the concepts that interpret them on the other. Of course, doctrinal statements are themselves bound to go on using symbol and metaphor, since no talk about God as the incomparable One can do without them; but they use metaphor in an effort to fix meaning, to define and limit a range of possible understandings. Recent writing on theology and literature (by, for example, David Jasper and T.R. Wright) has formally acknowledged such a 'creative tension', but has seen its task to be that of commending metaphor and narrative as a means of talking about God which eludes reduction, leaving doctrine to look after itself.[31] Some studies have positively regretted the loss of open-endedness in the formation of doctrine.[32] By contrast, the approach of this book, and particularly of its final five studies, will be to stage a dialogue between doctrinal theology and the movement towards mystery in creative literature.

FOUR TYPES OF MOVEMENT TO MYSTERY

To suggest that imaginative literature is reaching towards a mystery needs, of course, immediate qualification. Poetry, drama and narrative show different ways of self-transcendence, and these forms cannot be simply classified by chronology or genre. Different periods *have* produced their own emphases, but it is probably better to think of different types of relation to mystery which may appear in any age. That is, we are classifying the ways in which the work of creative writers seems to be in search of the hidden reality which is our ultimate concern.

First we may notice a *correspondence* to mystery. An author who is writing within the framework of a widely accepted Christian view of the world, such as was characteristic of the medieval period, will deliberately make his work correspond to what is felt to be 'the' Christian story of the world. He will, in a sense, begin from the conviction that the mystery has been finally revealed, that the hidden meaning of the world has been unveiled. But if he is writing a poem, novel or drama rather than Christian doctrine, he will still be working towards that mystery in a playful way. He will naturally allow himself ambiguities and portray shifting half-identities.

In Langland's *Vision of Piers Ploughman*, for example, who is the Piers whom the dreamer is advised to meet on his journey to truth?[33] Is he the old Adam, the Christian believer, or Christ himself? The dreamer meets him 'painted all bloody' and 'right like in all limbs to our Lord Jesus',[34] but Piers has the force of someone only half-recognised. He is really the centre of a whole cluster of ideas about the relationship between God and humankind, a process rather than a person. The elusiveness of Piers sums up the uncertainty of the whole poem, which is like other medieval literature in being a search for experience (pref) to flesh out the authority (auctoritee) of books of doctrine. The dreamer believes that 'If I may live and look, I shall learn better'.[35] The poem contains expositions of the doctrine of the Fall, Incarnation, Redemption and Trinity, but it ends on a note of questing uncertainty as Conscience vows to walk through the wide world 'to seek Piers the Ploughman' who destroys the 'pride' of learning.[36]

A similar elusive identity attaches to Beatrice in the *Divine Comedy*, whom Dante dares to make so central to the Paradisial vision that at one point she is all that he can see.[37] Is she a Florentine girl, divine Grace, Theology, human Romantic Love or the Virgin Mary? She is and she is not. She is, as Charles Williams wisely says, 'a poetic image; being in a poem, she cannot well be anything else. . .'.[38] She is, however, Dante's 'way of knowing, and the maxim is always, 'Look; look well'. On the Way of love which the poet is inviting his readers to tread 'her eyes are his knowing', and can be ours. Williams also finds it striking that 'this great poet should have said so little in the ordinary speech of Christians; he omits so much that any small Christian versifier would have put in.'[39] In his own words we may say, 'being a poem, it cannot well be anything else'. The poem *corresponds* to the Christian mysteries, but is not afraid to be playful and experimental.

A second mode of approach to the mystery is characteristic of the period from the Reformation to the nineteenth century, though it is by no means buried there. The author proffers an *individual insight* into the heart of truth. Here, imagination creates a private world which claims nevertheless to be a view of reality, a particular perspective which opens up the whole meaning of the world outside. The author may actually be referring to a spiritual realm, as in Vaughan's 'I saw Eternity the other night', or he may be offering his view of *what really matters*, in the everyday world around us, as in the 'realistic novels' of Dickens, Eliot and Hardy. As Gabriel Josipovici has pointed out,[40] the Lutheran emphasis upon individual justification by faith results in art forms in which the element of personal expression joins with imitation of nature. The writer, with 'authorial authority' offers his inner feelings about the world that he assumes we all know and will recognise.

But doubts about whether we *do* all share a consciousness of the same external world may well lead to a third kind of quest towards mystery, the use of symbol as the *unique entrance* to the real world. In place of the author's own feelings and experience are placed symbols which, as W.B. Yeats maintained (following William Blake) are '"a representation of what actually exists really and unchangeably". . . . indeed the only possible expression of some invisible essence, a transparent lamp about a spiritual flame'.[41] In this approach, some images are understood as having gathered to themselves the passions of humanity throughout the years, and so stand as entries into the 'Great Memory'. They awaken hidden associations, start echoes within us and turn our attention to the essence of life. Yeats commends this symbolic imagination in Blake, noting that he preferred to call it 'vision'. His own poems teem with images, whose very birth he naturally can only describe in symbols; they are created in a 'dance' of memory, or in a journey across the 'sea' of generation which is split by a passion for love ('dolphin-torn') and troubled by the fear of death ('gong-tormented'):

> Marbles of the dancing floor
> Break bitter furies of complexity,
> Those images that yet

Fresh images beget,
That dolphin-torn, that gong-tormented sea.[42]

Doubts will arise, however, as to whether even symbol can provide a door into the hidden mysteries of life. T.S. Eliot records that 'Footfalls echo in the memory', and 'words echo' in the mind,

But to what purpose
Disturbing the dust on a bowl of rose-leaves
I do not know.[43]

Thus the novels and poems of our present age tend to yet another approach, deliberately drawing attention to their structure and style in order to be a *negative catalyst* for reality. By insisting that they are *only* making artefacts, crafted works of art, writers awaken their readers to the actual wonder of the world around them. In his perceptive study of modernism, Josipovici notes that 'the modern novel draws attention to the rules which govern its own creation, in order to force the reader into recognising that it is *not* the world'.[44] He goes on to suggest that by making clear that the imagined world has boundaries, the writer thereby 'reveals what cannot be spoken, the existence of the world beyond those limits'. The poem or story debunks itself as 'only a piece of art' to provoke the reader into his own creativity, and 'so to sense what lies beyond, the absolutely other, distinct from me and my desires'.[45]

An extreme form of this approach is adopted by the modern movement of structuralist criticism. The structuralist pays attention to the style and verbal 'rules' of the text, ignoring any reference that it may be making to the outside world, and therefore also setting the intention of the author on one side. The text is self-sufficient, and interest is in 'the signifier, not the signified',[46] in 'the code, not the encoded'. So criticism does not so much read *from* the work as construct a meaning *for* it, allowing it to create a 'dreaming beyond the text'[47] in the reader. The formalist critic Tzvetan Todorov finds a parable of this in a short story by Henry James, *The Figure in the Carpet*. In this tale a famous author rebukes a critic for failing to find the key to his work, the central pattern in the texture of the whole; according to Todorov, the point is that the secret figure *can never* be found. A definitive message cannot be extracted from a text, and the reader experiences the secret or essence of what is real, precisely through the absence of such meaning.[48]

There is no need to adopt a thoroughgoing structuralist approach to accept that the reality to which a work is striving can be found only in *encounter* with the text, in the very act of reading, and not in a series of propositions. In fact, we shall find that a Christian doctrine of revelation maintains something rather similar. It is, however, another matter to suggest that the text has *no* content of meaning of its own, and makes *no* reference to the world outside itself. As Derrida perceived, merely analysing the way that the parts of a work relate to the whole is in fact to find an inherent meaning.[49] Admittedly, the conclusion which he, and other 'deconstructive' critics draw, is that a text debunks itself by drawing attention to its inner flaws; nothing holds together, and the point of criticism is to detect inconsistency and self-contradiction rather than structural harmony. We can, however, gain insights from both structuralist and deconstructive critics about the open significance of texts without necessarily following their view that a text tells us nothing about the truth of the everyday world in which we live.

We may be helped in this direction by reflection on a novel by Umberto Eco, who is himself a specialist in the science of verbal signs (semiotics). *The Name of the Rose* sums up the fourth approach to the mystery of reality we have been exploring, and also hints at its limitations. Cast in the form of a detective story, it begins with an elaborate and apparently realistic preface in which the author professes to have found a medieval manuscript containing the ensuing story. As we have noted with previous examples, the ploy of setting a story within a story immediately breaks down the division between art and life, as we are not sure whether the narrator of the preface is Eco himself or a fictional author. The story relates a series of murders committed in a Benedictine monastery in 1327, and the central point is that the monk-detective finds the villain by accident. He certainly traces him through following up the signs left by the crimes, but they turn out in fact not to have been pointing to the murderer at all. There *is* no plot which has generated the signs, and the way the detective understands the signs has even led the culprit to generate a plot to fit in with the interpretation. There seems then to be no link between sign and event, between the name of the rose and the rose itself. The narrator who has shared as a novice monk in these events concludes, 'I leave this manuscript, I do not know for whom; I no longer know what it is about.'[50]

This assertion that there is always an unbridgeable gap between the sign – whether clues of a crime or marks on a page – and the thing signified, need not be as negative in effect as it sounds.[51] The point being made is that all pattern is provisional, and reaches to meaning beyond itself. The reader discovers through the progress of the story that the signs are in fact not completely without indirect reference; he has to act *as if* they tell the story of reality, in order to get further towards the truth. At one point the monk-detective roots this final lack of order in the freedom of God to make new choices:

> The order that our mind imagines is like a net, or a ladder, built to attain something. But afterward you must throw the ladder away, because you discover that, even if it was useful, it was meaningless. . . . It's hard to accept the idea that there cannot be an order in the universe because [such order] would offend the free will of God and his omnipotence. So the freedom of God is our condemnation, or at least the condemnation of our pride.[52]

Whatever the author himself intends, these words offer a profoundly religious perspective on the gap between verbal sign and reality. From the viewpoint of Christian eschatology, the gap is not simply caused by the inability of human words to express the infinite, but by the fact that there is no fixed totality of meaning and value to be found. Stories do not point to an eternally underlying and unchanging Logos, but to a Logos who is always to come, to a divine story-teller who is the God of the future, who is always free to do new things and bring new reality into being.

The detective story in general is a simple example of a story in search of a story, for the characters are looking for the hidden story which will make sense of the signs with which they are confronted. As Todorov points out, there is the story of the crime 'which is absent from the book but real', and the story of the investigation (or the plot) which is 'present but insignificant'.[53] However, nobody normally wants to read a detective story twice, unless they have forgotten the ending, because the hidden story is not a mystery at all but only a secret in which there are no further depths once it is unveiled. The 'whodunit' is thus usually only a mere shadow of a story, and has little literary merit; Eco has written a detective story that *can* be re-read, because it not only discloses a secret story but points to a truly hidden story (a mystery) which is never told. However, we do feel that the Story towards which the story transcends itself is about human experience of living in the world; in Eco's tale the motive of the murderer is to suppress a supposedly lost second volume of Aristotle's *Poetics*, whose theory that comedy inverts creation is felt to be too subversive of society.

Eco's novel, despite its attack on objective meaning, at least hints that the world created by the novel throws some light on the mundane world. More firmly, Paul Ricoeur insists that stories and metaphors, 'redescribe reality'.[54] Like models held with a 'critical realism' by scientists, the imagination forms a new world which has indirect reference to the world in which we live. This referential quality allows us to understand imagination as a mode of empathy, creating poems and novels which are 'extenders of consciousness' (Coleridge's phrase).[55] John McIntyre suggests that Wittgenstein's definition that imagination is 'seeing-as' should be taken in an ethical sense;[56] it is seeing as others do, involving a sacrificial participation. In fact, it is a kind of incarnation.

The 'Chroniclers and Song-Makers' who ostensibly narrate Doris Lessing's fable *The Marriage Between Zones Three, Four and Five* express this kind of immersion into the lives of those they celebrate. They are, aptly, telling a myth of incarnation as they relate the descent of Al-Ith, the Queen of an advanced spiritual civilisation, into a lower zone of existence characterised by more bodily emotions; marrying its King, she achieves reconciliation at the cost of becoming an alien to her own people.

> Describing, we become. We even – and I've seen it and have shuddered – summon. The most innocent of poets can write of ugliness and forces he has done no more than speculate about – and bring them into his life. I tell you, I've seen it, watched it. . . . Yet there is a mystery here and it is not one I understand: without this sting of otherness. . . . then nothing works or *can* work.
>
> . . . . and so now, in this footnote to Al-Ith's thoughts on that occasion I simply make my cause and rest it: Al-Ith am I, and I Al-Ith, and every one of us anywhere is what we think and imagine.[57]

So W.H. Auden observes in his poem about the experience of being a novelist that he must,

Among the just be just
Among the filthy, filthy too.[58]

It is through story and poetry that we discover the incarnational principle upon which (as McIntyre suggests)[59] the ethics of love depends, and which Christian faith affirms is a repetition of God's own creative and redemptive work. Indeed, as we shall see, it is also the character of revelation.

THE PARALLELS BETWEEN IMAGINATION AND REVELATION

The four types of movement towards mystery we have been exploring (correspondence, personal insight, symbolic vision and negative catalyst) appear at first sight to stand in strong contrast to the Christian enterprise of making and guarding doctrine. The movement *towards* mystery is playful and questing, and lays a stress upon the autonomy of the imagination to create something new, even where the writer is deliberately writing in correspondence to Christian faith. Conversely, the theologian is always bound to be responsible to what he believes has been revealed in a movement *from* Mystery Itself. Creativity here, it seems, must be secondary.

However, the gap begins to be narrowed when we consider more carefully what it means to claim that God has revealed himself, or spoken his Word, to us. In the first place, there are strong grounds for believing that divine revelation cannot essentially be the communication of propositions by God, but rather the unveiling of his very Being. In a phrase of Karl Barth's 'Revelation is the Person of God speaking',[60] not the sending of a message. Revelation can be nothing less than an encounter with the speaking God, where 'speech' is understood as self-expression, an opening and an offer of the divine Self. This must be so for a number of reasons.

First, if as human beings we possessed the actual 'words' of God we would be infringing his freedom and otherness. Like Moses demanding to know the 'name' of God (Exodus 3:13), we would acquire power over him, demanding that he conform to this proposition or the other. Second, all human words are conditioned by culture and environment, and cannot be simply identified with the divine Word. If this identification were made, with whatever sophistication, God would either have to limit himself to one language and culture, or else express himself so vaguely that he would not be involved in the particularities of human history at all. Third, if God did communicate directly in propositions a set of infallible statements would have to exist somewhere, and faith could therefore be verified and its nature as trust would be destroyed.

Finally, and perhaps most important, the Christian confession from earliest days has been that the divine revelation has been focused in Jesus Christ, so that God is believed to express himself directly in a person and not in a list of propositions and creeds. Some theologians (and I count myself among them) will find this consistent with their belief in a God who is himself essentially personal. While recognising that all human talk about God must be analogical, since God cannot be included in a class with other beings, they find that personal language is the most adequate for expressing both the transcendence and immanence of God. While such talk cannot be literally accurate, it does actually *refer* to the reality of God. Other theologians, who believe that it is a more accurate analogy to speak of God as Being-Itself, nevertheless affirm that Being cannot be less than personal, and includes the power of personality.[61] Thus, although they prefer to speak of revelation as the self-unveiling of Being-Itself rather than a personal disclosure, they affirm that such revelation will, in our experience, take its most heightened form through a personal life.

We must therefore understand all concepts and propositions of Christian doctrine to be response and witness to revelation, not revelation in the immediate sense. The Bible also, as human words, can only be witness to the Word of God. However, since it is witness to primordial revelatory events, and above all to the Christ event, it can become the place where past revelation is repeated in the present. It can 'become the Word of God'[62] for the reader or hearer, a place of encounter with the same God who unveiled himself to Abraham, Isaac and Jacob, and who finally disclosed himself in Christ.

It can be readily seen that such a view of revelation has parallels with the various uses of the imagination which I outlined above. It has some affinities with the 'structuralist' view that all literary forms open a new world to the reader through encounter and living interaction with the text rather than directly through any concepts it contains. Moreover, even in the 'correspondence' model, we noticed that creative writers do not simply embroider doctrinal propositions but invite the reader on a journey of experience which is quite open-ended. The claim of other authors to a personal insight into the true nature of reality might be over-confident and over-subjective, but at least it puts truth into the area of personal knowledge and draws attention to the disclosure of being that happens within relationships. This is the achievement of the Lutheran Reformation, and the emphasis upon justification by faith.

Even more strikingly, the stress that some writers place upon symbol as *entrance* into new dimensions of reality, and not merely illustration of it, has a parallel with the use of symbol in Christian doctrine. Although all human words can only point by way of analogy to the unique being of God, some images are felt to have an intrinsic relationship to the reality they express and so (in the words of Paul Tillich), 'participate in the power of the divine to which they point'.[63] They act as media of the Spiritual Presence, not because of their own nature, but because they are used by the divine Spirit for a place of revelation. Tillich speaks of being 'grasped' by a symbol, which opens up new vistas both of ultimate reality ('the Holy') and the human spirit. Symbols are not arbitrarily invented (as mere signs are), but are rooted in the human psyche and emerge within particular human cultures, though it must be admitted that the way they appear has not as yet been satisfactorily explained either sociologically or psychologically.

Christian doctrine cannot, nevertheless, be totally relative to the culture of any one time. The symbols in which belief is framed cannot be merely passing and disposable expressions of an inner experience. There must be some *continuity* from age to age as well as an adaptability to new circumstances. In the first place, this is because the doctrine or 'teaching' of a community helps to supply communal norms and identity through its constant character, appealing for some kind of fidelity. From this standpoint we might distinguish between the 'doctrine' of any religious group and its 'theologies', which may be highly varied in the explanations they offer about the nature of reality. But even 'theology' ('God-talk'), must show some continuity as well as novelty if it is to be responsible about its subject. After all, it is supposed to witness to a God who has an internal self-consistency and faithfulness, and it is meant to create a response to God which is consistent in some way with his character. For these reasons, Christian doctrine and theology, its teaching and its talk, show 'a presumption in favour of the maximum amount of visible continuity' (S. Sykes).[64]

Undeniably, there is a contrast here with the free enterprise of the imagination in the arts, but we should also not miss an important parallel. When theologians ask where the core of this continuing identity is to be found in Christian teaching, many today will appeal to the authority of a *story*. I have remarked that Christian doctrine cannot be merely expressive of an inner experience, but we have already seen that neither can it be based upon a set of propositions which have supposedly been revealed by God. It has, indeed, been often held that the core of Christian doctrine resides in a number of truths given in biblical times, which have the seeds of all future development of thought within themselves; truth unfolds through the ages, according to this view, like an oak growing from an acorn. But such an approach is too static, and does not allow for real change and for leaps of new insight into God's purpose for the world. Rather, we may find the abiding substance of Christian doctrine neither in religious experience nor in a 'deposit' of truth, but in a story – the story of Jesus in the context of the biblical narrative of God's dealings with his people Israel.

We have seen it to be an insight of modern literary criticism that the story itself has power to shape the imagination of the hearer; the story can be understood as a kind of 'grammar' which enables the reader to speak a language in which he would otherwise be dumb. So the story of Jesus, as G. Lindbeck suggests,[65] does not so much give expression to an inner experience as make certain experience and feelings possible. The story of Jesus gives structure to human life for those who live within it. From a slightly different angle, S. Sykes notes that while Christian thinkers have always been engaged in disputes about the content of truth and doctrine, this very phenomenon makes clear that there *is* 'one thing' that is being argued about, that there is 'an essentially disputed concept'. What constitutes the fact that 'the players are all in the same game', suggests Sykes, is nothing other than the attention given to the story of Christ, to his 'performance' on the stage of human history.[66] Once more, then, we can see a parallel between the theological appeal to revelation and the use of the imagination in literature; in both cases there is a story which calls for attention in its own right, which demands that we notice it, and take account of it as it is. We are not to treat the story as a storehouse for our own preconceptions.

However, if the story with which Christian doctrine is concerned, and which it affirms as *the* story which makes sense of all others, is to be the *same* story through every age, there have to be some agreed concepts connected with it. In the first place, the achievement of Jesus is to be understood in the context of God and his relationship to the world; the story of Jesus is about someone who is open to the purpose of a heavenly Father. But even this God-context must have what Sykes calls 'boundaries' of thought.[67] Here Lindbeck speaks of 'rules', similar to rules of grammar which regulate the use of the vocabulary of a story.[68] Doctrinal formulations themselves act as 'rules' for a way of life, but these change from age to age; underlying them are some permanent rules reflected in all true doctrine. Sykes' 'boundaries' and Lindbeck's 'rules' have a striking similarity; Sykes refers to the concept of a God who is alone Lord over beginnings (creation) and endings (death), which might be understood as an expansion of Lindbeck's rule of monotheism. Both affirm the concept of a God who can initiate something new in history.[69]

Such propositions are not revelation itself; they are 'second-order propositions' or 'second-order rules of speech' (Lindbeck).[70] But Christian theologians are bound to show an allegiance to them, as providing the context for the story of Jesus and ensuring that the story remains the same story. Story and propositions are response to the self-revelation of God, which comes to a focus in the person of Jesus Christ. Thus, there is an indissoluble difference between the place of story in doctrine on the one hand and in literary imagination on the other; Christian theologians, working from belief in revelation, are moving within restraints that are not laid upon the novelist. Imaginative writers may, nevertheless, recognise their own kind of limits and tensions, as the next chapter will show. It also remains to be shown that there is not only a parallel, but actually a *union* between revelation and imagination.

2
The Creative Dialogue

'The ideas of Christian theology are too simple for eloquence, too sacred for fiction, and too majestick for ornament'.[1] Thus Samuel Johnson heads a notable list of literary figures who have protested against the attempt to mix poetry and doctrine. If poetry be regarded in the Augustan manner simply as a matter of decoration ('What oft was thought, but ne'er so well expressed')[2] as Johnson himself assumed, then such a mixture would indeed be paying faith an unwanted compliment. But other literary critics, well aware of the creative power of image and story, have objected to the blending of theology and literature on precisely those grounds. Originality and creativity, urge such critics as C.S. Lewis and Helen Gardner, have no place in doctrine.[3] Their convictions seem to be consistent with my observation in the previous chapter that Christian theologians, appealing to revelation, and writers employing imagination understand themselves as working in two rather different directions. The first are following a movement *from* a mystery towards image and story, the second from image and story *towards* a mystery.

However, while recognising a different emphasis in these two crafts, we have also found striking parallels between them. Now I believe we should venture one step further, starting from a basis in Christian doctrine; we may find the explanation for these parallels in an actual *relationship* between divine revelation and the human imagination. Only a theological idea about this relationship can cope with the accusation that the novelty of literary imagination has nothing to do with hearing the Word of God.

THE UNITY OF REVELATION AND IMAGINATION

One poet and literary critic of the nineteenth century, S.T. Coleridge, actually appeals both to movements to and from mystery in his writings, and from him we may glean a clue to their unity.

When thinking about the nature of poetry, he lays stress upon the first movement, speaking of the creative power of the 'Secondary Imagination'.[4] The Primary Imagination uses images to grasp the world around us, not in a mere passive receptivity but in a kind of repetition of God's own work of creation. In perceiving the world we share in the creativity that God has already exercised, and yet the Secondary Imagination transcends even this. Images can create a new world that has not yet appeared, giving us a new experience of the wholeness of life beyond the isolation of separate things. Both modes of imagination are to be distinguished from mere 'fancy', or a copying and decorating of objects from the world around. Fancy is like a mirror held up to nature, and works largely through memory, joining reflections together. Imagination is like a lamp rather than a mirror; it makes light. Above all, the Secondary Imagination has the power to create something new; like the moon, it sways the tides of the world.

But in his more religious writings, Coleridge seems to think in another manner, affirming the power of the 'Reason' to *know* the spiritual world.[5] Here he has taken up and modified Kant's distinction between the Reason and the Understanding. In Kant's view, as we have seen, the mind throws up ideas of a transcendent reality (such as God, the eternal Self, the Unity of the Universe) but as tools of perception these ideas only function in a 'regulative' way;[6] they supply a motivation or spur to the Understanding in its investigation of the physical world around us. But for Coleridge, these ideas actually 'constitute' reality; just as we know objects in the world of the senses through our Understanding, so through our Reason we can know the spiritual world. This is because we receive God's revelation of himself through our Reason. Thus there is a poetic intuition (the Secondary Imagination) and a religious intuition (Reason). In the first we use our wills to move out playfully towards a mystery, willingly suspending our disbelief. In the second we use our wills in religious commitment, joining our will to our Reason to produce faith. We take the responsible choice of commitment to what our Reason receives from God.

Though some critics have felt there to be a clash between poetic imagination and religious knowledge in Coleridge's work,[7] Coleridge himself has a way of bringing the two kinds of intuition together. He thinks of the human personality as being indwelt by the creative spirit of God; in the metaphor favoured by the Cambridge Platonists, we are illumined from within by 'the candle of the Lord',[8] and this is why we can be little creative lamps in our turn. However, although Coleridge inclines to such Platonist language, his fundamental thought is much more in terms of the encounter of human with divine personality; we can say 'I am' because we are in fellowship with the Almighty 'I am' – or rather we can make this fellowship real by a decision of our will.[9] We can move beyond the world of 'It is', the world of objects around us, into the realm of the personal or the world of the 'I am'. Thus the movement of the imagination, pointing to mystery, is part of the movement of God's own self-revealing Spirit.

The later notebooks of Coleridge are full of what he calls 'polar logic', by which he finds a triune shape about the way we know ourselves in the world, not only reflecting but interacting with the triunity of God. Yet even in an early poem like 'Frost at Midnight' (1798) all the basic elements of his theological thought are present. As the poet sits in his cottage at Grasmere, rocking the cradle of his infant son, he contemplates the film of heat fluttering on top of the steady thin blue flame of the embers. His mind, he muses, is similarly moved by the divine Spirit in all of nature:

> Whose puny flaps and freaks the idling Spirit
> By its own moods interprets, every where
> Echo or mirror seeking of itself,
> And makes a toy of Thought.

At first this account of the poetic mind actually sounds less like Imagination than mere Fancy, with the poet simply receiving and assorting the images of 'the numberless goings on of life' in 'sea, hill and wood' which the Spirit impresses upon him. But as the poem develops we find that the divine Spirit is also prompting the mind to an active work, to a speaking the creative word of God after him. All seasons will be sweet to his son because, wandering like a breeze by lake and mountain, he will see and hear

> . . . . The lovely shapes and sounds intelligible
> Of that eternal language, which thy God
> Utters, who from eternity doth teach
> Himself in all, and all things in himself.
> Great universal Teacher! He shall mould
> Thy spirit, and by giving make it ask.

'And by giving make it ask': this last phrase could stand as a pithy summary of a great deal of modern theological thought, where God's revelation of himself within human experience is understood to be the basis for the human quest after the mystery of God. If God were not giving himself in the first place, we would not ask after him. We reach after the mystery of final reality because we have already been grasped by it. As Paul Tillich expresses it, we have ultimate concerns because the Ultimate – Being Itself – is already participating in our existence. We are already seized and held by the Spiritual Presence, and what we think to be our autonomous reason is in fact linked to the 'Depth' of reason; so God is in our asking of the questions as much as he is in the answers.[10] Symbols thus open up a way into that Reality which is already present in our experience, though in a hidden way.[11]

A modern Catholic theologian, Karl Rahner, observes that the human spirit appears to have a natural openness to the infinite. A person experiences himself as a 'transcendent being', able to go on asking questions endlessly about his existence: 'the infinite horizon of human questioning is experienced as a horizon which recedes further and further the more answers man can discover'.[12] In fact, however, Rahner maintains that this openness to mystery can never be separated from God's own openness to us in gracious self-communication. The movements of grace and nature are always bound up together, so that God's offer of himself to us is prior to all our freedom and self-understanding.[13] To be a person, a spiritual being, is actually to take part in 'the event of a supernatural self-communication of God'. Though framed in the language of modern existentialism, this conviction is very close to Coleridge's hope that God would 'by giving make [thee] ask'.

However expressed, by Coleridge in the nineteenth century, or by Rahner and Tillich in the twentieth, there is a theological perspective here upon the sense of mystery which we articulate in image and story. The reaching of the imagination towards a new world is the result of God's reaching towards us. The work of the creative imagination is in fact one kind of response to revelation. Though the phrase 'general revelation' can be misleading[14] it is useful enough in this context, and conceptual clarity is gained if we distinguish it from 'special' revelation. The term 'special' here points to the experience that some events 'stand out' as decisive moments of disclosure, insisting that they be noticed and demanding a whole reorientation of life from the participant. Such moments of revelation to individuals can be 'primordial', leading to the founding of communities which share in the revelation through remembering and recalling it. At the centre of special revelation, Christians find the 'final' revelation of God in the life of Christ and the historical events surrounding it. 'Final' indicates of course not 'last' in time, but a completeness in the light of which all other revelations are to be interpreted.

The distinction between 'general' and 'special' revelation is also preferable to the distinction made in medieval theology between 'natural' and 'revealed' theology. The earlier pair of concepts assumed that a certain, low-level knowledge of God could be obtained through the natural capacities of human mind. It was thought, for example, that unaided reason, by reflecting upon the appearance of the world, could deduce that God existed and was One; but reason had to be supplemented by the higher knowledge gained through revelation if we were to know that God is Trinity. There is no need to rehearse in detail the problems with such a 'natural theology', problems which have become painfully obvious since the Enlightenment. Arguments for the existence of God based upon rational argument simply do not work; moreover, a theological view of the finite limits and sinfulness of the human mind entails that God must always take the initiative in revealing himself if we are to know anything of the Infinite.

In contrast to a natural theology, the concept of 'general revelation' thus affirms that God is present in his world to disclose *himself* within nature and human life. The idea is not that God leaves messages or propositions about himself embedded in the natural world which can then be 'picked up' by the receiving apparatus of the human mind. Rather, he unveils his own being through the vehicle of human and natural events. Nature is a place of encounter with the living God, not a dead-letter drop. Thus the term 'general' must not be taken to mean either a general principle deducible from the structures of nature, nor a 'generalised' revelation; all revelation, wherever it happens, will be a self-disclosure of the personal God to persons.

Anyway, if we are to claim the literary imagination to be one type of response to 'general' revelation, it is clear that such revelation *could not be* a communication of propositions. Obviously, many creative writers do not understand themselves to be responding to divine revelation, and it would be untrue to their experience to suggest that they had a religious *faith* without realising it. It is, however, consistent with experience for a Christian theologian to interpret their work (even if they do not) as one kind of response to God's offer of himself, in encounter between divine and human personality. For such response might take a wide variety of forms in human life, some involving conscious faith and others an unconscious awareness of the infinite, some more intuitive and others more discursive, some accepting and some rejecting the divine offer. Not only the creative imagination, but the moral sense and even the very quest for the meaning of life can be interpreted as response to revelation. Within this perspective, human beings are what they are because they hear the 'Word' of God spoken deep within their minds.

Yet this theological perspective does not in itself provide us with tools of practical criticism in considering the link between Christian doctrine and literature. It gives us a theological justification for making the link between imagination and revelation, but does not itself give us a way of 'reading' which is distinctively Christian. We have, it seems, two sets of stories and images. On the one hand there is the Christian story of God's self-revelation in the history of Israel and Jesus Christ, which can be reflected upon with the propositional language of doctrine. The work of theology is to speak responsibly about this human experience of God, responding to revelation with finite words and concepts which we believe to be appropriate analogies, yet which fall short of the divine reality. On the other hand there are the profusion of stories and images which express the self-transcendence of the human spirit, reaching out to mystery and ever-open horizons.

Both sets of stories open up a sense of the differing elements of order and newness within our everyday lives. We can claim, as a matter of theological understanding, that the two stories interact in the ever-present grace and the universal self-revelation of God. But, in practice, what difference does this make either to the making of doctrine or to the critical reading of literary texts?

THE DIALOGUE BETWEEN DOCTRINE AND LITERATURE

In searching for a relationship between theology and literature, we must beware of denigrating the arts, by treating them as a happy hunting ground for mere 'shadows' of Christian truths. All too often Christian apologists have attempted to turn the great secular writers into crypto-Christians, witnessing to Christian themes unawares and even verifying Christian truth through this witness, as a kind of natural theology of literature. A little scene from Samuel Beckett's play *Waiting for Godot* should stand as a warning against the quest for Christ-figures in literature that theologians often indulge in:

VLADIMIR: But you can't go barefoot!
ESTRAGON: Christ did.
VLADIMIR: Christ! What's Christ got to do with it? You're not going to compare yourself to Christ!
ESTRAGON: All my life I've compared myself to him.
VLADIMIR: But where he lived it was warm, it was dry!
ESTRAGON: Yes. And they crucified quick.[15]

In the view of Beckett's tramps, they can compare themselves to Christ in the sense that they are the true suffering servants; they are the type of whom he is the anti-type, the pale reflection, the mere 'shadow'. If then we believe that all use of story and symbol which reaches towards transcendence is in fact a response to divine revelation, what practical conclusions can we draw from this which will respect literature as creation in its own right?

All creative writing, since it is concerned with human experience, is occupied with themes that also occupy Christian faith and theology. The movement of the human spirit towards self-transcendence is bound to overlap with the theological understanding of the human spirit as being grasped by transcendent reality. As long as we do not pretend that the secular writer is actually making the jump from one dimension to the other, then the Christian perspective upon revelation allows the Christian thinker to set any writer's use of metaphor, symbol and story side-by-side with those from the Christian tradition, together with the Christian concepts which (as we have seen) 'delimit' them. It is this method of juxtaposition we shall be following in the five studies that make up the second half of this book. The practical result should be two-fold, illuminating both the theology and the literature. While no synthesis is made between the two, they can have a mutual impact upon each other, as there is an 'opening of horizons' between them.[16]

In the first place, this enterprise should help to shape Christian thinking. Christian theologians are always being faced with decisions about the meaning and expression of belief. How shall the multiple meanings to which the metaphors and stories of faith give rise be reduced and confined within concepts of belief? There are alternative ways of thinking about the deepest issues of faith, even when the theologian is aiming at consistency with past development of doctrine. For instance, should Christian love contain elements of *eros* (self-fulfilling love) as well as *agape* (self-giving love)? We shall return to this question in a critical study of the novels of D.H. Lawrence. Theological ideas can be influenced by an imaginative presentation of the themes with which both theology and literature deal and of the symbols they share. A portrayal in a novel or poem of some facet of human experience will alert the theologian to aspects he may otherwise neglect or fail to see at all. It may tip the balance when the theologian wavers in judgement. The movement in the dialogue between doctrine and literature here is *deductive*, the theologian drawing from an exegesis of the literary text.

But the hermeneutical principle of 'open horizons' works both ways. Christian belief and doctrine can provide the reader, in an *inductive* manner, with a perspective for interpretation of literary texts; as T.S. Eliot observes, 'To understand anything is to understand from a point of view'.[17] This does not imply that we attribute a religious intention to the writer when it is not there, though as a matter of fact most Western literature has been influenced in some way by the Christian tradition. Blake called the Bible 'The Great Code of Art', indicating the extent to which the thought patterns of Western art have been shaped by its language, images and stories. The theologian can thus help the literary critic to place a religious symbol in its context, and this will contribute to exploring the meaning of a text, which (as we have seen) cannot be reduced to authorial intention.

But beyond any such underlying traces of the biblical tradition in a text, the Christian reader will be alert to patterns of human experience that he might well have missed if he had not become familiar with them through the Christian story. Though structural critics have perhaps neglected the intention of the author and his historical setting in favour of the 'grammar' of the narrative itself, they have rightly drawn attention to common features or 'rules' in the way that stories are shaped and have their effect. The reader soaked in the images and stories of the biblical tradition will notice depths and dimensions in other stories too. Further, as we shall see in the following studies, the disciplined attempt of theologians to achieve a coherent grasp of these patterns of human life from a Christian viewpoint can make the reader sensitive to inconsistency and strains within the literary text. It can help him to identify at what point the text (whether in character, plot or world-view) falters in promoting a suspension of disbelief in the reality it depicts. This does not, of course, simply verify or legitimate the Christian understanding of the world. Rather, the reader is employing the skills of a literary critic in a way consistent with his theological view of a general revelation of God in human art, without subordinating the one to the other.

FINDING THE DIALOGUE WITHIN RELIGIOUS WRITING

The theologian's familiarity with Christian images and their development in particular cultures should also enable him to discern the kind of dialogue that might be going on between religious tradition and creativity *within* certain texts. As I have been suggesting, the reader may bring such a dialogue *to* any text, but some writers are themselves engaging in it already. Here the theologian ought to be able to distinguish between a dialogue that has a general 'religious' character, and one that has the characteristics of a particular 'religion', in this case the Christian faith. The latter style of writing holds new images and stories consciously *in tension* not only with traditional symbols, but with the concepts of belief that have been formed to interpret or 'delimit' them. In reading we can sense the stretching of mind and feeling, the tautness and even the stress which comes from holding together the movement *from* mystery and the movement *to* mystery. There is a kind of literature in which the writer feels a demand laid upon him by values and truths which have been preserved and expressed by a community of faith through the ages, and which have come alive for him in the present. Some particular experience of revelation in the past, whether to Abraham, Moses or Christ, has gone on being remembered, re-experienced and reinterpreted within the community which resulted from it, and the writer places himself within that succession and that debt.

What we may call more generally 'religious' writing may use Christian symbols and even come into dialogue with Christian doctrines, in the service of expressing a reality which in some way transcends what can be empirically verified by sense and rationality. But it does not manifest the tension that comes from allegiance to a particular way of delimiting the images. There is, of course, a shifting boundary between these two types of religious writing, but in the series of studies which occupy the second half of this book, we may tentatively classify Lawrence, Murdoch and Golding as 'religious' novelists while Blake and Hopkins may be called not only religious but 'Christian' poets.

If we are using the latter sense of the word 'religious' then we must surely agree with Helen Gardner that 'the peculiar interest and the peculiar beauty of religious poetry lies precisely in the fact that the poet who writes as a religious man does write in fetters'.[18] At the same time, however, the writer is freely exploring and wrestling with this reality from the resources within himself. He can take an image or story and playfully let it carry him where it will; artistic creativity has its own autonomy in expressing the artist's imagination, feeling and personality. This movement towards mystery may take the modes, as I suggested in my previous chapter, of 'correspondence' and (or) 'individual insight'. But then the writer and the reader are compelled to live within the tension generated by the received and the newly-created symbols. Helen Gardner rightly points to this dialectic when she speaks of 'an interaction of aesthetic and religious ideals'.[19] Coleridge had earlier defined the polarity as being between 'religious adherence to the past' and 'the mighty instincts of . . . free agency'.[20]

Coleridge himself presents us with many illustrations of this kind of tension and dialogue from within Christian belief. His poem 'The Rime of the Ancient Mariner' reflects the Christian story of the Fall (a theme to which I want to devote much of the next chapter), and ends with an explicit appeal to the grace of God to which the guilty conscience can surrender itself in relief:

> He prayeth best, who loveth best
> All things both great and small;
> For the dear God who loveth us,
> He made and loveth all . . .

But the symbols with which the poem proceeds appear to have a life of their own, and cannot be simply translated as representing various aspects of Christian doctrine. Why should the dreadful sin of the mariner be depicted as the shooting of an albatross? Why should the experience of guilt be described as falling into the power of the nightmare 'life in death', who 'thicks men's blood with cold', sailing by on a skeleton ship? Who is the 'Polar Spirit' who 'loved the bird that loved the man/Who shot him with his bow', and who demands vengeance? Why should the experience of God's grace be described as the dancing of shining watersnakes upon the surface of the sea?

These symbols are not allegories of a simple pre-existing meaning. In exploring the human psychology of guilt, the poet is allowing his imagination to reach out towards a mystery with the use of symbols, and these interact in an unpredictable way with the basic doctrinal idea of the voyage of a fallen soul away from the grace of God and back again. We notice also (returning to a theme of the previous chapter) that there is a story within a story; the wedding guest is halted by the glittering eye of the mariner and compelled to listen to the story. He asks, 'Now wherefore stopp'st thou me?', but that of course is the question of every reader as well. The story is not just the story of the mariner; we are fascinated by it because it is our story, because we can recognise in it our predicament and the hint of grace that can meet it.

In this ballad Coleridge allows explicit reference to Christian beliefs (prayer, penance, the cross of Christ and the love of God) to interact with his own use of symbolism. At the same time, however, he is using what C.S. Lewis has called 'the oblique approach',[21] leaving the reader to infer the connection with Christian story and symbol for himself, rather than thrusting it at him. One vehicle for the oblique method is to use other mythologies than the Christian story, so that we suddenly see new dimensions in each through the other. In his poem Coleridge draws upon half-remembered stories of ghost-ships and mutinies at sea to suggest the picture of a mutineer against God and the ghostly experience of guilt, 'alone on a wide, wide sea'. Even more indirect is a poem by T.S. Eliot which also takes up the image of the sea for the spiritual quest, and which again draws upon another mythology than the Christian one to express Christian truths. Eliot's poem 'Marina'[22] draws upon the Shakespearian mythology of the play *Pericles*. In 35 lines the only explicitly religious word is 'grace', and this is used equivocally; Eliot summons up images of our mortality which

Are become unsubstantial, reduced by a wind,
A breath of pine, and the woodsong fog
By this grace dissolved in place.

In Shakespeare's play, Pericles loses his wife in a storm at sea in the very act of giving birth to their daughter, Marina. Sixteen years later he is tricked into believing that Marina too has died. In grief he sails off into a storm, but is driven by the wind to the very country where she is, so that he gains landfall and his daughter at the same time: 'Thou that wast born at sea, buried at Tharsus/And found at sea again.' Thus, as Eliot reuses the myth, death is overcome by a voyage through death into life, the battered ship being our own bodies.

Bowsprit cracked with ice and paint cracked with heat.
I made this, I have forgotten
and remember.
The rigging weak and the canvas rotten
Between one June and another September . . .

In his poem Eliot evokes a landfall in a newly-discovered land which is to be reached through death; yet this land is strangely familiar, to be greeted like a loved and long-lost face. The lost 'daughter' and the new country blend together, suggesting a new kind of life which is supremely personal, and which we have already greeted in many experiences without really recognising what it is.

What seas what shores what granite islands towards my timbers
And woodthrush calling through the fog
My daughter.

The traditional Christian image of a heavenly or spiritual country as the goal of life is brought into interaction with an image which is exploratory and tentative – the finding of a daughter. The poem therefore evokes the experience of revelation, which is always encounter with Personal Reality. It is also a paradigm of the way that the openness of an image demands the reader be drawn into the text; but then, as I have already suggested, encounter with a text through imagination is not unrelated to revelation.

Eliot can also in his poetry enter into dialogue with more conceptual forms of belief; in *Four Quartets* we find such statements as 'prayer is more/ Than an order of words' and 'Sin is Behovely, but /All shall be well' (a quotation from Julian of Norwich) and declarations of the paradoxical belief that life comes through death ('to be restored, our sickness must grow worse').[23] A poet is free to make his dialogue *both* with developed concepts of Christian belief, *and* with Christian story and symbol in the raw state where its expansive echoes are as yet unlimited by concept (as in 'Marina').

The theologian too is always dealing, as we have seen, with the interaction of primary forms of faith (metaphor, symbol, story) and systematic statement. Truly, the doctrinal theologian is more bound by tradition, and is working towards formulating some certainties of belief in the way that a poet or novelist is not. However, this is not certainty in the scientific sense; a set of religious concepts will convince if they have an inner consistency, a coherence with the external world and general human experience as they are perceived to be by the present culture, and (as John Coulson insists, following Coleridge and Newman) if they are credible to the imagination.[24] The judgements a theologian makes are therefore bound to be influenced by being drawn into a text where dialogue is already going on.

HOLY SCRIPTURE AND THE DIALOGUE

The Christian scriptures of Old and New Testament hold a peculiar place within the dialogue I have been describing. On the one hand they lie at the foundation of the doctrinal tradition with which the Christian writer or critic comes into dialogue. But on the other hand they provide a wide range of *examples* of the dialogue, since the biblical writers are themselves in creative tension with the religious traditions of the communities to which they belong.

Some writings might be placed towards the 'doctrinal' end of the spectrum, insofar as they show a considerable continuity with the text or oral tradition they have received and which they are now applying to their own situation. The theological school which produced the books of Chronicles, for example, has certainly adapted and modified the earlier books of Kings, but has felt an obligation to retain as much as possible of its source material. In contrast, other writings are more ready to come into conflict with earlier tradition, or to modify it in ways that appear shocking at first; in their creative dialogue with the story they have received, they look more like imaginative literature. Hosea, for example, is speaking to people who relied upon the great story of the Exodus from Egypt as a guarantee of God's favour to his people; to shake their confidence he has to turn the story upside down, warning that Israel must retrace her footsteps back into a new Egypt:

> When Israel was a boy I loved him;
> I called my son out of Egypt;
> But the more I called, the more they went from me . . .
> Back they shall go to Egypt,
> the Assyrian shall be their King.
>
> (Hosea 11:1–5, NEB)

A century later Jeremiah is speaking to people who rely upon another great story for their security, God's choice of Jerusalem for his dwelling-place:

> You keep saying, 'This place is the Temple of the Lord, the Temple of the Lord, the Temple of the Lord!' This catchword of yours is a lie; put no trust in it. Mend your ways and your doings . . . (Jer. 7:4–5, NEB)

In this relationship to tradition they display a double aspect of both openness and closure. The literary forms of story, poem and wise saying are always opening meaning up by resisting reduction to any final pattern; they reflect the uncertainty of life and keep the future open. At the same time, the biblical writings show a drive towards the making of a unified story and a single meaning; they announce fulfilment and the finding of purpose. Here Gabriel Josipovici distinguishes between the approaches of Old and New Testament, which he finds characterised respectively by openness and closure; he maintains that while the Old Testament writers tell stories and urge us to remember, the New Testament insists that we should understand (with the honourable exception of Mark, and with Paul as the worst offender). History is meaningful for both Old and New Testament, but 'the difference is that the NT claims to know what that meaning is, whereas for the most part the Hebrew Bible merely claims that there is a meaning'.[25]

Of course, once it is claimed that all that is written is fulfilled in one person, as Jesus is portrayed as saying to the disciples on the road to Emmaus (Luke 24:25–7), then there is a centralising of meaning, and everything becomes part of a single story. However, both openness and closure of meaning are surely characteristic of *both* Testaments, and though there is a shift of emphasis in the New Testament with an identifying of Jesus with the divine Wisdom,[26] the whole range of biblical literature supports the conclusion by an Old Testament scholar that 'God fulfills his promise in unexpected ways.'[27] A promise, as we have already seen, places limits on meaning;[28] but unlike the crystal-ball gazing of prediction, there is still an open gap between promise and fulfilment which does not fix the future. The prophets claim to have stood in the divine council and to have heard the Word of the Lord, but they express their oracles in metaphor which has an open-ended and ambiguous quality about it. As the New Testament scholar George Caird shows, biblical writers use, for example, end-of-the-world language to refer to events which are decisive turns of event within history.[29] When Jeremiah speaks of the earth as mourning, the hills moving to and fro, and the darkening of the sun and moon, he is foretelling the invasion of a foreign army (Jer. 4:24–8). But this very language prevents any exact prediction of events.

Similarly, the prophets reuse old oracles of former prophets and find new meaning within them for their own time. For example, Hosea's promise to the Northern Kingdom that their coming captivity would be ended by Yahweh's enticing of them into a new honeymoon period in the wilderness (Hosea 2:14–23) was not fulfilled, since Assyria destroyed their national identity; the prophets in the South who took over the oracles of Hosea after the wreck of the Northern Kingdom therefore applied the promise (and the warnings) to their own Kingdom of Judah (see Hosea 11:12). Then in Judah's own later exile in Babylon, the prophet 'Isaiah' is coping with the ancient prophetic promise about the unfailing continuity of the Royal House of David, in a situation where it seems highly unlikely that there will ever again be a Davidic King; he interprets the promise of an 'everlasting covenant, my steadfast sure love for David' as now being democratically extended to the whole people, who are themselves to be the new David (Isa. 55:3–5).

Even when a past promise *has* been fulfilled (or closed), often in a surprising and unexpected way, this does not mean it is dead; the fulfilment is itself a promise, pointing forward to new possibilities. Jeremiah was believed to have promised that the Exile would only last for seventy years; the later apocalyptic writer of Daniel, disappointed at the low state of his nation after it did indeed return to its homeland, interprets this as seventy weeks of years (or 490 years) and so promises an imminent *real* ending to exile in his time, with an entrance upon new national glories (Daniel 9:1–2, 24–7). It is in line with this reuse of fulfilled oracle that Matthew adopts the ancient promise that 'a young woman shall conceive and bear a son' (Isa. 7:14); Isaiah of Jerusalem was expecting such a period of peace and prosperity in the immediate future that people would call the new royal child 'God is with us', and Matthew finds unexhausted fulfilment in a child of his own time (Matt. 1:23).

The narratives of the history writing show the same oscillation between the tracing of purpose and an openness of meaning. Kierkegaard, for instance, finds the ambiguities of the story of Abraham's abortive sacrifice of Isaac to be so dense that he retells it in four different versions: 'No one was so great as Abraham and who is capable of understanding him?'[30] Yet the priestly writer is also making a definite doctrinal point; God not only does not require human sacrifice, but has established the whole system of animal sacrifice to cleanse away the sin that the nation is powerless to deal with itself (Genesis 22:12–14). In fact, the narrators of stories in the Old Testament often claim an omniscience about the inner motives and intentions not only of the human characters but also of their divine Creator. In the story of Joseph, sold as a slave into Egypt and exalted to be Pharaoh's Vizier, the narrator can pass the judgement of God upon human action as Joseph says to his guilty brothers, 'You meant evil against me; but God meant it for good.' (Gen.50:20) As Robert Alter points out, in his study of Old Testament story-telling,

> the biblical narrator, quite unlike the prophet, divests himself of a personal history and the marks of individual identity in order to assume for the scope of his narrative a godlike comprehensiveness of knowledge that can encompass even God himself.[31]

However, while the story-tellers may assume an omniscient view of the human stage, they share this knowledge with their readers in a highly reticent way, alluding to meanings and motives rather than stating them directly. In the story of Joseph, for example, we do not know for a while how he is reacting to the presence of his brothers, who have come as suppliants to an Egyptian Lord they do not recognise (Genesis 42). Is the trick he plays upon them to be a kind of revenge or a way of stimulating their repentance? Until he weeps, we do not know; perhaps we *never* know the whole truth, for the style of the narrator hints at 'the density and the multiplicity of any person's motives and emotions' (Alter).[32] How much less can we, the audience, plumb the depths of the divine Actor's purpose?

There is, then, a dialogue between openness and closure in a range of Old Testament literature, and the same dialogue is evident in the New Testament. Meaning has certainly been centralised in Christ, yet we are being drawn into a real life with all the indeterminacy this involves (as Josipovici himself admits, at least with regard to Mark's account). This goes a long way to justifying David Jasper's characterising of the New Testament as a 'confused, baggy monster of a novel'.[33] The ultimate meaning is in a person, and so this closure at the same time is always an opening. Jesus is certainly the final agent of the Kingdom; but the rule of his Father can only be evoked with a stream of images – buried treasure, lost coins, mustard seed, explosive yeast, a dinner party, a dragnet bursting with fish. We respond to a succession of metaphors which, as Coulson puts it, 'never settle into a mere finite definition'.[34]

The preferred title for Jesus in the Synoptic Gospels is 'Son of Man', possibly a choice stemming from Jesus himself; so we are presented with a deliberately enigmatic self-description, hovering between such different meanings as 'Everyman' and the heavenly champion who wins God's victory (Daniel 7:13–14). While the title does foreclose meaning in claiming a central place for Jesus in the coming of the Kingdom, it is open enough to require the hearer to make his own decisions; in a similar way the hearer is forced back upon himself by the silence of Jesus on trial, when his judges demand that he identify himself.[35] This silence persists even in the Fourth Gospel (John 19:9); elsewhere this evangelist has Jesus openly proclaim his identity as the true Son of the Heavenly Father ('I am in the Father and the Father in me'),[36] and yet here too he speaks of himself in images which appeal as much to the imagination as to reason: 'I am the bread of life . . . the light of the world . . . the good shepherd . . . the true vine'.[37] At the same time this 'I am' formula hints at the self-proclamation of God in the promise oracles of Isaiah of Babylon ('I am God, and also henceforth I am He'),[38] which themselves reuse and reinterpret the ancient revelation of the divine name as the elusive 'I am who I am' (Exodus 3:14). As the one through whom God is revealing himself, Jesus is thus presented as fulfilling all expectations, but in a way that leaves an openness for understanding.

The story of the death and resurrection of Jesus certainly does claim to sum up the whole previous history of God's covenant relationship with his people. Here is the final tragedy of human God-forsakenness, and the ultimate creating of a new situation that overcomes it. The ancient prophetic promise that God would restore his people's life 'in three days' (i.e. a short period; Hosea 6:2) is now seen as foreshadowing the period between Good Friday and Easter Sunday. Yet fulfilment does not evacuate the promise. Instead of a 'fairy-tale pattern'[39] in which the resurrection simply cancels out the cross, the continuing contradiction between cross and resurrection generates a promise which opens out a real future. For the New Testament writers understand the risen Jesus as still having a future in which new things will happen; as the Apostle Paul envisages it, he will hand over the Kingdom to the Father, and what his own resurrection promises will be fulfilled in the resurrection of all humanity and the renewal of the cosmos.[40] Jürgen Moltmann aptly concludes that 'what happened between the cross and the Easter appearances . . . points beyond itself, and even beyond Jesus, to the coming revelation of the glory of God'. Thus the titles which express the enigmatic identity of the risen Christ 'are not hard and fast titles which define who he is and was, but open and flexible titles, so to speak, which announce in terms of promise what he will be'.[41]

The story of Jesus promises an eschaton which, as a real future, must have the characteristics of unexpectedness and surprise. Thus, as Wolfhart Pannenberg rightly insists, this new creation and its prolepsis in the resurrection event can only be expressed in metaphor.[42] However, these open metaphors and flexible titles are dynamic in effect, 'stirring'[43] us to anticipate the coming kingdom through endurance of suffering and works of liberation in the present. Promise also prompts us to anticipate fulfilment through telling a unified story, and by making concepts which provisionally delimit its meaning.

The theme of promise and fulfilment in Old and New Testament thus both closes and opens meaning at the same time. The interpreter places boundaries around meaning which has been left open in previous generations, and yet this very act opens new possibilities for his successors. It is within this ongoing process that scripture lays an obligation upon any writer who lives within the community of faith, although the theologian will be unifying and systematising in a way that the poet will not. The claim made by the text is not that it cannot be fallible, but that it cannot be ignored. As I have already proposed, the Bible with its various literary forms (including prophetic oracle, history, hymn, wise saying, and law code) is witness and response to revelation. It is not revelation itself, which is nothing less than the self-unveiling of the personal God. All literature, I have suggested, is some kind of response to revelation, but for Christian believers the Bible has the authority of being first-order witness (but not, of course, necessarily eye-witness) to the event of Jesus Christ, whom faith recognises as the centre of divine revelation and fulfilment of promise.

Scripture, then, demands to be always taken into account in the making of doctrine through the ages, and also provides an essential storehouse of images and stories for the creative writer who stands within the Christian tradition. Although the living God is free (as Karl Barth insists)[44] to choose whether to unveil himself or to remain hidden, scripture may be expected to be a place of encounter with the self-revealing God.

As Christian doctrine enters into dialogue with scripture it will, as we have seen, tend to delimit meaning. The emphasis will swing towards closure, and yet since it can only anticipate final meaning it retains an openness. The Creed of Nicaea–Constantinople (AD 381), for example, defines Christ as *homoousion* (of one being) with God the Father. This abstract concept forecloses the experimental language of the New Testament, which only quests towards the idea that the earthly sonship of Jesus has something to do with the *being* of God by naming him as 'Wisdom' and 'Word'. Yet the idea of *homoousion* needs the further doctrine of the eternal generation of the Son from the Father, and though the early theologians denied that this generation was merely a metaphor for being created, it clearly remains a metaphor with some open meaning; unlike human generation, for instance, it involves the father in not only begetting but also birthing (a mother image), so that Hilary can speak of the Son as coming forth 'from the womb' of the Father.[45] Any attempt to talk about God and his self-unveiling will thus stretch human words, making them work in odd ways. God cannot be the conclusion of a logical proof, or be described literally.

The gap between promise and fulfilment has a further implication; it leaves room not only for the creative freedom of God, such as Eco's monk-detective proposed,[46] but also for the free response of human beings. One theological way of taking this freedom seriously is to affirm that God has chosen to limit his omnipotence and omniscience, passing over to his creatures a freedom to contribute to his project of creation.[47] He has, we may say, a purpose but not a blueprint for the future. While George MacDonald suggestively described the 'image' of God in human beings as 'imagination', he unfortunately restricted its scope to discovering what God had already created.[48] That God fulfils his promise in unexpected ways leaves room for true originality in human as well as divine imagination; this, as I have already suggested, takes the form of incarnation into the lives of others. So even the fulfilment of divine purpose in the incarnate Christ has the character of promise, of beginning as well as end.

3

The Shape of the Story

If we are to set the Christian story in a dialogue with other stories, we need to be able to sketch its outline. The central moment of the 'plot' is incarnation, when the continual immersion of God into the pain and joy of his world comes to its deepest point in the estrangement of the cross of Jesus and the victory of his resurrection. God, the great creative artist, freely submits to entry into the 'sting of otherness' without which 'nothing works or can work', as Doris Lessing has her poets say about the experience of their craft.[1] As a journey of identification with the human situation, drawing together the scattered and broken pieces of life, incarnation is a movement of both revelation and divine imagination.

But how shall we sum up the *wider* plot? As we have seen, the Christian gospel claims to interpret the whole of reality from the key of this event. The New Testament presents Jesus as the fulfilment of the Old Testament; his life and death impose a coherent pattern upon its many images and stories. Later, a cycle of medieval mystery plays, embracing the history of the world from the fall of the angels to the last judgement, was staged on the day of *Corpus Christi*. As one scholar suggests, this vast canvas supplied the context for the enfleshment of Christ; to play the whole drama of human life was 'to *celebrate* the Corpus Christi sacrament, to explain its necessity and power'.[2] But how then shall we describe the shape of the whole? By what set of concepts can we reduce the chaos of human life to an order in which the story of Christ is central? If we are to have beliefs (doctrine) as well as faith, we must necessarily delimit the sprawling mass of experience.

A U-SHAPED CURVE?

Many religious people carry around a short outline of the Christian story, which we may describe as Paradise, Paradise Lost and Paradise Regained. A brief form of it might run like this: 'Once upon a time there was a man called Adam who was perfect and blessed in every way. Then he fell away from God through disobedience and the whole human race fell into calamity with him. The Son of God came down into the disturbed human situation, to restore humankind to its original state of perfection.' This shape of the story seems to be established by the Bible, which begins in Genesis with the Garden of Eden containing the Tree of Life (Gen. 3:24) and ends in the book of Revelation with a Heavenly City, at whose centre is the Tree of Life whose leaves are for the healing of the nations. (Rev. 22:2) We seem to move from the loss of the Tree of Paradise to a regaining of the Tree of Heaven, by way of the Tree of Golgotha, prefigured by the 'rod out of the stem of Jesse' (Isa.11:1). This is the kind of shape to which Donne appeals in his 'Hymne to God my God, in my sicknesse':

> We thinke that Paradise and Calvarie,
>   Christs Crosse, and Adams tree, stood in one place;
> Looke Lord, and finde both Adams met in me;
>   As the first Adams sweat surrounds my face,
>   May the last Adams blood my soule embrace.[3]

Expressed as a diagram, the story would be what Northrop Frye calls a 'U-shaped curve': from perfection down to alienation and back up to perfection again, the final glory restoring the lost glory. In his book on the Bible and literature, *The Great Code*, Frye identifies this curve as the basic narrative line of the Bible. Influenced by structuralist criticism towards finding a 'grammar' of the text, he discovers the curve to be both the total shape and the pattern for many shorter cycles of experience on the way:

> The entire Bible, viewed as a 'divine comedy', is contained within a U-shaped story of this sort, one in which man, as explained, loses the tree and water of life at the beginning of Genesis and gets them back at the end of Revelation. In between, the story of Israel is told as a series of declines into the power of heathen kingdoms . . . each followed by a rise into a brief moment of relative independence.[4]

In his recent book, *Towards a Christian Poetics*, Michael Edwards discerns the same shape of story, referring to a 'ternary' pattern which proceeds 'from the Garden of Eden, through a fallen earth . . . to the higher Garden of Paradise'.[5] So he suggests, as a Christian theory of poetics, that the search for a story in creative literature is actually a search for the lost world of Eden:' . . . story is born, as another world to be reached for out of this fallen one'. Stories, Edwards suggests, lament and counter the fall, an argument based upon what he believes to be the self-evident fact that 'we cannot imagine stories in Eden'. In a perfect existence, communication (he argues) would be identical with reality, and so there would be no need for stories in which an event was created and a form imagined: 'the need for story comes with the exile from Eden'.[6] As it is, imaginative story leaps beyond our real world, which itself offers only the dull story, 'There was a fall from Eden'.

As we shall see in the next chapter, this view of the Christian story results in a particular view of comedy and tragedy. But here we must immediately challenge the basic assumption that this is the *only* possible form of the Christian story. Indeed, Josipovici points out that although earlier ages read the Bible as a romance beginning and ending in a garden, and although we find the romance 'full-blown in Spenser and Milton', nevertheless 'even as Spenser and Milton were writing, the Bible was ceasing to be seen in this way'.[7] In fact, the U-shaped story is a conceptual construct imposed upon Scripture, a useful teaching tool in an age when lessons were contained in stained glass or the mystery plays, but which ceased to grip the imagination once it was perceived that the Bible was a collection of different documents, and that it was only a matter of traditional arrangement that the book as we have it begins with the Genesis story of the human fall and ends with the heavenly City of the book of Revelation.

A fall from primal perfection is basic to the U-shaped sequence, but in this regard as in others (as 'deconstructive' critics have usefully insisted),[8] the Old Testament 'refuses pattern'. When we read the Old Testament as a whole, we notice in the first place that there is a startling failure to refer back to the story of a fall in Eden when biblical writers are reflecting upon the human predicament as they know it in their experience. There is not a single direct reference in the Hebrew scriptures to the story of Adam and Eve outside Genesis 3.[9] Generation after generation of prophets and priests are painfully aware of disruption in human life, and often profess themselves puzzled by the perverse behaviour of God's people. Why should a people upon whom God has lavished such care turn against him? 'Sons I have brought up/ But they have rebelled against me', says God in perplexity through Isaiah of Jerusalem (Isa.1:2). But the explanation is never given that it was something to do with the crime of one man in the past, Adam. Indeed, in the development of post-Old Testament Jewish thought about the origins of sin, it seems that the first story to be fixed upon as an explanation, perhaps in the early second century BC, was the unholy union of angels and women narrated in Genesis 6. It was not until a century later that the Adam narrative of Genesis 3 began to supplant the angel story as the official 'fall' narrative.[10]

The fall story of Genesis 6 also shows that the Old Testament knows no neat sequence of an angelic fall as the first downward stroke *preceding* the fall of Adam and helping to explain it, a myth developed in later Judaism (partly under the influence of Zoroastrian dualism). Indeed, we find traces in the Old Testament of a progressive and continuous fall of the angels *during the course* of human history. It seems that in an attempt to explain the existence of the gods of other nations, the belief emerged that Yahweh had placed the nations under the rule of members of his heavenly court, or the 'sons of God' (Deut. 32:8–9); however, these guardian angels had become corrupted through worship offered to them, and had ceased to act justly (Psalm 82:2). It is these that the Apostle Paul seems to have in mind when he speaks of rebellious 'principalities and powers'.[11] It ought hardly to be necessary to add that the text of Genesis 3 does not identify the snake with the 'Satan', that this particular member of the heavenly court does not appear until right at the end of the Old Testament period, and that when he does he is still exercising the legitimate role of God's public prosecutor, if in a sinister and over-zealous way.[12]

Is it then the New Testament which has rough-hewn these Old Testament loose ends into the shape familiar to the reader of Milton? Josipovici believes this to be so, and identifies the pattern of fall and rise as another case of the New Testament's saying 'understand' where the Old Testament simply says 'remember'.[13] Certainly, New Testament writers present the story of Christ as unifying all stories of relationship between God and humankind, and so portray him as the New Adam. Despite this, they do not present a pattern which fixes meaning rigidly into a sequence of past fall and present recovery. Although the Adam–Christ typology is widely present, there is actually only one direct reference to the ancient *sin* of Adam (Romans 5:12–21).[14] Two more texts (one Pauline and the other from Pauline circles) give a passing mention to a variant Rabbinic tradition that Eve was sexually seduced by the serpent (2 Cor. 11:2–3, 1 Tim. 2:14).[15]

Rather then, various New Testament writers depict Christ as the New Adam in order to incorporate his story into the wider story of human history contained in the Old Testament, and to draw us as readers into his life. Mark's story of the temptation of Christ in the wilderness among the wild beasts may be contrasting him with Adam, who named the beasts and yet failed under temptation.[16] But this narrative requires us to become involved because we feel Jesus to be in a real struggle, presented with alternative methods by which he might conduct his ministry of bringing in the Kingdom. Again, Jesus in Gethsemane passes the test in a garden where Adam failed, but his plea that the Kingdom might come some other way than through drinking the cup of suffering, and his agonised silence, witnesses to the reality of the struggle and the open-endedness of the conflict. As Jasper remarks about other gospel narratives, Jesus is not a stock hero from a fairy-tale, but is always 'slipping out of focus' so we are made to feel a 'perpetual sense of reaching out to a universe of discourse which is here only hinted at'.[17]

It is the Apostle Paul whom Josipovici singles out as the real culprit in foreclosing meaning with his use of the fall story, projecting (as he believes) upon history the downswing and upswing of his own spiritual rebellion and sudden conversion experience. But even in Romans 5:12–21, Paul's interest is less in a plan of history (and not at all in any scheme of inherited guilt such as Augustine read into the passage), than in the possibility here and now of leaving the old humanity whose representative is Adam, and being involved in a new humanity whose head is Christ. W.D. Davies aptly comments that 'For Paul, the sin of Adam is the sin of everyman.'[18] A new solidarity is being offered in place of the old. The stress is upon participation, which we have seen to be a characteristic of imagination; so this passage leads into a description of sharing in the death and resurrection of Christ through the rite of baptism.

The passage certainly shows that Paul believed in a historical Adam whose sin marked the beginning of a long entailment of human sinning. But he does not simply bind the causation of our own sin here and now to Adam's act as does Augustine. His account contains at least two statements which burst open any view of original sin as a tight cause–effect linking. First, he remarks that although sin came into the world through one man, death 'spread to all men *inasmuch as* (*eph ho*) all men sinned'. Thus he insists, paradoxically, upon our own responsibility for a fallenness in which we are entangled. Augustine reduced this paradox by reading in his Latin text '*in whom* (*in quo*, reflecting a corrupt Greek text *en ho*), i.e. in Adam, all men sinned'. Second, Paul insists that the free gift of grace in Christ is 'not like the trespass'. He can say 'as in Adam, so in Christ' but he immediately adds 'not as'. Like all metaphors, the comparison with Adam 'is and is not'. As Ernst Käsemann comments, primal-time and end-time are not 'stages in history', but 'confront each other' in a sharp antithesis.[19]

Now, I am not denying the growing popularity of a one-point fall and a U-shaped story of human history in Jewish literature from the first century BC onward, nor the lengthy development of it in later Rabbinic writings and Christian theologians such as Augustine. Our main concern is with the form that the Christian story should take for us now, which will enable us to hold 'beliefs' which (though limiting the possibilities of meaning) are consistent with an imaginative faith. Here it matters that a reading of scripture also supports another dialectical shape, one which was overlooked in past ages of Christian tradition but which actually has a firmer place in the Bible as a whole.

THE LINE OF TENSION

The present literary form of the first two chapters of Genesis portrays a dialectic in human existence. The account of creation in Genesis 2:4–25, which scholars generally reckon to be the older, presents man as a creature made from the dust of the earth (2:7). The stress in the account of chapter 1:1–2:3, probably coming from later Priestly theology, is of man and woman made in the image of God (1:27). So there is a dialectical contrast in human life: human beings are both dust of the earth and image of God, both limited by their environment and free over against it. The editor who wove the two stories of creation together obviously thought that both dimensions were important, and that they made up the unique tension in which human beings live. We are both free and limited; we can reach out beyond ourselves and our world, and yet we are finite. Like God we have a freedom; we are not bound by our world in the way that animals are. If a man is born in the forest he is not obliged to be a woodcutter, trapped there like a forest animal in its natural habitat; he can become something else – a nuclear physicist, perhaps, examining the very molecular structure of wood. He can also reach beyond himself in time, travelling into the past in memory and into the future in hope. He is, as the theologian Wolfhart Pannenberg expresses it, 'open' to the world and to the future.[20] We have already in past chapters reflected upon the human ability for self-transcendence through the imagination. Yet like the animals we are limited by the world around us, conditioned by the 'hidden persuaders' of which psychology and sociology make us aware. We are influenced and shaped by our genes, by our inner complexes, by the outer circumstances of our society, and in the end we are bounded by death.

Modern Christian theologians have been greatly impressed by this tension in which human beings live. Reinhold Niebuhr speaks of the tension as being between freedom and finiteness, and in a similar way Paul Tillich refers to the dialectic between freedom and destiny, John Macquarrie finds a polarity between possibility and facticity and Pannenberg describes a tension between central ego and environmental involvement.[21] They all point out that the result of this tension is *anxiety*; if we were completely free like God, or completely conditioned like the animals, we would not be anxious. But because we are caught between freedom and limits we become anxious, and we seek to resolve this anxiety. There are two resolutions of this dialectic; the authentic way of trust in God who is making our personalities through this process, and the inauthentic way of finding our own securities in life. The inauthentic way can be called sin, or a failure to trust.

Humankind is fallen because as a matter of fact it fails to take the way of trust. In this way of thinking, while creation and fall 'coincide', the fall is not therefore a structural necessity of creation. But the 'original fact' is that all human beings do in practice fall into estrangement, a riddle that we shall have to discuss more fully. The tensions are so acute that we are tempted to take the easy way out, of making our own concerns final, of finding our security in something less than God. So we make 'idols', out of our careers or our possessions or our political ideologies, making (as Tillich puts it) our 'ultimate concern' of what is less than ultimate. Another characteristic of this predicament is what Macquarrie aptly calls 'an existential imbalance'.[22] In our anxiety and quest for security we tip over to one side or other of the two poles of our existence; we either ignore our limits and posture as gods, or we give away our freedom and succumb like animals to the forces that squeeze and determine us.

This theological account of human beings finds the basic dialectic of fallenness not in a scheme of glory and fall from glory, but in a scheme of glory and limitations. In this second pattern, fall is the continuous *outcome* of the dialectic, but an outcome that can be replaced by a new harmony. Actually, this kind of tension can already be seen in the fall story in Genesis 3, which therefore stands as a typical expression of our human existence. In the story, Adam and Eve are free, sharing fellowship with God, and yet they also have limits: 'We may eat the fruit of any tree in the garden, except for the tree in the middle of the garden; God has forbidden us either to eat or to touch the fruit of that . . .' (Gen. 3:2). Commenting on this passage, Claus Westermann notes that the prohibition is 'a clear expression of the limit which is the necessary accompaniment of the freedom entrusted to humanity'.[23] This tension of freedom and boundary leads to anxiety, experienced as temptation, which the human pair try to relieve by asserting themselves against God rather than by trusting in his word: the temptation comes in the form: 'You will be like Gods, knowing both good and evil.' But the result is not a healing of anxiety but an increase of it, in the form of despair and fear.

Now, it is true that this reading of the story is quite a modern one, owing much to the nineteenth-century Danish thinker, Søren Kierkegaard, and his own sense of alienation.[24] But each age will discover the story for itself, and the dialectic of freedom and limitation is certainly within it. It seems, in fact, to be more clearly present than the dialectic former ages found there of an original perfection and fall from bliss. After all, the picture is very far from a primal perfection from which there is a sharp fall downwards; there is a serpent in God's creation which is capable of doubting God's word, and the human pair are in a state that may be innocent but is also immature, since they do not yet know the difference between good and evil and have not yet tasted of the tree of eternal life. As Paul Tillich comments upon this masterly narrative by the Hebrew story-teller, 'The symbol "Adam before the Fall" must be understood as the dreaming innocence of undecided potentialities. . . . it is not perfection.'[25] Commentators have often noted what seem to be untidy and discontinuous elements in the story – the tree of life plays a curiously minor part, the theme of

God's jealousy seems discordant and there are unresolved ambiguities about his warning that the human pair would die if they ate the fruit. Alerted by insights of 'deconstructive' criticism we may treat these elements as more than embarrassing appendices left over from different sources; the untidiness provokes a sense of 'sacred discontent' with myth,[26] and invites us to become involved in the tensions of the story to find a meaning that does not exist without us.

We can detect the basic dialectic of freedom and limitation throughout the Old Testament story, and (as Josipovici suggests), wherever the human desire comes up against its own limits, 'language gives out . . . and we arrive a kind of knowledge of what it is like to be a human being'.[27] Israel is constantly placed in boundary situations – the wilderness wanderings, the new environment of Canaan with its already-existing agricultural religions, the pressure of the superpowers of the time (Egypt, Syria, Assyria, Babylon, Greece, Rome). The sad history of Israel is its failure to trust God in the tension between its freedom and its limits. It continually seeks to rid itself of its anxiety by making its own security, its own false alliances in defiance of the prophetic word of God, and so meets disaster. This pattern is just as prominent as any U-shaped pattern of success, failure and restoration. After all, the Deuteronomic history of the Kings of Israel presents periods of success as only temporary respites in the process of sin in one generation leading to disaster in another, not as restorations;[28] what is constant in this cycle is Israel's lack of trust in God. The prophet Isaiah sums up the whole tragedy when he urges King Hezekiah in vain to put confidence in God rather than in an offensive alliance with one superpower (Egypt) against another (Assyria), when he is caught in the tensions between them:[29]

> In returning and rest you shall be saved;
> In quietness and trust shall be your strength.
> And you would not, but you said,
> No! We will speed upon horses. . . .
>
> (Isa. 30:15–16)

It is significant that while Northrop Frye attempts to squeeze the prophetic type of word into a U-shaped mould, he does not venture to do so with another literary type in the Bible, the wisdom sayings. This genre of literature, he admits, thinks of the human situation not as a curve but 'a kind of horizontal line formed by precedent and tradition and extended by prudence'.[30] His verdict that wisdom literature was simply a preparation for the (presumably more advanced) prophetic genre is not, however correct. The flowering of wisdom literature after the return from exile in Babylon actually seems to have been a way in which Israel coped with what was felt to be a failure of prophetic vision.[31] The wisdom perspective upon the world focuses precisely upon the tensions between human freedom and limits. On the one hand the wise man observes patterns in the natural world and patterns in human behaviour, and is fairly confident that he can steer his way through the complexities of life with the help of the guidelines he formulates and passes on, often in the form of proverbs. His maxims represent order won from the chaos of life. But on the other hand, he recognises limits to his wisdom; however much he observes, calculates and deducts, there are unknown factors which he never gets under his control. The wisdom writers have a humility in the face of hidden factors that they have not reckoned with; they realise they cannot know the whole story about the world.[32] Only God knows the whole, and so they also speak of the 'fear of the Lord as the beginning of wisdom'.

> The plans of the mind belong to man,
> but the answer of the tongue is from the Lord . . .
> A man's mind plans his way,
> But the Lord directs his steps.
>
> (Prov.16:1,9)

A man has a thought in his mind, but there is an element of unpredictability about how that will emerge as a spoken word. Or, a man may plan how he will walk, but something may trip him up. Similarly there are elements of the unknown about the achievement of happiness (16:20), victory in battle (21:31) and the choice of a right wife (19:14). The wise man has confidence in his control over experience, yet at the same time he knows his control has limits. Though different from the prophetic experience of hearing the word of God, this is no less a religious stance in life. It is a humility before God.

THE PROMISE OF NEW CREATION

The biblical promises of final salvation, whether in the Old Testament prophets or the New Testament writings, certainly offer images of a new creation to come. The last things are described in terms of the first, or in more technical theological language, 'protology is eschatology', or in the rather more memorable phrase of T.S. Eliot, 'in my end is my beginning'. The healing of the cosmos is portrayed in such paradisial images as the tree of life, the water of life, and a harmonious relationship between humankind and the animals: 'The calf and the young lion shall grow up together and a little child shall lead them'. (Isa.11:6)[33] In the New Testament message about Christ, he is portrayed as the true image of God, recalling the creation of Adam in the image of God, and is identified as the last Adam and the new man.[34] All this imagery could be understood as pointing to a U-shaped pattern, in which glory of the original creation is first lost and then recovered. Northrop Frye claims that the prophetic perspective is to see man 'in a state of alienation . . . at the bottom of a U-shaped curve. . . . It postulates an original state of relative happiness, and looks forward to an eventual restoration of this state, to, at least, a "saving remnant".'[35]

But imagery of 'beginnings' can also point to a different pattern – that of the perfecting of creation in a new beginning, in which the tensions that belong at the centre of creation will be resolved in harmony instead of the present disruption. Paradisial images for the future therefore equally support the second kind of dialectic – of freedom and limit – in human existence. Theologians are increasingly becoming discontent with the idea of a static eternity in which personalities no longer grow and develop. There is a crucial distinction to be made here between perfection, in which a personality may be perfectly related to all the reality there is, and completion. Thus we may conceive of an eschaton of perfect incompleteness, a 'continuing consummation'[36] in which there is always new reality to come, and where creative tensions no longer lead to alienation.

It is in line with this that the pictures of the new creation are no return to a lost dream-world, but claim a superiority to the old creation, and a radical transformation of it. As we have already noticed in St Paul's typology, the second Adam is better in every way than the first Adam, for while the first was made a 'living soul', the last is made a 'life-giving spirit' (1 Cor.15:45). The light of the heavenly bodies will be much stronger than at first (Isa.30:26), or there will be no need for them at all as God himself (and the Lamb of God) will be the light (Isa. 60:19f, Rev.21:23). Again, consistent with the idea of developing the first creation is the Jewish belief that some things were set aside in the creation for the last times. Thus, the light of the first day is said to be reserved for the righteous in the age to come, and the mighty creatures Leviathan and Behemoth are reserved for a celebration meal.[37] In the Letter to the Hebrews, the Sabbath rest of the seventh day of creation is seen as not yet entered upon, but reserved for the people of God in the last days (Heb.4:3–6).

If we take a U-shaped pattern of glory, loss of glory and regaining of glory as fundamental to human life, then we shall fit the work of the redeemer into the curve. Matching the human history, Jesus is portrayed as descending from glory to the bottom of the curve, and then ascending again taking humankind with him back to glory. Divine incarnation is thus understood as a rescue quest of the divine hero into the lower world of darkness, extracting fallen souls and returning them to their proper sphere of light. Now, the pattern of the descent and ascent of the divine Word is certainly present in the New Testament, especially in the Fourth Gospel,[38] but it is not quite the systematic story that later Christian (and especially Gnostic) tradition has made it. For instance, in the New Testament the virgin birth and the resurrection are never coupled as means of entrance and exit of the divine redeemer in a neat U-shaped pattern. Again, the 'rescue quest' pattern gained a great deal of its attractive colour from the later Christian addition of the descent of Christ into Hell, and the harrowing of souls from their prison there. This is not part of the primitive redemption story in the New Testament, and gained a grip on the popular imagination through its vivid literary form in the so-called Gospel of Nicodemus.[39]

Frye usefully diagnoses a basic assumption of the scheme in which a divine hero descends and ascends:

> The quest of Christ can be thought of as a cycle because, however important for man, it involves no essential change in the divine nature itself.[40]

But once we understand incarnation as a work of divine imagination it must involve a sympathetic participating in human life, and we must therefore question the Greek philosophical tradition of an impassible God. If we follow the dialectic of freedom and limitation within human existence, then we shall see the work of the redeemer as an entrance into human tensions, and 'descent' will be understood as an image for a depth of empathy which does not leave the hero unchanged. This pattern is basic to the New Testament picture of Christ, whose story is one of suffering and obedience. In the gospel story Christ is portrayed as entering into the alienation that has resulted from the human failure to trust God within the tensions. He identifies himself with his sinful nation by being immersed into baptism for repentance, he eats and drinks with the outcasts of society and is crucified between two thieves (perhaps terrorists) in utter forsakenness. In St Paul's account of the gospel, Christ comes under the horizon of 'sin, law and death'.[41] But within these tensions and this estrangement Jesus remains in trusting obedience to his father; 'in obedience he accepted even death' (Phil.2:8). Likewise, another author comments: 'Son though he was, he learned obedience through what he suffered'. (Heb.5:8) As the truly obedient son he therefore enables us to make his trust in God our own, leading us into a harmony of life in place of destruction. This is not a path which returns the divine hero to the same state from which he started.

> It was clearly fitting that God . . . should, in bringing many sons to glory, make the leader who delivers them perfect through suffering. (Heb.2:10)

THE RIDDLE OF THE FALL

Though the anxiety arising from the tensions of human existence is unavoidable, this does not mean that the fallenness which results from it is a logical necessity of creation. Such are the pressures upon human beings, stretched between their freedom and their limitations, that it is inevitable in practice that they should fall towards inauthentic life. In *fact* there can never be creation without fall. But this move away from the Good is still a 'leap', and not simply part of the structure of the world. This view is well expressed by Paul Tillich, who speaks of the fall as 'the original fact':

> Creation and fall coincide. . . . God creates the newborn child; but if created, it falls into the state of existential estrangement.

This is the point of coincidence of creation and the Fall. But it is not a logical coincidence; for the child, upon growing into maturity, affirms the state of estrangement in acts of freedom which imply responsibility and guilt. Creation is good in its essential character. . . . the leap from essence to [estranged] existence is the original fact. . . . it has the character of a leap and not of structural necessity.[42]

Tillich's compressed statement makes clear that the theologian is wanting to keep several truths in play at once. He has an underlying belief in the goodness of God as creator, and so is reluctant to say that God actually makes beings in a fallen state. Moreover, he notices that we have a sense of moral responsibility and genuine guilt which we blunt at our peril; it is part of being human to feel that we *need* not have done what we so bitterly regret. Further still, if fallenness were a necessary part of creation, there would be no hope for redemption, for the transforming of life through response to God. Indeed, the very concept of being 'fallen' implies that we can rise higher, that we are not what we *can* be. On the other hand, however, we have to be realistic in recognising that sin is a universal fact, not an occasional problem. The phenomenon that has to be explained is what we feel as an inherent tendency to decline from the good. We are aware of a constant bias towards wrongdoing, sympathising with St Paul's cry, 'The evil I do not want to do, that I do.'[43] The poet Gerard Manley Hopkins feels himself torn by the same dilemma: 'heart . . . O unteachably after evil, but uttering truth.'[44]

We have to admit that there is an irreducible element of paradox in all this, though Tillich himself prefers to use the term 'riddle'. The fall is the given Fact, but not a 'structural necessity'. Though the fall was not an event at one historical moment, he suggests that it can only be 'half-way demythologised';[45] it has to be told as a story which happened 'once upon a time', in which we ask 'and what happened next?', to make clear that the fall is *not* a necessity. Similarly, the theologian Reinhold Niebuhr states that 'sin is. . . . inevitable, but not in such a way as to fit into the category of natural necessity', and that 'sin is natural for man in the sense that it is universal, but not in the sense that it is necessary'.[46] John Macquarrie speaks of the fall of nature and humanity as 'unavoidable possibilities'[47] – the phrase itself catching the heart of the paradox.

We can, of course, labour to make this paradox reasonable, though we can never reduce it to a rationality. We might, for example, suggest with the philosopher John Hick that for human beings to be truly free and to grow as responsible persons they must be confronted with a real moral challenge.[48] Thus God has to put us into a situation where it appears easier to resolve our anxieties in some other way than trust in him. To open ourselves in trust, forsaking all the securities we rely on and breaking all false idols, needs a 'courage to be'; it is a demanding path, a truly 'narrow way'. Moreover, once human beings *have* turned away from trust in God, sin will accumulate in social life and so provide extra pressure on succeeding generations. This at least begins to explain why we are prone to slip from a situation of anxiety into one of sin. In the weakness of our finitude, constrained by our limits and facing the threat that we may cease to be, we take what seems to be the easy way out.

The pattern of a U-shaped curve, taken as a literal historical sequence, attempts to *remove* the element of riddle altogether by placing the fall at a single point in history, as a dropping away from a world of pristine perfection. This places all the weight on to human guilt and removes the paradoxical element of inevitability as far as Adam was concerned. As St Augustine proposes it, God was not at all responsible for the situation, because he placed Adam in perfect communion with himself and gave him gifts of grace to strengthen his natural weakness.[49] But the question arises as to why, if he enjoyed unhindered bliss, Adam should have wanted to fall away from God at all. Augustine can only register this as a mystery, and insists that sin is inevitable now for us, as Adam's descendants, because we simply inherit a bias towards wrong resulting from his primeval crime.[50] This, however, produces the further problem as to how the original sin is transmitted from Adam to us; Augustine suggested it was passed on through the carnal excitement accompanying the sexual act of procreation,[51] a theory which had the most unfortunate (though hardly surprising) result of leading the Church to a negative view of sexual relations.

Any reduction of the human predicament to a concept thus contains the element of riddle; the question is only where the riddle is to be most appropriately located. The idea of a fall which is 'inevitable but not necessary' delimits and systematises an experience of evil whose complexity can be better expressed in a story. But the conceptual belief is at least consistent with the story it aims to interpret. The present literary form of the first three chapters of Genesis, whatever their sources, has an inevitable flow from creation to 'fall'. As Josipovici comments, the theme of creation as 'division' (God separates light from darkness, sea from land, and so on), which is only potentially threatening in the first chapter, drives forward into Chapter 3 where the serpent introduces division which is really destructive.[52]

FREEDOM AND LIMIT IN DOCTRINE AND LITERATURE

At the beginning of this chapter we enquired what this Christian story might be which we are to place alongside the other stories that are told in literature. In the past, the U-shaped story of predicament and salvation has served us well, but it does not fit so well into the way that novelists and poets perceive the human situation today. There is no longing for a lost Paradise, a nostalgic yearning for the return of a golden age. Modern writers are certainly well aware of a massive disruption within human existence, a universal unease to which they are quite likely to attach the image of 'fallenness'. They are often aware that they are telling stories in order to evoke a world in which there is healing instead of disintegration. But there is no evidence that they are looking for a lost paradisial world in which there was, and will be, no need for stories, because everything there is perfectly complete, as Michael Edwards suggests. The new world they evoke seems to be a story-telling world, and if we move beyond the constraints of a U-shaped curve, we can see that there is indeed no reason why the Creator should not go on being eternally creative, completing his original creation in ever new ways.

In fact, the analysis that many contemporary writers make of human life is precisely of a tension between freedom and limitation, and they find the human predicament to be a failure to keep a balance between these elements. This is most obviously the case in the so-called 'existentialists' such as Jean-Paul Sartre and Albert Camus. They are impressed by the ambiguity of human life, free in so many ways and yet also conditioned. Camus, for example, appeals to the myth of Sisyphus in Hades, bounded by his everlasting task of rolling the boulder up the mountain, but each time free to scorn the gods on his way down to start all over again.[53] The conclusion to which secular existentialist writers come is that human life is simply absurd; faced by the tensions of our freedom and our limits we should simply give up the attempt to find any inherent meaning there. Human life is a great cosmic joke. It is the given fact that we live in alienation from ourselves and others, but having faced up to this realistically, we can dare to take some action to assert our freedom and dignity. There *is* no meaning, but we can ourselves *make* meaning. In Sartre's novel *Nausea*, the hero records in his diary all the random events of his day, and his state of nausea comes from his inability to find any kind of purpose or pattern in their giddy movement. All is contingency – it just happens – and there is no stability of necessary being. Because he nevertheless has a freedom he contrives to experience his life as an adventure; he seeks to live as 'the hero of a novel', imagining that some important event is awaiting him around the next corner. It never happens. His moment of illumination comes sitting under a chestnut tree in the Public Gardens, when he realises that the tree just *is*, like himself. 'The word Absurdity is now born beneath my pen. . . . how can I put that into words? Absurd: irreducible . . .'.[54] He has realised that 'adventures are in books'; life will not yield up an explanation, and so the book ends with a decisive act to *make* meaning. He decides to write a novel 'above existence' and 'hard as steel'. In the book itself he fails to do so, though we may say that Sartre himself has!

When we place the Christian story beside this, we find that Christian faith also recognises the phenomenon of 'giddiness'. It finds the same polarity between contingency (what just happens to us) and imaginative freedom. But faith has another perspective; it affirms that this tension is not all there is; life is not just absurd, for the tension points beyond itself to God. There is the gift of grace available to live harmoniously within the tensions, if we will only trust. The tensions are not a cosmic joke, but the means by which God is making free human personalities. So the Christian dialectic of freedom and finiteness can be brought into meaningful dialogue with the secular story, where it would be quite artificial to fit in a fall from the grandeur of Paradise to misery.

It is, however, not just the Continental existential tradition of 'absurdity' that recognises a polarity between freedom and limit. In succeeding chapters of this study we shall be exploring the 'line of tension' in a range of English-speaking writers from William Blake to William Golding. Here the title of the whole book is deliberately ambiguous. We shall be tracing their handling of this particular theme, and its relation to other human concerns such as love, truth and beauty; but at the same time we shall be holding a dialogue between their own imaginative freedom, and the limits which Christian theology creates as it develops concepts of doctrine. The two strands interweave, of course, and the expansiveness of the title is perhaps apt for a study in which we are much concerned with openness of meaning.

4
Comedy and Tragedy: the Shakespearian Boundary

Towards the end of Shakespeare's play *A Midsummer Night's Dream*, the amateur actors, who are possibly the most incompetent the world's stage has ever witnessed, propose to put on 'a most lamentable comedy'. Similarly, they promise 'very tragical mirth', to which the Duke responds:

> That is hot ice and wondrous strange snow.
> How shall we find the concord of this discord?[1]

But what the rude mechanicals do hilariously badly, Shakespeare himself does amazingly well. Although this scene is a satire on the tragi-comic style used by other contemporary dramatists, Shakespeare himself is always crossing the borderline between comedy and tragedy, finding 'the concord of this discord'. His tragedies contain notes of triumphant joy, and his comedies include dark strains amid the festivities. He brings clowns and kings together, and undertakes the task with which Berowne is challenged at the end of *Love's Labour's Lost*, to 'move wild laughter in the throat of death'.

In the last chapter we surveyed two possible patterns of the Christian story, a 'U-shaped curve' and a 'line of tension', and now we must observe that they result in a correspondingly different approach to the fundamental genres of comedy and tragedy. We should be able to assess the value of each pattern by seeing which one best includes the comic and tragic dimensions perceived in human destiny by Christian faith; equally, we should see which pattern provides the best critical perspective on the human arts of comedy and tragedy. I am selecting Shakespeare's work as a paradigm because of all English writers he has most profoundly brought the two modes together, continually exploring the shifting boundary between them.

Shakespeare shows us that comedy and tragedy are two views of the same universe. If all stories remind us that we, the readers and audience, are in quest of a story for our lives, he makes clear that it is not simply either comedy or tragedy. Reduced to their barest levels, a comedy has a happy ending and a tragedy has a sad one; we approve the ending of one, and regret the other, wishing it could have been otherwise. But our reaction to such drama as Shakespeare's is a mixture of feelings, focused in his phrase 'hot ice'. In this way Shakespeare anticipates the mood of modern drama, as practised by authors as various as Strindberg, Chekhov, Brecht, Beckett, Ionesco and Stoppard. Their common approach is an irony which arouses a continual shift of feelings and perspectives in the minds of the audience. Ambivalent responses towards the characters are produced by sudden swings from comedy to pathos. Characters like Shakespeare's Cleopatra, Strindberg's Miss Julie, Brecht's Azdak and Beckett's clowns alternately win sympathy and provoke detachment, or even repulsion. The plays demand a perpetual and sometimes bewildering reorientation of 'modes of attention',[2] which fits our sense of an unformed world. It seems that straight tragedy can only flourish in a society where there is a strong sense of an accepted moral structure, and so a common agreement about what makes 'a great man'; in an age like ours which has embraced the flexibility of a situation ethic, tragicomedy evokes a more recognisable world.

But then, this more complex shape of a story also reflects the Christian world-view. The Christian story is basically a 'divine comedy', as Dante entitled it; it ends well with a new creation. But there are also tragic elements within it; there is cross as well as resurrection, and in the vision of the Seer of Patmos the lamb in the midst of the throne still has the marks of slaughter upon him (Rev. 5:6). It seems that resurrection does not wipe out death, but absorbs it into life. The question then is which alternative pattern of the Christian story best illuminates the kind of blend of tragedy and comedy, laughter and tears, with which Shakespeare confronts us.

THE HEALING ART OF COMEDY

The comic spirit is one of confusion and healing. Comedy disturbs the fabric of life through magnifying its disorders, but it thereby brings a new harmony. Healing comes through a deliberate wreaking of havoc. It is as though the surface of things has to be blown wide open by a joke in order to find the truth hidden deep beneath. Why this should be so begins to find an answer when we look at one device which is omnipresent in Shakespeare's comedies, and which has the ambiguity of tragic overtones, that of pretence.

The comedies of Shakespeare revolve around what the Elizabethans called 'practising', or tricks of deception played by someone on an unsuspecting victim.[3] In particular, Shakespeare is fond of presenting what we would now call 'role-playing', or the assuming of a strange identity. In comedies such as *Twelfth Night* and *As You Like It*, the heroine herself pretends to be someone else and so causes all kinds of exquisite complications. Viola pretends to be a page-boy, and so is ideally placed for the Duke Orsino to fall (unconsciously) in love with her. Rosalind also pretends to be a young man and so gains the opportunity to hold several amusing conversations with the hapless Orlando about the painful experience of being in love. In other comedies, the main characters do not *take* a role; they have it thrust upon them by others. Mainly they are tricked into playing the part of a lover; they are enticed into assuming this identity but then, profoundly, they actually *become* the role they play. Shakespeare might achieve this by means of a magic trick; the pairs of lovers in *A Midsummer Night's Dream* are first enchanted, with the aid of some potent flower-juice, into playing the part of frantic lovers with the wrong partners, and then Demetrius is magicked into love for the right one. Or it might be a psychological trick; the violent and abusive Kate in *The Taming of the Shrew* is tricked into being a loving wife by Petruchio's always addressing her as if she were in fact 'gentle' and 'low-voiced', so that at last she becomes the part that was forced upon her. Or it might be a trick of game-playing; Orlando is persuaded by 'Ganymede' to play a charade of talking with him/her as if she were his 'very, very Rosalind' (which of course she is), so that Orlando plays at being Rosalind's lover while becoming it in truth.

We notice that in all these cases, the persons who are tricked into playing a role (Orsino, Orlando, Demetrius, Kate) become it because it was really theirs all the time. The part belonged to them; they needed to discover it, or to explore it more deeply. To take another prime example, Beatrice and Benedick of *Much Ado About Nothing* are tricked by a simple fraud; though they are sworn opponents in a 'merry war' of words, they are hoaxed into courting one another by being made to think that each is pining away with love for the other. So they respond, at first out of a sense of being flattered, but then with a growing reality of love. At the end, when they discover they have been tricked, it does not matter in the least; they have become the roles they were playing. Benedick still maintains to Beatrice that 'by this light, I take thee for pity', and Beatrice holds her position that she yields 'partly to save your life, for I was told you were in a consumption', but they refuse to be parted. (V.4.91–6) They have discovered what was true all the time about their relationship. This plot then highlights the basic pattern of comedy in Shakespeare's work. Harmony and healing can only come through confusion, of which one form is pretence. It actually needs tangles, such as those produced through role-playing, to unwind complicated human relations. For reality lies deeply beneath the surface, and not in appearances.[4] The only way to get to it is to mine deeply with an explosive charge of confusion.

Comedy then, as practised by Shakespeare, does not fit well into a U-shaped curve of story. The perspective of the U-shape assumes that the disorder into which a comic plot plunges is the loss of a previously happy world; this lost world is supposedly recovered at the end, when disorder has been defeated. But in Shakespearian comedy there is already something fundamentally disturbed, long before the beginning of the action of the play. Families have been broken by shipwreck or jealousy, and minds are broken by an unhealthy love or a suppressed love. *Much Ado about Nothing* begins with a disorder in relationships, an absorbing mockery between two people which is a kind of disease. On the other hand, *Twelfth Night* opens with the solipsistic desires of a man who is obsessed by the very notion of being in love, regardless of object: 'If music be the food of love, play on!/ Give me excess of it . . .'. If comedies are a search for the human story, then they do not reflect a past paradise which has been lost. Understood as a comedy, the Christian story of human life fits best into the shape of a line in constant tension, with voyagers who are constantly losing their balance and falling into distortions, either of self-assertive freedom or surrender to their conditioning. Comedy promises that this disorder can be healed, that a balance can be gained, opening up a new world. Comedies assure us that the end does not merely restore some lost beginning, some bygone paradise; there is something surprising and new about the healing, since it is an opening of awareness to a process that is continually developing, though as yet often unseen.

Comedy shows us that healing comes from immersion into disorder. The movement of comedy is from an initial disorder in the state of things, through further disorder caused by comic confusion, and so to a kind of new order. It is as if the world has to be turned upside-down to show that it was the wrong way up all the time. To penetrate to the truth a little mystification is needed. If we bring this pattern into dialogue with the Christian story, we recall that the drama of redemption is about God's immersing himself in Christ into the disturbance and estrangement of human life in order to bring healing. In comedy, disorder brings healing in at least two ways. In the first place, exaggerating the situation helps us to see it for what it is. Corruption is exposed by making it worse and so ultimately ridiculous. In Shakespeare's great cast of comic characters, the academics are more pedantic, the melancholics more world-weary, the lovers more blind, the governors and stewards more ambitious, the money-lenders more greedy, and so on. In the Christian story, the 'foolishness' of the cross of Christ consists in its invitation to the powers of evil to overreach themselves there. The hostile powers defeat themselves by doing their worst, and being taken captive in the very moment of apparent triumph. This insight is expressed in the little comedies which the Christian Fathers produce in their reflection upon the meaning of the cross; the Satan is caught on the fish-hook as he swallows his prey, or is snapped in the mousetrap as he reaches for the tasty morsel.[5] Though these myths have the form of a trick, they surely reflect the experience that evil exposes itself for what it is when it launches its worst attack, and being caught out in the open can now be coped with: 'You shall know the truth, and the truth will make you free' (John 8:32).

But the disorder of comedy also brings healing in another way, to which Shakespeare's comedies draw particular attention. As we have already seen, love and understanding actually *develop* through the tangles of the situation, which has been produced by a trick or a set of mistakes. The confusion within which characters are caught enables them to express their feelings in a way which is powerful and creative through being indirect rather than clear and open. The ironic way they speak actually copes with the complexity of their emotional responses and enables them to explore each other's minds. Viola, disguised as a page-boy, can speak of her love to the Duke with a depth and subtlety that communicates with him at an intuitive level, and prepares him for the moment when she is revealed as his 'fancy's queen':

VIOLA: . . . . My father had a daughter lov'd a man
As it might be, perhaps were I a woman,
I should your lordship.
ORSINO: . . . . But died thy sister of her love, my boy?
VIOLA: I am all the daughters of my father's house,
And all the brothers too: and yet I know not.
(*Twelfth Night* II.4.107–22)

As Viola confesses something she knows not, so Beatrice and Benedick do in their conversation with each other:

BENEDICK: I do love nothing in the world so well as you: is not that strange?
BEATRICE: As strange as the thing I know not. It were as possible for me to say I loved nothing so well as you, but believe me not; and yet I lie not; I confess nothing, nor I deny nothing . . .
(*Much Ado About Nothing* IV.1.267–72)

Within the framework of their misapprehension they are feeling for a truth with their intuitive senses that their conscious minds will not acknowledge; in their ambiguous use of the word 'nothing' they could either be saying that they value each other at nothing, or more than anything, and they are moving within themselves from one meaning to the other. It seems that love cannot be recognised without a bit of chaos, for love does not operate with normal sight and rational intellect. In Renaissance iconography Cupid is depicted with a blindfold, since:

Love looks not with the eyes, but with the mind
And therefore is wing'd Cupid painted blind.
(*A Midsummer Night's Dream* I.1.234–5)

Love does not rely upon the appearance of the senses, but employs a more intuitive sight. Beatrice thinks she can see clearly when she scorns love and marriage: 'I have a good eye, uncle: I can see a church by daylight.' But appearances can mask reality; comic mistakes can help to unmask it.

In what way does this healing confusion of comedy throw light on the Christian view of the human comedy? It would be absurd to draw the therapeutic conclusion that we should play tricks on each other in order to find the truth of our relationships; dramatic comedy uses this technique so that we can experience confusion vicariously, and so come to a sharper awareness of our own hidden feelings through an exaggerated situation. But it does indicate that the anxiety of our own 'line of tension' can be creative as well as a temptation to fall. Magnifying the tensions and polarities of life, however it may happen, can actually bring us to see the imbalance in which we exist more clearly. This begins to move us towards a theodicy, in which the goodness of a Creator who sets us in the midst of such pressures of finite freedom is justified. But to live in such tension involves the risk of creation, that we shall try to resolve our anxieties by false means, falling from the good into greater estrangements. This is paralleled in the dramatic comedy of Shakespeare, where the devices of pretence have a dark underscoring to them. Here we begin to cross the boundary between comedy and tragedy, for in the comedies as well as the tragedies, people are hurt even by the pretences that are meant to be genial. There is a dangerous side to 'practising', not only when undertaken by comic villains like Don John, or by tragic villains like Iago, or by half-hearted villains like Iachimo, but even when it is used for the best intentions by romantic heroes like Viola.

In *Twelfth Night* Viola works a trick upon the whole of Illyria; by putting on the clothes of a page-boy she touches with confusion every level of this already disturbed society. But she does not use her disguise to manipulate others; she carries it like a cross,[6] sensitive to the pain which it causes her and those whom she deceives: 'Disguise, I see thou art a wickedness' (II.2.26). She can only wait, in the suffering of patience, for time to untangle matters: 'It is too hard a knot for me t'untie' (II.2.40). We may have less sympathy for the predicament of Olivia who falls in love with the supposed Cesario, feeling as we do that pride and posturings at grief deserve some kind of check. But we do feel for Viola herself, and for the generous sea-captain who mistakes Viola for her twin brother Sebastian and suffers the sting of apparent ingratitude. The comic sub-plot, in which the ambitious Malvolio is fooled into believing that Olivia dotes on him (a more bitter version of the device used in *Much Ado About Nothing*) reflects the same theme: Malvolio is damaged more than is proper for a jest: 'He hath been most notoriously abus'd' (V.1.378). This play focuses on the narrow line between pretence and abuse that runs everywhere in the comedies.

As one of the so-called 'problem comedies' that swing in a grotesque manner between comedy and tragedy, *All's Well that Ends Well* typically shows up the dark side of pretence. We are uncertain about how to react to Helena who manoeuvres her reluctant husband into consummating the marriage by a bed-trick, admitting as she does the 'wicked meaning in a lawful deed' (III.7.45). But to some extent all Shakespeare's comedies are 'problem comedies'. Even in a play full of courtly games and verbal jests like *Love's Labour's Lost*, the charades result in a failure to take real love seriously, reducing it to mere 'bombast and . . . lining to the time' (V.2.773). There is a hint of pathos in the judgement that time is now too short 'To make a world-without-end bargain in' (V.2.781).[7] The comic disorders that can expose the gap between appearance and reality can also widen it dangerously, to the point where no happy ending can entirely close it. In proper tragedy, of course, the gap is deliberately played upon. Iago, for example, persuades Othello that Desdemona is not what she appears to be, quoting her ability to deceive her father for Othello's sake as evidence of her natural duplicity: 'She that so young could give out such a seeming. . . .' (*Othello* III.3.213) In another 'Problem Comedy', Troilus sums up the tragic irony of finding that the gulf between appearance and reality is unbridgeable: 'this is, and is not, Cressid' (*Troilus and Cressida* V.2.146).

Through the device of 'practising', the comedies disrupt a situation to get at the hidden truth; tragically, this may leave damage that can never be repaired. But these ambiguities belong to the 'line of tension' which the characters walk; to understand the pattern of comedy as a curve which goes down and up in simple sequence can never encompass these ambivalences. Tragic strains are set within the bounds of laughter, and this is particularly characteristic of the endings of the plays, where there is always a hint of something unreconciled. But before we take note of the patch of darkness that lingers as the comedy closes, we ought to get things in proportion; the predominant mood at the end of a comedy is that of harmony and reconciliation. Comedies typically end with a marriage, revelry, feast or a dance as the misunderstandings have been scattered. The happy ending of a comedy awakens us to the blessed end of the cosmic story for which we are searching; through laughter it opens up the promise of a better world, and protests against the fallenness of the present. For comparison, two little biblical comedies of 'an unlikely birth' also end in a joy which opens up the future, though the Old Testament story of Sarah gives an ironic twist to her laughter which is not present in the New Testament story of Elizabeth.[8]

But if we were to adopt the 'U-shaped curve' as the pattern of the Christian story, we would have to say that the endings of comedies are finally illusory; they may foreshadow the new creation, but 'they are not the real world', as Michael Edwards puts it, advocating the U-shape of the story.[9] The real world will be the restoring of the Paradise of the past, the recovery of Eden. So Edwards goes on to say that, 'if we could move beyond this world we should no longer need to laugh'. However, if the 'comic' shape of the Christian story is not the return to a past, accomplished perfection but a healing of distortions that develop along a continual line of tension, then all comic visions actually contribute to that new creation. There is no return to a beginning whose character is already formed, but a working towards an end that has something new about it, and which takes up into itself all the values which the human spirit has produced. The happy endings of these works of art are not in themselves the new world, but they will be included within it. Every happy ending, every new world made through laughter, is building a weight of glory which shall finally be revealed.

Nevertheless, as I have already indicated, Shakespearian comedies do not end in total sweetness and light. In the midst of the feast he introduces a note of doubt; a shadow falls. Nearly always, for instance, there is someone excluded from the charmed circle of the dance; there remains an outsider who cannot or will not be reconciled, a witness to the darker strains of life which cannot be tidied away. There is Malvolio, vowing, 'I'll be revenged upon the whole pack of you'. The melancholy Jacques excuses himself from returning to the gaity of the court '. . . to see no past-time I'. Shylock does not belong, despite his enforced baptism: 'I pray you give me leave to go from hence.' Don John refuses to be integrated into the carnival of Messina: 'I had rather be a canker in the hedge than a rose in his grace; let me be that I am and do not seek to alter me.' Like Caliban in *The Tempest* he remains testimony to the fact that some exclude themselves from human nurture. The dance is never complete, and its patterns are the poorer for those who are absent. But there are other shadows too. Deep emotions have been aroused, and strains shown up in relationships which threaten to break out into new trouble in the future. Such couples as Claudio and Hero, Antipholus and Adriana, Jessica and Lorenzo, will need to be wary. Don Pedro seems constitutionally unable to find his life's partner ('Get thee a wife, Prince'), and the conflict for Prospero lies all ahead in Milan, now that he has left the island where his book and staff gave him absolute control.

Above all in the comedies, the shadow of death presses in. Despite all the harmonies that art and music can give, the final boundary remains, giving urgency to passing time and bringing to nothing even 'the great globe itself,/ Yea, all which it inherit' (*The Tempest* IV.1.153). We are constantly reminded that death breaks the dance. At the end of *Love's Labour's Lost* the pageant and games are dissolved by the arrival of the messenger with news of death: 'The words of Mercury are harsh after the songs of Apollo'. Even in a farcical comedy like *The Comedy of Errors*, the ravages of time are underlined; the reuniting of a mother with her lost children seems like a new birth, but it cannot wipe out thirty-three years of birth-pains and extended labour (V.1.400). How much less can the sixteen years of married love be regained, which Leontes has lost through his jealousy; in the very moment of restoration and 'resurrection' of his wife from apparent death, Leontes is forced to remark: 'Hermione was not so much wrinkled, nothing/ So aged as this seems' (*The Winter's Tale*, V.III.28).

Now, what can these strains of darkness tell us about the Christian comedy, and what light can the Christian story throw upon this shadow at the end of comedy? If we adopt the pattern of a U-shaped curve, there seems no logic within the comedy itself for anything less than complete healing. The movement is simply upwards. We would have to say then, as Edwards does, that the tragic shadow in comedy points us once again to the truth that the new world opened up by the comedy is not real. Comedy is drawing the spectator or reader into 'a fictive world, as the place where a dynamic – of destroying and recreating, purging and transforming – can be fulfilled', but it also sends the reader away. 'It subverts itself', argues Edwards, showing that it is 'only a metaphor of religious events'.[10] Comedies, on this view, are only a pale reflection of the archetypal Divine Comedy, and they show it by self-destructing.

But if we adopt the alternative shape of the Christian story, a line of tension that can be resolved in ever-new harmonies, then there is an internal logic for the possibility of a touch of tragedy in the ending. Even the bliss of spiritual fulfilment can become an occasion for loss; even the beatific vision can include waste. The universe is on an 'adventure' which 'reaps tragic beauty', as A.N. Whitehead expresses it.[11] For if the end is not merely a static repetition of the beginning, but through the desire of God has something open about it, then some potentials that could have been actualised will not be so, and for some actualities to be realised will require the sacrifice of other potentials. If God has limited himself in giving a genuine freedom of action and choice to his creation, then the manifold possibilities of the universe can only be realised through a cooperative response of the creation. God may then, through the persuasion of his love, bring about the harmonious dance of the new creation, but the precise measures and turns in the dance will depend radically upon the rhythms of his world. That may indeed mean a sense of tragedy for God, in his knowing that the creation has missed opportunities he held out to it, though the creatures may themselves be thoroughly satisfied with the vision of God.[12]

Thus, if we place the structure of comedy alongside the Christian comedy we see a difference; in the Christian story, the tragedies of wasted time and spoiled relationships are felt not so much by the characters as by the Author. But there is still a profound continuity in the touch of darkness among the healing laughter. The shape of the Christian story alerts us to these strains in comedy, as they in turn prompt us to reflect again upon the meaning of 'consummation' in the Christian Comedy. Conversely, we find that tragedies – especially those of Shakespeare – end with a touch of triumph amid the dark. Death is presented there as the final disorder of life, the last enemy, yet it can be made to serve the promise of life, if it is approached in the right way. As we shall see, this confirms our conclusions so far, but from the opposite side of the tragi-comic boundary.

THE TRIUMPH OF TRAGEDY

Tragedies end with a waste of life and expense of spirit that we regret. We wish that things could have been otherwise, though we have also been convinced by the progress of the drama that in practice they could not. Viewed from the perspective of a 'U-shaped curve', the major pattern of tragedy is a fall from greatness to misery, and the motivations for the tragic fall are either the force of destiny or some flaw in the character of the hero, or a combination of both. The tragedy of Classical Greece highlights a sinful flaw, such as *hubris*, in an otherwise exceptional person, while medieval tragedy tended to emphasise the wheel of Fortune. According to accepted theory of tragedy, the plunging to disaster of an important person, such as a King, universalises the tragedy and helps to release the emotions of pity and fear in the audience. In particular, we may say that watching the public death of a great human personality enables us to face up to the fact of our own death, which is likely to be insignificant and accidental.

All these insights doubtless contribute to our experience of tragedy, and help to explain why we enjoy watching someone dying on a stage, but it is another matter to systematise them into a 'U-shaped curve' and then to insist that this is an exclusive theory of tragedy. It might be urged that the picture of a great man fallen upon hard times is an accurate reflection of the Christian story of Adam; it has been suggested that since Adam fell from greatness into misery, we create tragedies because they remind us of this fall.[13] From the perspective of the Divine Comedy, a tragedy is therefore an incomplete comedy, since it has taken the participant only down one side of the curve to the valley of the shadow of death at the bottom. Similarly, it might be regarded as an inverted 'U', where the hero rises to a peak of achievement before plunging into catastrophe.[14] But we find that, as a matter of fact, Shakespeare's tragedies do not neatly fit into this dialectic of glory and degradation. As we have already noted, he stands at the beginning of a modern consciousness about 'great men' which tragi-comedy reflects by evoking an ambivalent attitude towards its heroes. We only have to be alert to these ambiguities, of course, to see them present already in some form in Classical Greek and medieval tragedy, as J.L. Styan shows in his comments on Euripedes and the mystery plays.[15] Even Northrop Frye, who firmly identifies a U-shaped structure in the biblical narrative, has to admit that the biblical writers actually have a distinct lack of interest in heroic achievements of 'great men', taking an ironic view of their claims and concentrating instead on the moment of collapse.[16]

Shakespearian tragedy shows us another kind of dialectic, which can accommodate the note of tragi-comedy, both in evoking an ambivalent approach to the leading characters, and in allowing a slight affirmation of triumph even in the midst of death. Tragedy consists, not so much in a fall from greatness to disaster, as in a failure to live successfully in the tension between self and society. His tragic heroes are people who have a certain freedom over against their environment, in perceiving some truth or value which challenges custom. They have a vision of how things are which contradicts appearance and convention, and they create friction with their surroundings for a while; but they are unable to hold to the vision they glimpse, or to build anything substantial upon it. They cannot hold the balance between their freedom and their limits. Like Hamlet, they may have the uneasy feeling that they should be acting on their insight that 'the time is out of joint' (*Hamlet* I.5.189), but they never really make their own decisions to get started. Like Lear, they may not question the system at all until it is too late to do anything but learn from being reduced to absolute zero. Having required his daughters to quantify their love for him, he now protests against a widespread ethic based upon mere calculations: 'O *reason* not the need . . .' (*King Lear* II.4.266). Or they may, like Richard II, betray their own vision; though he has a vision of sacral kingship out of joint with the new, pragmatic power of the times, he himself gives away his identity as King through his money-raising leases: 'Landlord of England, art thou now, not King' (*King Richard II* II.1.113).

This last example makes clear that the audience often has an ambivalent attitude to the value held by the tragic hero; while ready to admit it contains a dimension which society ignores at its danger, the audience may at times side with the society with which the tragic hero is in conflict. While Antony, for example, regards his passion for Cleopatra as 'the nobleness of life', it is judged by efficient Roman society as lust, dotage and folly; the audience may well find a grain of truth in both views, depending on its inclination to poetry or politics. So the spectator shifts in mood between sympathetic involvement and detachment. The 'comic interludes' of Hamlet's gravediggers, Macbeth's Porter, Cleopatra's Clown, Lear's Fool and Juliet's Nurse are not just light relief; they help to create a sense of shifting perspective, changing our expectations and alerting us to the need for flexible reactions.

The love tragedies provide the most obvious example of a conflict of values between hero and society. As in the comedies, the insights of love can penetrate beyond merely superficial appearance, but in the tragedies the protagonists fail to sustain them in face of the hostility of their society. The circumstances are unpropitious. Further, the love-tragedies exhibit a particularly intense form of this pattern of conflict; in a kind of swinging movement, the hero begins with a new vision which is at odds with his society, relapses back into the old perspective, and then attempts unsuccessfully to recover his former height of vision. It is the relapse that prompts the catastrophe, since the characters cannot live on two levels of world-view at once, and each destroys the other.

For example, when Othello woos and marries Desdemona, his love challenges the outward forms and conventions of his society. He is a black African, a commoner and a soldier, while she is a white Venetian, and a sophisticated noble lady. Her father can only explain an act which seems to him 'against all rules of nature' (*Othello* I.3.101) in terms of witchcraft. The tragedy of Othello lies in his failing to hold to his intuitive perception of Desdemona, and relapsing into the prevailing view of his world; prompted by Iago, he accepts the verdict that the match is such an unlikely one that she is bound to betray him in the end, and he lets the outward evidence of his senses (the handkerchief) convince him against the inner knowledge of his faith. Judging that Desdemona's love for him is 'nature, erring from itself', he capitulates to the surface view of things expressed by Iago:

> Not to affect many proposed matches,
> Of her own clime, complexion and degree,
> Whereto we see in all things nature tends;
> Fie, we may smell in such a will most rank,
> Foul disproportion; thoughts unnatural.
>
> (III.3.231)

Similarly, Romeo, from the perspective of his love for Juliet, begins by challenging all the conventions of his feuding society by tolerating the insults of Tybalt. But he loses his grasp on the new vision when Mercutio is killed: 'O sweet Juliet,/ Thy beauty hath made me effeminate' (*Romeo and Juliet* III.1.112). He capitulates to the old vendetta between the houses of Montague and Capulet, kills Tybalt and so catapaults himself into tragedy. From that relapse flows all the haste which brings them finally to the 'dateless bargain with engrossing Death'.[17] Likewise, Antony begins with an intuitive vision of his love with Cleopatra in Egypt:

> Let Rome in Tiber melt, and the wide arch
> Of the rang'd empire fall! Here is my space,
> Kingdoms are clay: our dungy earth alike
> Feeds beast as man; the nobleness of life
> Is to do thus . . .
>
> *(Antony and Cleopatra* I.1.33–7)

But he betrays his vision when he swings back to Rome to recover the old values of political power: 'These strong Egyptian fetters I must break/ Or lose myself in dotage' (I.2.114–15). The political bargain he makes by marrying Caesar's sister will mean tragedy when he swings back again to Egypt and Cleopatra, as he must. As Wilson Knight perceives about both Antony and Cleopatra, there is 'a strange see-saw motion of the spirit, an oscillating tendency, back and forth'.[18]

So all these tragic characters oscillate from one side of their line of tension to another, 'to rot [themselves] with motion'.[19] They lose their balance, alternately asserting their freedom and capitulating to the limits of their environment. What is needed is not for them to ignore all limits in the confident freedom of their vision; that is the tragic pride of forgetting creaturely finitude.[20] What they fail to do is to keep the vision clear while taking account of their boundaries as they are. We cannot altogether blame them, for the pressures of their world make their fall practically inevitable. Yet death, when it comes, gives them an opportunity to affirm the vision they have lost. At the very moment of catastrophe we find again in Shakespeare's plays the moving boundary between tragedy and comedy. Death is a waste, and yet there is a moment of triumph in it. As Othello stabs himself, he recalls his valour in the little story of his smiting of the Turk, and reasserts his love for Desdemona:

> I kiss'd thee ere I killed thee, no way but this
> Killing myself, to die upon a kiss.
>
> *(Othello* V.II.359–60)

Thus, in the act of dying he affirms the values of valour and love that he had perceived beneath the surface and failed to live by.[21] Similarly Antony and Cleopatra, while betraying their love for each other in life, attain fidelity in death: now, claims Cleopatra

> I am marble-constant: now the fleeting moon
> No planet is of mine. . . .

> The stroke of death is as a lover's pinch
> Which hurts, and is desir'd.
> *(Antony and Cleopatra* V.2.238, 294)

In a different setting, Richard II has squandered his kingdom and now lost his crown to a usurper, so that he does not know who he is any longer; yet in the face of death this nameless one can assume again the name of King whose glory he once felt deeply, claiming that his killers have with 'the King's blood stained the King's own land' (*King Richard II* V.5.110).

Of course, we must get matters into perspective, as the Clown does at Cleopatra's theatrical death, remembering that he once knew a woman 'something given to lie'. A bystander at Othello's dying speech observes, 'All that's spoke is marr'd', and T.S. Eliot underlines this by remarking that Othello sounds like a man on the brink of eternity trying to cheer himself up. After all, since the tragic hero is to die, nothing can spoil the affirmation he or she is making. Truly, if it were not for death's coming the hero might betray the vision again; Cleopatra would again pack cards with Caesar, and Richard would again put his sacral charge of kingship up for leasehold. But this is just the point: since death *has* come, it can be used to fix the vision into a monument of art which will survive death itself. Death can be used to defeat itself, and the mutability of time is overcome in the moment of its apparent victory. Death makes the story immortal. Tragedy then suggests that to die well, in a way that summons up those values by which one wanted, but failed, to live is to make death serve one. It is to make a pattern and a story that will heal time itself. At the end of *Romeo and Juliet* the Montagues and Capulets who have now been reconciled by the deaths of their children, raise a golden monument to their memory; but the real monument is the story, whose vision can never be lost. The word lives in the grasp of death.

How, then, shall we understand this note of achievement within tragedy, in the light of interaction between the Christian story and other stories? If we take the 'U-shaped curve' as the normative pattern for story, then there seems no real reason from within the structure of tragedy itself for the note of hope that appears at the end. The victim ought to be left at the bottom of the curve. The story of a fall from greatness to misery is complete in itself. If tragedy is either the first two moments of a U-shape, or an inverted U-shape, then we can hardly append a further movement upwards towards harmony without destroying the pattern of tragedy altogether. Michael Edwards, in his theory of Christian poetics, can only suggest that tragedies like those of Shakespeare *add* a movement towards transformation because this witnesses to the human hope of a story in which there is a final harmony and a new creation.[22] So tragedy is said to 'move beyond itself' in quest of a new world, tracing 'the dialectic of the Bible'. It witnesses, despite itself, to the comic structure of the Christian story where there is a resurrection beyond the cross.

But such a critical Christian appraisal imposes a perspective upon tragedy that does not arise from within the tragic story itself. If we consider instead the pattern of a 'line of tension', then the movement towards fulfilment and triumph in tragedy is integral to the whole sequence. If the disaster is caused by a failure to hold a vision of value in the midst of the tensions of life, then the possibility is there for death to defeat itself. At the very moment when the tensions are finally resolved in death, the vision can be affirmed. Death which seems to triumph has over-reached itself and lost its prey. Within the context of a work of tragedy, this affirmation can only take the form of the story itself, as a monument of art. Christian faith reaches beyond this, though in continuity with it, in its hope of resurrection when God will bring all that is hidden to light. The possibilities that were never properly realised because of the pressures of human life can be fulfilled in the life of God. The tensions of our tragedy are 'preparing for us an eternal weight of glory' (2 Cor.4:17).

The Christian story maintains that this glory is possible because we can share in the story of Christ, participating in his death and resurrection. He is the greatest tragic hero in the sense that he suffers the ultimate catastrophe, participating fully in human loss and disintegration: 'My God, my God, why have you forsaken me?' He cannot, it seems, use the occasion of death to recall the vision of his life. He can only (according to the earliest traditions as recorded in Mark 15:37) make a desolate cry. Yet he transcends tragedy since, unlike other tragic figures, his whole life up to the point of death has been one of holding to the vision of ultimate worth, trusting in his father in the midst of the tensions of life and in the midst of conflict with the values of his society around him. The shape of tragedy therefore gives us a means of understanding the vicarious nature of the death of Christ; he alone suffers a death in which no opportunity can be found to affirm the vision, yet because he alone sustains that vision throughout life, death cannot hold him:

> But God raised him up, having loosed the pangs of death, because it was not possible for him to be held by it. For David says concerning him: 'I saw the Lord always before me . . .' (Acts 2:24–25)

From the other side of Easter, the meaning of the cross now can be seen; though the experience was one of utter estrangement, God was in it and using it as his final reconciling act. Thus the evangelists can now tell the story from this perspective of faith, and present the drama as more like the triumphant moment of a tragedy; the words of the dying Christ affirm the values of forgiveness, compassion and trust by which he lived, and which brought him into conflict with the structures of his world (Luke 23:24, 43, 46; John 19:26–27, 30). The two presentations – the sole cry of forsakenness, and the affirming sayings – are both true, in their own way. It is only because Christ experienced the situation as utter desolation that *we* can perceive that, in fact, his death summed up the self-giving of his life.

The cross is no mere preliminary to resurrection (as is perhaps suggested by the U-shaped pattern), and the interweaving of the two is made clearer by our experience of tragi-comedy. Tragedy reflects our sense of the disorder of life, but consoles us with the promise that death can be accepted and perhaps even conquered. Comedy consoles us with the assurance that there *is* order and purpose in the whole, but warns us that death remains as a finite boundary. Each overlaps with the other, bearing witness to the Great Story of the God who includes both pain and bliss in his own life.

Part II
Holding the Dialogue

5

William Blake and the Image of the City

Within the dialogue between literature and Christian doctrine, William Blake (1757–1827) is an outstanding example of what I have described as the 'Christian writer'.[1] While showing a commitment to the images and stories of faith he has inherited, he feels no inhibition about playfully creating and exploring new ones, and rejoices in the tensions that arise between old and new. The glowing illustrated books which he composed and engraved were too disturbing for his time, and it is perhaps only today that Blake is attaining his deserved recognition as a revolutionary in the cause of the imagination. We must then first explore the way he himself deliberately engaged in the dialogue, especially relating to Christian ideas of human fallenness, and then (as with all creative writing) we must set his achievement within our own critical dialogue between the text and theology.

THE FALL AND RESURRECTION OF THE CITY

To enter Blake's new world of imagination, we must always be aware that he loved the City; first and last he was a Londoner, a child of its streets and common life. In his epic poem, *Jerusalem*, he manages to work nearly all the addresses at which he had lived in London into one passage, depicting the ruined human state as a city in need of renewal:

> We builded Jerusalem as a City & a Temple; from Lambeth
> We began our foundations, lovely Lambeth. . . .
> I see London, blind & age-bent, begging thro' the streets
> Of Babylon, led by a child; his tears run down his beard . . .
> The corner of Broad Street weeps; Poland Street languishes;

To Great Queen Street & Lincoln's Inn all is distress and woe.
(Jerusalem, 84.11: K.729)[2]

This spiritual map-making and personified geography enables Blake to portray salvation as the resurrection not simply of the *body*, but of a *city*. He is forming a new constellation of biblical and traditional images, and a bright star in the firmament of symbols is his own city of London. There is already a wide biblical context for the startling conjunction of the images of a body and a *single* building (a temple), relating both to the human being in general and to the resurrected Christ in particular (as, for example, in Psalm 118:22, John 2:19–22, 1 Cor. 3:10–17); Blake draws on this background when he records his vision that:

I also stood in Satan's bosom & beheld its desolations:
A ruin'd Man, a ruin'd building of God, not made with hands.
(Milton, 38.15: K.529).

There are also scriptural personifications of cities such as Babylon and Jerusalem: 'The Jerusalem above is free, and she is our mother.' (Gal.4:26)[3] Blake freely extends this personification so that old and familiar pictures are suddenly filled with new meaning: when the Lamb of God is nailed upon the Tree of Mystery, 'Jerusalem saw the Body dead upon the cross. She fled away . . .' (*The Four Zoas,* 8.331: K.349). Further, the Pauline metaphor of the church as 'the Body of Christ' makes clear that there is an overlap between the individual identity of the risen body of Christ and the whole redeemed human community; this new humanity can also be portrayed as one holy building or temple (Eph. 2:16, 21–22). Though Blake learned from both Jacob Boehme and Emanuel Swedenborg about the corporate existence of humankind, united in one divine Person, the germ of this is present in the New Testament concept of living 'in Christ', who is the new Adam.[4]

Now, working from all these received materials, Blake brings the Christian symbols of the resurrection of the body and the City of God together into one focus, and also (as we shall see) into interplay with other images and stories created more from his own imagination. In particular the received image of the heavenly city comes into remarkable interaction with the image of his own city; the Jerusalem he is building is a spiritual London, which is at the same time a kind of resurrection body. The ideal city of 'arts and manufacture', which can only be built through the imagination and forgiveness embodied in Jesus, is 'Golgonooza the spiritual Four-fold London eternal'. (*Milton*, 6.1: K.485) Perhaps, as one critic suggests,[5] the name Golgonooza is meant to awaken echoes of a 'New Golgotha'. The new man, crucified with Christ at Golgotha and risen thence with him, is a holy city; every individual lives in such social harmony with the other that in the eternal Golgonooza,

> . . . every thing exists & not one sigh nor smile nor tear
> One hair nor article of dust, not one can pass away.[6]

For to say that Blake loved the city must be qualified; he loved what he believed to be the true city. He saw the actual city of London as broken by squalor, and by injustices done to the poor by the industrial revolution.[7] The walls of the churches were now blackened by soot, but an even greater blot was the sweeping of soot from chimneys by the bodies of the children who were forced to climb them:

> How the chimney-sweeper's cry
> Every blackening church appalls;
> And the hapless soldier's sigh
> Runs in blood down palace walls.
> ('London': K.216)

Blake had been happy and productive in Lambeth, and with its etymological meaning 'House of the Lamb' it becomes a key point in his vision of the spiritual renewal of London. It is the place where 'the secret furniture of Jerusalem's chamber' is made. Yet in Lambeth there was also Bethlehem Hospital for the insane, where the treatment was cruel even for the time. Bethlehem had become Bedlam, 'Dens of despair in the house of bread' (*Jerusalem* 31.26: K.657). The social horrors of industrial society and the exploitive conditions of the new factories readily spring to mind when we read Blake's protest:

> And was Jerusalem builded here
> Among these dark Satanic mills?
> (*Milton*, Preface: K.481)

But when Blake speaks of the 'Satanic mills' he is thinking of something even more fundamental than the evil of machines; he is pointing to an inner state of mind which has been expressed outwardly in this dehumanising technology; there are mills of the mind. For Blake this was the rationalism of the Enlightenment period, influenced by the scientific calculations of Newton and the mechanistic philosophy of Locke. In Blake's view the age of Reason was the age of Law which had imprisoned and stifled the free creative imagination: man has made his machines in the image of his mind. In the poem 'London', Blake relates his experience of walking the streets of the City and tracing 'marks of weakness, marks of woe' in every face, which have a deep, underlying cause:

> In every cry of every man,
> In every infant's cry of fear,
> In every voice, in every ban,
> The mind-forg'd manacles I hear.

The human being has shackled his intellect within the laws of science and empiricist logic; he has exalted Reason and lost his spiritual freedom. In terms of our theological exposition of fallenness in Chapter 3, he has lost his balance amid 'the polarities of his finite freedom'. What Blake sees is that when we think to free ourselves from all limits by the mere use of reason, we end up by capitulating to the limits of law. In asserting the control of our intellect over the boundaries of our world, we have in fact lost the true freedom of our imagination. The story Blake is telling is a version of the human 'line of tension'; it is the story of domination by an idol of our own making, rationalism, and it opens up the hope of a resurrection through the spirit of imagination.

Blake works out this human imbalance through his image of the city as a body. For instance, the two states of mind, imagination and rationalism take architectural form, symbolised on the City landscape by two great churches. He saw Westminster Abbey with its Gothic architecture as a monument to the imagination, while St Paul's Cathedral was a monument to the natural religion of the Enlightenment, to Newton's Pantocrator, to the Workman God of a mechanistic universe. In his poem, *Jerusalem*, Plate 32 shows the dome of St Paul's belonging to the symbolic figure Vala, and Westminster Abbey being guarded by the figure of Jerusalem. In

Blake's mythology, Vala and Jerusalem are the two wives of the Giant Albion, who is Britain and Everyman; Jerusalem is the spiritual soul, and Vala is natural humanity. The proportioned architecture of St Paul's expresses the reason of the natural man, while the Gothic lines of Westminster Abbey express the life of the Spirit. The human aim should be to build Jerusalem, the 'human form divine', through the power of the imagination. Jesus, the Lamb of God, is Man brought to true unity with himself; he is corporate humanity, possessing pure imagination, and Jerusalem is his bride.[8]

In Blake's view, then, the outward expression of the inner 'dark Satanic mills' was not only industrial society. It was also the uniform style of neo-classical art and architecture, a regularity which imposed restrictive law upon art as science imposes law upon our perception of the natural world. He was convinced that Grecian form was barren 'mathematical form', while the Gothic style was 'living form'.[9] It is living because it is neither a mere copy of nature nor at the other extreme a searching for a regular pattern of ideal beauty, but instead finds the 'typical nature' of different things; so it expresses characteristic human emotions and feelings. Adopting our theological concepts, we might say that it neither leans towards subservience to the limits of finitude, nor seeks ambitiously to transcend them absolutely. In consequence, Blake found the mark of the Gothic – or imaginative – style in the flowing line, giving a firm boundary and controlling disorder, but at the same time having a freedom to move and to wander. Blake called it organising the Spirit within a 'bounding form', and good examples are the wandering vines and foliages which ornament and frame the text in medieval missals, or the decorations of Gothic stone-masons who freely extend the stone into a disciplined complexity like the interweaving branches of trees. Blake's own illuminated books are greatly influenced by this style, with interlacing borders, and the spaces between filled with insects, birds and fishes. He believed that this 'living form' of Gothic art, which is omnipresent in the flowing draperies of his figures, was the truly Christian art. In his myth-making, Blake claims it was brought to Britain by Joseph of Arimathea, who was 'One of the Gothic artists who built the Cathedrals in what we call the dark ages';[10] since Blake prop-oses that Joseph was visited by Christ himself after his resurrec-tion, we see that the context for the famous lines from the Preface to *Milton* is actually a theory of art:

And did those feet in ancient time
Walk upon England's mountains green?
And was the holy Lamb of God
On England's pleasant pastures seen?

But in the Age of Reason, on the landscape of the 'dark Satanic mills', an inner legalism has imposed itself outwardly in the bleakness of industrial society, and in a uniformity of art which claims to be following so-called 'classical' patterns. In fact, Blake judges that Western Europe has misinterpreted truly classical art, overstressing the mathematical style, and neglecting the living line.

BLAKE AND THEOLOGY

Arising from Blake's view of the loss of balance in human life is a certain concept of God. He believes that the supremacy of Reason is also evident in the religion of his time, which envisages God as the supreme law-giver. The theology of the Deists rests upon conceiving God as the First Cause of a universe which runs henceforth by mechanical laws; God as the supreme law-giver imposes order and so, Blake complains, limits the energy of desire and imagination. The God of natural theology is a false God; he is the 'Nobodaddy' of a fragmentary poem by Blake, the ill-tempered old father in the sky.[11] Blake felt that the Jews of the Old Testament period had at times fallen victim to such a concept of God when they depicted him as imposing the tablets of stone, with their laws, upon Moses. For Blake, stone is often a symbol of rigidity; the imagination petrifies when Reason imposes its laws upon it. But the cosmic law-giver is an illusion; he is a mere projection of human reason, the sort of God that human reason would make for itself. Indeed, he is nothing other than Satan. The true God is Jesus, the human imagination which is divine; the energy of the imagination is far superior to the moral rules which so-called religion teaches:

The tigers of wrath are wiser than the horses of instruction[12]

Nobodaddy appears in *Songs of Experience* as 'Starry Jealousy' and 'Selfish Father of men', chaining delight.[13] He takes final shape in the mythological epics as 'Urizen', a deity who uses Newton's scientific instruments to measure the deeps: 'He formed golden compasses'. Having entered the 'state of Satan', he is '. . . Newton's Pantocrator, weaving the Woof of Locke'.[14] Urizen is, of course simply human reason which has been allowed to deify itself and construct a world under the dominion of law; his name suggests both 'Your Reason' and a constricting 'Horizon'.

. . . Satan, making to himself Laws from his own identity,
Compell'd others to serve him in moral gratitude and submission,
Being call'd God, setting himself above all that is called God;
And all the Spectres of the Dead, calling themselves Sons of God,
In his Synagogues worship Satan under the Unutterable Name.[15]

Now, the biblical theologian may object that Blake ascribes a religion of legalism too simply to the priests of the Old Testament, in his enthusiasm for the Hebrew prophets and the New Testament evangelists.[16] But modern Christian theology is certainly in accord with Blake's basic thrust of protest against an inflexible God of law within Christian dogma, and his rejection of a cosmic dictator. It will no longer be scandalised, as were Blake's contemporaries, by his underlining of Christ as the Sabbath-breaker.[17] Christian theology has recently become aware that certain concepts of God are dead, for there has been a massive revolution against the God of classical rational theology, who is the 'unmoved mover', completely unaffected by the process of the world. St Paul's insight that the true divinity of God is seen in the weakness of the cross (1 Cor. 1:18–25) has been recovered, especially by the movement for 'Theology of the Cross' in current German theology; theologians such as Jürgen Moltmann have spoken of God's opening his trinitarian life to include all the suffering of human history.[18] The movement of Process Theology has conceived God as one who moves the world by vulnerable persuasion rather than coercion, and who is in turn influenced by it, so that God is not the dominating Monarch but 'the fellow sufferer who understands' (Whitehead's phrase).[19] The unmoving, apathetic God of Greek philosophy has been unmasked as a creation of human wisdom. The human mind thinks a God ought to be 'wholly other', but in the light of his humility in Christ, 'such beliefs are shown to be quite untenable, and corrupt, and pagan' (Karl Barth).[20] The absolute ruler is an image of God which is dead.

The so-called 'Death of God' theologians in the 1960s went further than this perception, however, and proposed that *all* images of God are dead in our age. They maintained that we do not have any way of thinking about God; he is effectively absent from the modern world which no longer needs the idea of divine causation to explain reality, and which has ceased to be aware of God as a factor in human experience. We must, they concluded, simply wait in silence about God, and hope that he might return to human consciousness at some time in the future.[21] One prominent thinker in this school, Thomas Altizer, appealed to Blake for support of this idea. Taking up Blake's text that 'God is Jesus',[22] he understands Blake as saying that God has sacrificed his own Self, his objective identity, and has immersed himself into the human imagination. Combining Blakean symbols with aspects of Hegel's thought about the self-negation of God, Altizer conceives God as annihilating his own primordial essence for the sake of 'the human form divine'. The figure of the Satan in Blake's myths is, maintains Altizer, simply the dead body of the erstwhile transcendent God who has sacrificed himself.[23] This notion of an objective world-ruler, though now illusory, has been given reality by religion and has become increasingly tyrannical as it has become the focus of all denials of human life. The 'dead body' of God has gone on decaying in Christendom, but the time will come when it reaches such a peak of nothingness that it will be revealed for the alien and empty thing it is, and being stripped bare, its power will be broken. The self-sacrifice of God will be completed when, in the light of that epiphany, we too will be able to annihilate our Selfhood or our self-righteousness, resulting in a flowering of a new spirituality of human passions and imagination. Like Milton in Blake's poem, we shall be able to address the Satan who lurks in the 'shadow' of our deadly Selfhood:

> . . . . Know thou, I come to Self Annihilation.
> Such are the Laws of Eternity, that each shall mutually
> Annihilate himself for other's good, as I for thee.[24]

Thus, in the Neo-Blakean theology of Altizer, the modern consciousness that 'God is dead' is in fact the darkness before the dawn. It heralds the realisation that an objectively existing God is strictly 'nothing', an oppressive emptiness.[25] However, Blake himself is surely not concerned either to deny or affirm the actual existence of a transcendent God;[26] he is concerned to expose the *false* God created by human consciousness, and to reveal the true divinity of the human imagination, represented by Jesus. In Blake's view there is no transcendent Father except the one who can be known in his image, which is the 'human form divine'; to try to know any Almighty Father *in himself* is to end up with 'Nobodaddy' or the false God of rational theism.

As we shall see, then, the drama of the Satan makes more sense as the story of the disturbance of the human psyche and its yielding to Selfhood than as an actual self-annihilation of a heavenly Father. Altizer identifies the Satan as the 'empty shell' of God's objective existence; but for Jacob Boehme, to whom Blake is greatly indebted, the Satan was the 'empty shell' of God's wrath.[27] Northrop Frye comments that Boehme's Satan is 'very like Blake's Selfhood',[28] and we must notice that Blake's notion of Selfhood is not 'self' in the mere sense of self-existence, but 'self' in the sense of a self-righteous legalism. Though Boehme has his own original scheme of a conflict between the principles of fire and light in God, or wrath and love, he is partly reworking the biblical and Lutheran theme that the Satan is the prosecuting counsel for the law that condemns humanity, and which is overcome by the love of God.[29] What is dead and God-forsaken here is not God's own existence as an objective reality, but his existence in the character of wrathful law. In all this, Blake is not concerned with a literal history in the divine being, but with constructing myths for human experience. His prophetic message is that one particular concept of God is dead; that is, we must realise that human reason has been allowed to supplant the imagination and construct a world under the dominion of law, whether the laws of Moses, neo-classical Art, Newton, Locke or Deistic religion.

Blake's scheme cannot, of course, simply prove Altizer to be wrong. But when we set up a dialogue between Blake's work and the making of doctrine, it must have some impact upon the theological question about the relation between the symbol of the Satan and God. Though in a different way from Altizer, other theologians have also proposed an integration of the symbols; some, for instance, following Jung's view of the Satanic shadow within the archetypal image of God, have explored notions of a dark side in God.[30] By contrast with such ideas, Blake's poetic drama locates the Satan firmly in the context of human fallenness, and the coherence of his picture of fall, Satan and God ought at least to influence theologians in their decision-making.

More generally, his poetry allows us to *experience* the tensions of finite freedom which the theologian conceptualises. The story which Blake has to tell is the imprisonment of humankind through the domination of rational law, and release into new life through the power of the imagination. Throughout his work he tells this story in different ways, bringing such received symbols as resurrection and the City of God into interplay with his own images and stories; each version allows us to explore the loss of balance in our existence, and to discover how the elements of our limits and our freedom become confused. At the same time the theologian has questions to ask about this imbalance, together with concepts of God related to it, and his questioning offers a hermeneutical tool for understanding Blake's imaginative world. In particular, we shall be following this two-way movement in four versions of Blake's story, beginning with what often seems to be the most accessible one.

THE EXPERIENCE OF THE GROWING CHILD

In his *Songs of Innocence and of Experience* Blake presents a number of lyrics which are simple enough for children to listen to, and yet which are too profound for any adult to understand completely. They chart the growth of children from a state of innocence and joy into the maturity of experience, which means both sexual awareness and the sense of being under the yoke of law. Children are pictured as moving into the bondage of moral and social rules, though there is just a touch of hope that they might finally move beyond this into the free creativity that was promised in their childhood.

> O! he gives to us his joy
> That our grief he may destroy . . .
> ('On Another's Sorrow', 33: K.123)

It is this creative spirit that has been stifled by law and by the imposing of a false sense of guilt. Significantly, in telling the story of growing up Blake frequently sets it in the context of the city, drawing pictures from the children in the streets of London, scene of his own childhood. We have already noticed the link made between sooty church walls and child chimney-sweeps in the poem 'London', and there is a further lyric entirely devoted to the sweeper who is 'a little black thing among the snow', sent out to work by his parents while they go to church to pray.

In both parts of the collection there is a poem called 'Holy Thursday', and a comparison of its two versions is revealing. The version in *Songs of Innocence* (K.121–2) appears to approve of the way that the children of the charity schools of London are taken to a special service in St Paul's Cathedral, led by 'grey-headed beadles'. But when we recall Blake's view of organised religion and his aversion to the 'high dome' of St Paul's in particular, we shall not miss the irony in this account. The children are being regimented, marched in formation to church in the uniform of their schools ('walking two and two, in red & blue & green') and all mainly to advertise the charitable souls of those who presume to set themselves up as 'wise guardians of the poor'. Here are children under law, both social and religious. In their state of innocence, they ought to be playing spontaneously 'on the Ecchoing Green' that features so often in these lyrics. As it is, they express their creative spirit by freely 'like a mighty wind' raising to heaven the voice of song, and by turning their disciplined walk into a flow like the waters of the Thames. What Blake really thinks of this scene and the 'aged men' is set out without irony in the other version of the lyric 'Holy Thursday' in *Songs of Experience*:

> Is this a holy thing to see
> In a rich and fruitful land,
> Babes reduc'd to misery,
> Fed with cold and usurous hand?
>
> Is that trembling cry a song?
> Can it be a song of joy?
>   (K.211–12)

Blake is full of wonder (and some incredulity) that the children in St Paul's can preserve their spring of joy even under such conditions. In 'A little boy lost' the changing of intuitive love into a moral and social law is finally destructive of the vision; when the child confesses that he cannot love others in the same way as himself, and that he loves God just as much as he loves all things in nature, the priest condemns him by the moral law 'And all admir'd the Priestly care':

> The weeping child could not be heard,
> The weeping parents wept in vain;
> They strip'd him to his little shirt,
> And bound him in an iron chain.
>
> (K.218)

In another lyric, the Church imposes a sense of guilt with the onset of sexual awareness:

> I went to the Garden of Love,
> And saw what I never had seen:
> A Chapel was built in the midst
> Where I used to play on the green.
>
> And the gates of this Chapel were shut
> And 'Thou shalt not' writ over the door. . . .
>
> (K.215)

One of the lyrics warns that the creative energy of childhood, if suppressed like this, will break out in terrible and violent forms; 'The Tyger' both admires and fears the power of the imagination which cannot be finally tamed – not even by the God of the Deists with his mathematical and technical skills:

> Tyger! Tyger! burning bright
> In the forests of the night,
> What immortal hand or eye
> Could frame thy fearful symmetry?
>
> . . . And what shoulder, & what art,
> Could twist the sinews of thy heart?
>
> (K.214)

This then is the first way that Blake tells the story of the building of the spiritual city which is also the resurrection body of humanity. We can learn from the springs of joy and creativity in children, especially the children in the streets of our city, and stop the inflexible application of laws which damages the imaginative life. Living through the alternating freshness and sickness of these lyrics should have an effect upon a theology of human fallenness; the theologian should be prompted to ask what kind of doctrine, when held, brings the guilt which is *felt* in these lyrics to be a false one. What appears to be oppressive is not a genuine sense of responsibility that comes with maturity; as poems like 'The sick rose' and 'A poison tree' show, Blake is well aware that anger and lust lead to estrangement. But what is unhealthy is simply the imputing of inherited guilt to children by their elders who are made uncomfortable by the way they are 'happy and dance and sing'. Blake's vision of innocence in childhood is not a sentimental and naive view of children's 'goodness': he is quite ready to describe a self-willed baby as struggling with its parents 'like a fiend hid in a cloud'. Rather, what Blake observes and admires in children is their capacity for joy and imagination even under the worst conditions of poverty and exploitation.

Such a vision of 'the human form divine' does not fit in well with a 'U-shaped curve' of human history, where the image of God in humanity is either destroyed or at least badly damaged. Blake clearly does not appeal to a U-shaped pattern in the orthodox shape of a fall away from an initially perfect material creation. However, he does admittedly draw upon other forms of a U-shaped story of human fallenness. Influenced by the tradition from Paracelsus,[31] he thinks of the fall of Adam as being a pre-mundane fall of an angelic being from a purely spiritual existence into a material world; this fall from Paradise is also the context for the fall of the Satan. Further, Blake has been impressed by the Neo-Platonist account of birth as a continual descent of all human souls from a pre-existent spiritual state into the body.[32] Both the 'Paracelsian' and 'Platonist' views of fall into bodily existence stress the openness of the human spirit to a transcendent sphere; in imagination it reaches beyond its limits to the infinite realm to which it belongs and of which it has a dim recollection. Though these two fall stories are not strictly compatible, the former kind has stamped the imagery of Blake's 'prophetic' books, and the latter underlies some of the symbolism in his *Songs of Innocence and of Experience*. For example, the pair of poems 'The Little Girl Lost' and 'The Little Girl Found' portray the girl as wandering through desert places and seeking a place to sleep in; finally she is carried by lions, leopards and tigers to sleep safely in their cave. On the one hand she is falling into the 'sleep' of her budding sexual maturity, dwelling among the passions ('among tygers wild'); but this story also recalls the Neo-Platonist scheme of the prior fall of the soul into the sleep of life, through the cave of generation:

> While the lioness
> Loos'd her slender dress,
> And naked they convey'd
> To caves the sleeping maid.
>   (K.113)

Now, the result of employing these different kinds of fall stories as stuff for poetic images is to present fall as a simultaneous dimension of creation. It does not really matter, within Blake's poetry, that his Paracelsian and Neo-Platonist views of human fallenness are not fully consistent with each other, nor with the remnants of the Genesis story that are still present. He is using these various mythologies to express a sense of the human consciousness as being caught here and now between the pulls of freedom and limitation.[33] His multiple myths qualify and modify each other, and so turn our attention away from any 'once upon a time' of a garden towards the desert of the present, which can '*become* a garden mild' in that futurity when the earth awakes from its sleep, and

> Shall arise and seek
> For her maker meek.
>   (K.112)

The contribution which art is making here to theology is to allow the maker of doctrine to *feel* the effect of what Tillich (as we have seen) calls 'half-way demythologization'. There is, as John Macquarrie aptly expresses it, a 'limit to de-mythologizing'[34] in any religious discourse. Where myth is present (I am not here adopting the view that *all* talk about God and his activity in the world ought properly to be called 'mythological')[35] the myth can never be treated as a kind of husk to be entirely discarded when the kernel of 'meaning' has been threshed out. When an interpretation which illuminates human existence has been found, the story must still be retained since it keeps meaning open, and the meaning of transcendent reality can never be finally stated. In the case of the myth of the fall there is the further limit to de-mythologising, in that telling it as a story with an inner sequence makes clear that fall is not a logical necessity of creation. It is, as Tillich puts it, an irrational 'leap' into estrangement, even though it is the 'original fact' that created beings always do attempt to resolve their tensions in this way, so that creation and fall coincide. This is the risk of creation, and the 'riddle of the fall' that we have been exploring.[36] Now, while a theologian will conceptualise the Eden story like this, Blake's poetry provides a kind of testing-ground in which through a variety of myths the theologian can experience both a de-mythologising in terms of a conflict within the human psyche, and yet also the indispensable nature of myth.

The movement between literature and doctrine also, however, runs the other way. The theologian asks *why* there must be a fall as soon as there is a physical, finite universe. The theological answer we have been unfolding is that fallenness derives from the tensions which created beings experience in being both free and limited. The theologian will, then, be alert to the way that Blake answers this question and this supplies a critical tool in reading him. Here we notice a possible ambiguity. Blake's use of the Neo-Platonic myth might give the impression that he presupposes the evil, or at least inferior, nature of matter as an explanation of the inevitable drift towards non-being. The view that finite existence is inferior to an essential, spiritual world is not part of Christian theology; it also fits uneasily with Blake's own positive evaluation of the part the body plays in the life of the imagination. We shall find other traces of this ambiguity about the status of the body and its senses, once we are alert to the question, and a theological perspective may (as we shall see) help in interpreting him here.

THE BIRTH OF REVOLUTION

A second way that Blake tells the story of the resurrection of humanity and the building of Jerusalem is through the theme of the birth of revolution. This is another manifestation of the Tiger, and though it is a political theme, Blake tells it in a highly symbolic form. In *The Book of Urizen* there appears a whole cast of mythological characters whose dramatic adventures are to fill the 'prophetic' books that Blake writes and illustrates with glowing plates during the next twenty-five years. These figures, not unlike the characters of a modern cartoon film in their flexible metamorphoses from one state to another, are in fact all part of the human psyche. They are the elements of a personality which has disintegrated. The story of the building of Jerusalem is thus the re-uniting of man, his

resurrection to wholeness. In Blake's image, divided Man is typified as the Giant Albion (also England) who is asleep, and needs to
awaken to find his unity, each man at harmony with himself and
the whole race of humankind. This is the Divine Family,

> Mutual in one another's love and wrath all renewing
> We live as One Man; for contracting our infinite senses
> We behold multitude, or expanding, we behold as one,
> As One Man all the Universal Family; and that One Man
> We call Jesus the Christ; and he in us, and we in him
> Live in perfect harmony in Eden, the land of life.[37]

Man is to be reunified through the power of the imagination,
which is embodied in Jesus. Though we can see the outlines of a
mythology here – the fall of Adam/Albion as microcosmic man
from a heavenly Paradise which is Blake's version of Eden – what
confronts us most strongly is Albion's present state of being at war
with himself. His psychological components rage against each
other as he sleeps, and if we cannot always understand exactly
what the imagery indicates, we certainly receive an impression of
the splitting of consciousness as we shudder our way from stanza
to stanza. Blake enables us to live in the most extreme way
between the tensions which can lead to imbalance in existence;
while a theologian can describe the situation, here it becomes our
experience. We know, as we read these poems, that we are being
disturbed. In *The Book of Urizen*, this disturbance is centred upon
the emergence of Orc, the terrible child of revolution.

In a parody of the days of creation in Genesis 1, Urizen creates
the universe, binding it together by the laws he reads from his
'Book of Eternal Brass'; he decrees

> One curse, one weight, one measure,
> One King, One God, One Law.
>   (4.7–8: K.224)

This is the God of the Deists, the God of Newton's physics,
'dividing and measuring space by space'. Urizen symbolises the
human faculty of reason, trying to control the world through
imposing the mechanistic laws of science and morality. Into the
space which Urizen creates are sucked eternal spirits, to be im-

prisoned within it. But Urizen too finds that he is bound within his own creation, and that his work has disintegrated into 'ruinous fragments of life'. Wrenched apart from the side of Urizen there emerges 'Los', who symbolises the human poetic spirit of imagination, and he tries to rebuild the shattered ruins of Urizen's work with his anvils and hammer. He pities the fallen and chained Urizen, with the result that Los himself further divides: there emanates from him a 'round globe of blood/trembling on the void', which branches out into fibres of blood, milk and tears, and takes shape as a shadowy female:

> All eternity shuddered at the sight
> Of the first female now separate
> Pale as a cloud of snow
> Waving before the face of Los
> (18.9: K.231)

It scarcely matters that we can find here a trace of the myth (as in William Law) that the original Heavenly Man was androgynous, or that we might detect a regrettable demotion of woman within the cosmic hierarchy. Blake is re-using the biblical picture of the splitting of woman from the side of man to allow the reader an experience of the dividing of the human psyche into its component parts. Reason and Imagination are split from each other, and then they both further divide into a shadowy image of themselves. Each character in Blake's cast is provided with a female counterpart, and regardless of the exact mythology being employed, the basic impression created is one of multiplying of disintegration. Again we experience the coincidence between creation and fall; as in Genesis 1–3, inevitably the diversity of creation slips into divisions.[38] The female emanation that ought, in the eternal state, to be a true 'contrary' to man has in fact become an unhealthy 'negation'.[39] Los's female shadow is called Enitharmon, and between them they beget a flaming child, Orc 'the terrible boy'. Orc is the spirit of desire, and when they try to chain him down, as the priest chained the boy in 'A Little Boy Lost', he becomes revolutionary.

> They took Orc to the top of a mountain.
> O how Enitharmon wept!
> They chain'd his young limbs to the rock

With the Chain of Jealousy
Beneath Urizen's deathful shadow.
                    (20.21: K.233)

The child's cries begin to awake the dead – who in Blake's time
are the masses in France and America. Urizen too stirs himself and
redoubles his efforts to bind the world in the nets and webs of
science and religion, using scales, 'massy weights', a brazen quad-
rant and golden compasses. While this drama recounts a fall in
primeval history ('he planted a garden of fruits'), at the same time
it is a retelling of recent political history. According to Blake,
revolution is the child of poetry; Orc is begotten of Los. Men of
imagination such as Tom Paine have tried to give poetic form to the
Age of Reason and the result has been an unleashing of destructive
energy. The more explicit political tracts which Blake writes at this
time (*America: A Prophecy* and *Europe: A Prophecy*) explore the
terrible energy of 'Red Orc'.

At this point in his thought, Blake appears to be relatively happy
with the response of revolution to the Age of Reason; later he
becomes more disillusioned with its achievements. He does have
some doubts which are communicated in the form of the myth: at
root it was a mistake for Los to try to repair the work of Reason,
trying to give it a poetic form rather than starting again.[40] But Blake
is a Republican and on the side of the oppressed peoples of France
and America. He approved of their revolutions, and it seems likely
that he was caught up in the crowd which burnt Newgate prison at
the time of the storming of the Bastille.

So we return to the image of the city. A pervasive image in these
political-symbolic poems is disorder in the streets, for the shattered human mind is a city which is divided against itself. Red
Orc runs wild through the streets of London, causing havoc and
dismay. Blake imagines the restive crowds and the fleeing of the
rulers from their seats of power, especially the guardians of unjust
law:

Above the rest the howl was heard from Westminster louder &
    louder:
The Guardian of the secret codes forsook his ancient mansion,
Driven out by the flames of Orc; his furr'd robes & false locks
Adhered and grew one with his flesh, and nerves & veins shot
    thro' them.

With dismal torment sick, hanging upon the wind, he fled
Groveling along Great George Street thro' the Park gate. . . .[41]

THE DRAMA OF THE CONSCIOUSNESS

Blake's interest, however, was not fundamentally in politics, but
with the spiritual life of Everyman. In his next great work, *The Four
Zoas*, he turns away from the panorama of history to the inner
history of the psyche, and London is the symbol for the state of
humankind in any age. Each person is a ruined city, and though
the scale of this poem is tremendous, it is a projection of the very
small area of a single mind. In Blake's *theory*, we recall, each mind
is inseparable from the whole spirit of humankind, and is actually
a microcosm of the universe, but the *style* is also characteristic of
Blake as a Londoner; since he was a city-dweller his art was not
fostered by the panoramic landscape, but by the individual
'human form divine'. He learnt to see the whole cosmos in small
objects; a single flower or tree in the townscape affirmed the
holiness of life no less than the vastness of nature.

> To see a world in a grain of sand
> And heaven in a wild flower,
> Hold infinity in the palm of your hand
> And eternity in an hour.[42]

Thus the third way that Blake adopts for depicting the building of
Jerusalem is through developing more directly the drama of consciousness itself. That which is begun in *The Book of Urizen* is
expanded in *The Four Zoas*. The cast of characters is completed, and
we are given a whole map of the human spirit. Orc (revolutionary
desire) is accompanied by a less extreme form of himself in Luvah
(the emotions), and to make up a quartet of major faculties Blake
adds Tharmas, or sensual, instinctive life. 'Four Mighty Ones are
in every Man'.[43] Los (or Urthona), Urizen, Luvah and Tharmas are
the Imagination, Reason, Emotion and Instincts, and following the
imagery of a city they are also located geographically; they should
occupy the places of North, South, East and West respectively.[44] In
the poem *Jerusalem* they are associated first with different areas of
London, and are then superimposed upon the whole map of
England by being identified with various cathedral cities.[45] These

characters of course all have their female counterparts, and although we may pass over other complexities of identity, we should notice that Los who appears in this world has an eternal form in 'Urthona'. We recall that the human imagination is the link with divine life; Los is the prophet of the imagination, and so when Jesus comes 'the Divine Appearance was the likeness & similitude of Los'.[46]

The four faculties or 'Zoas' (life-forms) are contained within the consciousness of the eternal Man, or the Giant Albion. As we have already noted, he has two wives – Vala or natural humanity (whom we may now identify as the emanation of Luvah) and Jerusalem, the spiritual soul. Blake sets these figures in whirling motion, depicting the splitting of consciousness and the possibility of its reunion through Jesus, who is total imagination. As we read we are immersed into a sea of conflicting currents, and are made to feel the tensions of existence in an acute way. Throughout, we notice, the two matrices of the quartet are freedom and limit: the North–South line asserts the transcendence of the human spirit over the world in Imagination and Reason, while the East-West line acknowledges the boundaries of the Emotions and bodily Instincts of the natural life.

Another way Blake multiplies disintegration is to provide each human faculty with a 'spectre' or shadow as well as a female emanation; the three make up a 'Trinity of frustration',[47] and the resurrection of man to unity will come though the redemption of the emanation and the annihilation of the spectre. The spectre is Selfhood, or the self in 'the state of Satan', divided from the eternal self. Since the Satanic sphere is characterised by egocentricity, hypocrisy and self-righteousness, the spectrous self is dominated by the power of reason, which makes the laws which limit energy, desire and forgiveness. Thus the spectre can be called Satan, and Satan can be identified with Urizen – though these are not simple equivalences.[48] The 'annihilation' of the Selfhood is really then a reclaiming of the self:

> . . . Los embrac'd the Spectre, first as a brother,
> Then as another Self, astonish'd, humanizing & in tears,
> In Self abasement Giving up his Domineering lust.
> (*The Four Zoas* 8.339: K.328)

There is no progression without contraries. Faced with our divided self we must accept it and recognise it as our own, rather than trying to execute it legalistically, pretending it has nothing to do with us. A power of self-justification cannot be dealt with self-righteously. In his later poem, *Milton*, this is portrayed in a mythical form when Milton refuses to annihilate Satan; while the Selfhood is to be annihilated, 'Satan' (as a state of being) is not.[49] The 'reasoning self' is to be reclaimed and subdued to the divine mercy, and then 'Satan, the selfhood, as a state, ceases to exist when any man perceives his error'.[50] The shifting identities of the 'spectre', and the complicated reactions the characters (and the reader) have towards it, help to foster the sense of a world of tensions, in which the Satanic state of separation is 'continually carrying on'.[51]

In *The Four Zoas*, Blake presents several versions of the fall, or the disintegration of a human being into his various energies, which cannot (as many interpreters have discovered) be reduced to a single chronological sequence. Events are presented in the form of dreams, songs and flashbacks. The bid of Urizen for sole rule in the cosmos of human consciousness is told first, for instance, as a response to the attempt of Luvah to purloin the fiery steeds of Urizen while he was asleep: 'Luvah siez'd the Horses of Light & rose into the Chariot of Day.' (1.264: K.271) Luvah flies up into the brain, intellectualising love and rejecting his proper partner of the instincts and sense of touch – Tharmas. It is thus hinted that Luvah, 'the Prince of Love, the murderer' (1.325: K.273) has killed Tharmas, recalling the slaying of Abel by Cain, which Jacob Boehme had regarded as the proper story of the fall. Consequently, Albion or the Eternal Man orders Urizen to take the sceptre of divine rule and suppress Luvah. Alternatively, however, the fall is told as a conspiracy initiated by Urizen, in which he *gives* his chariots to Luvah in the South while himself ascending the throne of Urthona in the North. In 'that deadly night/ When Urizen gave the horses of Light into the hands of Luvah' (4.113: K.300), the intellect tries to establish a realm of pure reason, separating itself from love. Subsequently, in either account, Urizen suppresses the now assertive Luvah who thus falls into the womb of Los-Enitharmon to be born as Orc and to be chained down as in the earlier epic. But we learn later, from another song, another version of the fall in which the Man fell when he became infatuated with Vala (natural humanity), begat Urizen, and then suffered the splitting away of Luvah from Vala (7.234–50: K.326).

Yet another story of dissolution can be told, echoing the myth of Adam and Eve. For the poem in fact begins not with Urizen but with 'Tharmas, Parent pow'er, dark'ning in the West', who separates from his emanation (Enion) with the onset of sexual experience; sex itself is not the cause of fall, but in the act they see each other as separate objects:

> Why wilt thou Examine every little fibre of my soul,
> Spreading them out before the sun like stalks of flax to dry?
> (1.47–8: K.265)

Consequently they feel shame and jealousy and find Urizenic moral law imposed. From this union there emerge the 'fierce children' Los and his female counterpart Enitharmon, who wander in a kind of Eden made by Urizen, suggesting that poetic imagination is born from sexual awareness and conflict. This account appears to be quite different from the birth of Los out of the side of Urizen, in the earlier epic. It can just about be fitted in as a sequel to Urizen's displacing of Urthona from his throne in the North in this poem, since that ends with Urthona (Los) and Enitharmon falling into the womb of Tharmas; but it can scarcely be reconciled with the birth of Enitharmon from Los as a globe of blood at the moment when Los tries to remake the shattered furnaces of Urizen, a sequence from *The Book of Urizen* which is repeated here in *The Four Zoas*.

These different versions are partly due to Blake's continual rewriting of the poem and its unfinished state. But they are also possible because of the shifting life of the consciousness; each faculty in turn splits from another, supplants another, and attempts to control the human being, proclaiming 'Now I am God from Eternity to Eternity' (1.319: K.273). Blake is not writing a story of fall and resurrection that follows any simple U-shaped curve. The theologian finds in his experience of reading the poem that he can never trace the ultimate cause or moment of the fall; it is simply the given fact, inevitable, arising from the tensions between faculties of freedom (Urizen, Los) and the limits of bodily life (Tharmas, Luvah), yet this is not felt to be incompatible with a sense of responsibility. Each faculty comes to repentance, including the spectre of Urthona who confesses that 'I am the cause/ That this dire state commences . . .' (7.403: K.330).

In this drama of the unbalancing of energies, reason (Urizen) has repressed desire (Luvah-Orc), and imagination has failed to prevent it; Los-Urthona has been thrown down from the starry heights. Here Blake dares to take the older poet, Milton, to task, and to correct his version of *Paradise Lost*. The story apparently told in Milton's epic is that God has cast down Satan and then sent his Messiah into the world to redeem humanity. But Blake believes Milton has been seduced by rational religion, as evidenced by his portraying of the so-called Messiah as a rational Governor of the universe. As a result the 'God' of Milton's poem is really the Satan, or reason deified, and the plot can be read as Reason suppressing the Desire which is truly divine. Blake finds this diagnosis supported by Milton's view of sex which, following Augustine, he presents negatively as a consequence of the fall. These ideas are too disturbing to be contained in the present poem of *The Four Zoas*, and Blake will have to start again with the poem *Milton* to work them out properly.

Thus Blake tells the story of man's disintegration; he now moves to an account of his reunion. Urizen enters into an unholy alliance with Orc, who becomes the serpent coiled round the Tree of Mystery; that is, legalistic religion uses suppressed desire for its own ends. Jesus, the Lamb of God, appears 'as One Man infolded/ In Luvah's robes of blood' and faces Satan, his shadow or Selfhood. He is then judged by the 'Synagogue of Satan in dire Sanhedrin' and nailed upon the Tree of Mystery by Urizen in league with Vala, who has become distorted as the Rahab of 'lovely delusive beauty'. Quickly we move to the last judgement and the general resurrection. That is, the sleeper Albion awakes, remembers his imagination, and calls upon Urizen to resume his proper functions. When Reason stops trying to suppress Orc (desire) then Orc burns himself out and becomes Luvah again, or the proper emotions. There is a great eucharistic harvest of humanity as life is remade through the winepresses of Luvah and the mills of Urizen, and man wears the garments of eternity:

Around the Eternal Man's bright tent, the little Children play
Among the wooly flocks. The hammer of Urthona sounds
In the deep caves beneath; his limbs renew'd, his Lions roar
Around the Furnaces & in Evening sport upon the plains.
They raise their faces from the Earth, conversing with the Man:
'How is it we have walk'd thro' fires & yet are not consum'd?
'How is it that all things are chang'd, even as in ancient times?'
(9.840–5: K.379)

The vision of Isaiah, that the lion and lamb shall lie down together, 'and a little child shall lead them' (Isa. 11:6) is given a rebirth of images against the background of Blake's earlier 'Songs of Innocence' about the lamb and the tiger. But the reader is bound to ask 'why the Eternal Man should ever wake at all.'[52] The reader therefore feels the impact of the revealing of the image of divine love and forgiveness in Jesus. Los had declared that Man had 'sunk down into a deadly sleep' because he was 'refusing to *behold* the Divine Image which all behold'; now the Man confesses that because the Lamb of God 'is *seen*' in the bosom of Jerusalem, 'I thro' him awake from death's dark vale'. The Daughters of Beulah confess to the Saviour that it is when 'in mercy thou appearest' clothed in Luvah's robes of blood that they '*behold* thee and live'.[53] For the theologian, there is fleshed out here the atonement theory of Abelard, that the revelation of divine love in Christ has power to kindle redeeming love in those who *see* it. Those who live through this drama will know that such a revelatory event has objective, creative effect and that this view of atonement cannot be dismissed as a 'merely subjective' arousing of emotion.

At the same time it should become clear that the speculations of Thomas Altizer about the death of God have been imposed on to Blake. Christ's actions to 'assume the dark Satanic body in the Virgin's womb' and to 'put off Satan eternally'[54] on the Tree of crucifixion are not parts of a process in which a transcendent God has supposedly sacrificed his objective identity. They are a graphic representation of the traditional view that Jesus gave up his own 'self' to death, or in the phrase of John Macquarrie, 'broke the last idol' which is one's own self.[55] In the view of Blake, the most pernicious form which the idols take is the curse of legalism (and the Apostle Paul says something similar in Colossians 2:14–15). A theological theory of atonement may propose that the cross of Jesus, in revealing the final breaking of idols, has power to enable the human person to break the idols of the self; once again, Blake's drama allows us to experience this happening.

All this the poem can do for the theologian. But the dialogue also runs the other way; theology can provide a perspective for the critical reading of the poem. Interpreters of Blake vary about his attitude to the physical body, especially in his later work. Los is prompted to tear down the heavens of Newtonian science and initiate the last judgement in the Ninth Night when he meets the risen Jesus:

But Jesus stood beside them in the spirit, separating
Their spirit from their body.

(9.4–5: K.357)

Does this view of the resurrection, together with Blake's description of redemption as 'putting off the dark Satanic body' (8.196:
K.346) mean a rejection of the material body in favour of a spiritual
reality?[56] Blake, after all, describes the human being as 'cavern'd
man', lit by 'five windows' (the senses) which are mere 'narrow
chinks'.[57] The echo here of Porphyry's cave might confirm a Neo-
Platonic view of the inferiority of the material world, and much of
the *The Four Zoas* tells of the exploring of 'dens of darkness'. The
weaving of the body through the looms of Enitharmon is portrayed
as a kind of torture; creation is destruction – 'a vast spine writh'd in
torment upon the wind'. But the theologian will ask *why* creation
and fall should coincide, and we have already seen that an answer
can be found in the tensions and inevitable imbalance of human
life rather than in any innate evil within matter. When we have felt
the coherence of the theological account, we will be the more likely
to treat the imprisonment of man in his cave of senses as an image
for the tensions between the Zoas, rather than as the cause of it.
That is, we will take the alchemical imagery of the cavern as
denoting a body in which we fail to use our senses *imaginatively* to
shape the world around us, and simply allow them to be imposed
upon by our environment.

Thus, we will be more likely to agree with those critics, such as
Thomas Frorsch,[58] who interpret Blake as hoping for the body to be
risen in this world. The putting off the mortal body is 'the putting
off the consciousness of the body as a natural object in geometric
space'.[59] As Blake expresses it, true freedom is 'the liberty both of
body & mind to exercise the Divine Arts of Imagination'.[60] Resurrection is the enlarging of perception to discover that 'every Minute Particular is Holy';[61] it is the sharpening of the senses, not the
abolition of them. Here Frorsch aptly refers to Blake's description
of the Eternals in the Council of God whose senses are fluid,
contracting to behold the multitude of particular things, and expanding to behold reality as a Whole –

As one Man, for contracting their Exalted Senses
They behold Multitude, or Expanding they behold as one,
As One Man all the Universal family; & that One Man
They call Jesus the Christ . . .[62]

Blake's finest vision of this risen body ends his poem *Jerusalem*, which is also the name of the emanation of the Eternal Man. The Four Zoas reappear as the four senses placed at the four compass points of this Man who is also a holy city: 'And every Man stood Fourfold; each Four Faces had: One to the West/ One toward the East, One to the South, One to the North, the Horses Fourfold. . . .' (98.12–13: K.745) The resurrection of the individual body and the body of society merge as each man converses with the other, 'Creating space, Creating time . . . which vary as the Organs of Perception vary' (98.31, 38: K.746). In a new cluster of biblical images,[63] Blake affirms that when the senses are renewed to perceive the one and the many, the body will flow in motion like four rivers or four chariots of fire converging:

> The Four Living Creatures, Chariots of Humanity Divine Incomprehensible,
> In beautiful Paradises expand. These are the Four Rivers of Paradise
> And the Four Faces of Humanity, fronting the Four Cardinal Points
> Of Heaven, going forward, forward irresistible from Eternity to Eternity.

THE JOURNEY OF A PILGRIM

The fourth way that Blake tells his story is through the spiritual journey of one person, John Milton, though Blake's own pilgrimage merges with it in considerable autobiographical detail. Since the journey is in fact a progress deep within the consciousness, through the fourfold universe of the Zoas, it is not so much a journey *to* the heavenly City, but *through* the Holy City of art where God dwells, Golgonooza 'Which is the 'spiritual fourfold London in the loins of Albion'. At the same time, because the 'mundane shell' is the human body, the journey is also the building *of* the City. Or rather, since Golgonooza is depicted as a kind of city-state, surrounded by fertile land, the journey is the cultivation of the city; the human harvest is to be reaped, and the human vintage pressed, 'from the vales of Lambeth'. The body and blood are to be nourished by the bread and wine of imaginative vision. Again we perceive the richness of meaning that develops from overlaying the images of city and body, now brought into further constellation with the picture of a journey. Further, the journey is actually a kind of fall – or at least a voluntary descent along the path of the human fall. For the pilgrim is John Milton, and whereas his epic *Paradise Lost* had begun by describing the fall of Satan from heaven, this poem begins in imitative style by describing the descent of Milton himself:

> Say first! What mov'd Milton, who walk'd about in Eternity
> One hundred years, pond'ring the intricate mazes of Providence,
> Unhappy tho' in heav'n –
> . . . . . To go into the deep . . .?
>
> (Milton 2.16: K.481)

In Blake's poem, Milton in heaven is prompted by a bardic song to realise that he has fallen into error in his attempt to justify the ways of God to men. He had been led astray by his reasoning faculty, which had attained dominance over him as the spectre, Selfhood or 'Satan'; for he had depicted God and his Messiah in the role of Governors of the cosmos according to Natural Religion. (See especially Book 8 of *Paradise Lost*.) The Song which alerts him to his error tells the story of the fall of Satan, in yet another version of the theme that reason has supplanted the place of the divine imagination. The Bard tells how Satan (this time depicted as the youngest son of Los) was not satisfied with his allotted task in the harvesting of humanity; his proper function was turning the mills of heaven, controlling the rules of nature as 'Newton's Pantocrator, weaving the woof of Locke'. But he wanted to drive the harrow of the Almighty, controlling the 'invisible and incomprehensible' laws of life which transcend mere reason, and which are associated with compassion and forgiveness. Los at first refuses; this task belongs to his eldest son, Palamabron:

> Anger me not! thou can'st not guide the Harrow in pity's paths.
> Thy Work is Eternal Death with Mills & Ovens & Cauldrons.
>
> (4.16: K.483)

When Los yields, the disastrous result of Satan's effort is to madden the horses of the harrow and disrupt the harvest; the laws of reason cannot impose order upon the elemental energies. There ensues the fall of the whole divine family into disruption, the confusing of the Zoas and Satan's own fall into 'a vast unfathomable abyss'. In the consequent universe of 'separation', Satan builds synagogues for the 'spectres' of rationality to worship his moral laws.

Thus the fall of Satan which Milton charts in his epic poem is in fact the ascendancy of moral and rational religion. A symptom of this, according to Blake, was Milton's fear of passion as shown by his ascribing of sexual desire to the fall. Urizen has suppressed Luvah. Thus Milton finds himself in heaven without his emanation or female counterpart who has been sundered from him, and scattered in the deeps (of Ulro). The counterpart is actually sixfold (Milton's three successive wives, and three daughters) and, called by the name of Ololon, is presented as a twelve-year-old virgin. She needs finding and redeeming, since passion sundered off from the whole personality distorts and is distorted.

In face of all this evidence to this grievous error, Milton offers to enter the universe of the Zoas to search for and redeem Ololon; he will descend into the deeps and suffer for her sake the death of his Selfhood.

What do I here before the Judgment? Without my Emanation?
With the daughters of memory & not with the daughters of
    inspiration?
I in my Selfhood am that Satan: I am that Evil One!
He is my Spectre! in my obedience to loose him from my Hells,
To claim the Hells, my Furnaces, I go to Eternal Death.
                                        (14.28–32: K.495–6)

So he will overcome his error by annihilating his spectre and redeeming his emanation. He is of course entering the depths of his own consciousness in order to be reunified with himself: the redeeming of the affections (Luvah) is also the humanising of reason (Urizen) through the power of the imagination (Los) in the arena of the natural senses (Tharmas). This is expressed vividly by a duel between Milton and Urizen when they meet at the Brooks of Arnon (19.6: K.500); while Urizen tries to freeze Milton's brain by throwing the icy water of reason upon it, Milton counters by moulding red clay around Urizen, sculpting him a form which embodies the other human qualities. At the climactic moment when he confronts Satan, Milton refuses to annihilate him in a spirit of hypocritical legalism; he knows that the state of Satan itself cannot be removed while human life lasts, but he reclaims his own Satanic spectre, which is his 'reasoning power', and so annihilates the Selfhood. (38.35: K.530) His strategy against Satan is

> . . . . to teach men to despise death & to go on
> In fearless majesty annihilating Self, laughing to scorn
> Thy Laws & terrors, shaking down thy Synagogues as
>   webs.

Finally he meets Ololon and reunites with her, exulting that contraries need not be negations. In the spirit of forgiveness and pity, which is Jesus, the struggle for mastery between the sexes can be overcome. In particular, Milton faces his sexual fears and casts off his previous false idealisation of woman as ever virgin; that figure flees with a shriek 'into the depths of Milton's Shadow.'

> I come in Self-annihilation & the grandeur of Inspiration
> To cast off Rational demonstration by Faith in the Saviour,
> To cast off the rotten rags of Memory by Inspiration,
> To cast off Bacon, Locke and Newton from Albion's covering,
> To take off his filthy garments & clothe him with
>   Imagination . . .

(41.2: K.533)

All this journey has nothing to do with a simple chronological sequence of a fall of humankind in primeval history, and its undoing by the descent of a redeemer. In the first place, Albion is already fallen, fragmented through his refusal to acknowledge that imagination is 'the divine body of the Lord Jesus' when the poem opens and before Satan makes his bid to drive the harrow of the Almighty. When Satan is described as the youngest son of Los, this is evidently a commentary on the most recent 'fall' of civilisation into the power of the new age of Reason. Further, while Milton descends to find Ololon who is scattered through the depths, she is actually already in heaven as a personification of the divine family, or corporate humanity redeemed. In the second book of the poem, she herself descends, following the track of Milton, to find *him* and show him true compassion. Clearly, we are dealing with the separation of male and female from each other, and the need of each to claim the other as part of himself or herself. Ololon

descends to redeem the 'shadowy female' (Rahab), the feminine
desire to gain power over the male through, for example, the false
use of pity.

> 'These tears fall for the little ones, the Children of Jerusalem,
> Lest they be annihilated in thy annihilation.'
> No sooner she had spoke but Rahab Babylon appear'd. . . .
> A Female hidden in a Male, Religion hidden in War. . . .
>   (40.15: K.532)

The contrary states of human experience, of which maleness and
femaleness are typical expressions, can become a struggle for
tyranny. Once again we see Blake expressing through his myths
the lack of balance which is fallenness. These multiple myths of fall
and descent encourage the theologian to half-demythologise, to
feel the necessity of reading myths in a literary rather than a literal
way, and at the same time to feel their indispensable role.

But even more disturbing to any simple U-shaped story of
human fall and recovery, is the identifying of Milton's journey
with Blake's own visionary journey, and the locating of Golgonooza as London. For Blake describes how Los unites with Blake in
Lambeth, and carries him off to a country cottage in Felpham to
'write all these visions /To display . . . the deceits of natural religion.' The journey of Milton, who was 'unhappy tho'' in heaven'
has its counterpart in Blake's decision to return from Felpham to
London.[64] Blake had enjoyed a heaven of financial security and
natural beauty in Felpham, but his artistic vision was gradually
being stifled. His patron Hayly, who had loaned him the cottage,
was well-meaning but insensitive; Blake gets his revenge for the
trivial commissions he plied him with, by depicting Hayly as Satan
in *Milton*. As Milton is moved to 'go into the deep', Blake is moved
to return to the only place where he can build Golgonooza, in
London. Before he leaves, walking about his garden he dreams
Milton's dream which is the dream of the sleeping Giant Albion.
The histories of Milton, the Four Zoas and Blake intersect in a
wonderfully intense way; on his track of descent into the fourfold
universe, Milton enters Blake's left foot. The sandal which Blake
wears on his walk contains 'all this vegetable world' (21.12: K.503),
for Milton's journey is Blake's own pilgrimage, as he opens himself
to the inspiration of the older poet whom he loved, though not
uncritically.

The encounters which Milton has on his journey are thus, at the same time, depicted as happening in Blake's country garden. Here Blake stands 'in Satan's bosom', into this garden Ololon descends, and here Blake experiences the triumph of the last judgement, when male and female have annihilated their Selfhood for the sake of each other, by being crucified with Christ. Resurrection happens when a person realises that the cross is not a punishment for the ancient sin of Adam finally inflicted by a legalistic God, but the redeeming power of sympathy and compassion here and now:

Then as a Moony Ark Ololon descended to Felpham's Vale
In clouds of blood, in streams of gore, with dreadful thunderings
Into the Fires of Intellect that rejoic'd in Felpham's Vale
Around the Starry Eight; with one accord the Starry Eight
   became
One Man, Jesus the Saviour, wonderful! round his limbs
The Clouds of Ololon folded as a Garment dipped in blood . . .
(42.7: K.534)

Even if we cannot follow all the details of Blake's symbolism, Blake succeeds in conveying to us the impression of states of mind, once divided and now united. He enables us to live in the spiritual city of Golgonooza within the streets of London, making us aware through his myths of the tensions within human life and the redeeming power of love.

6

Gerard Manley Hopkins and Mortal Beauty

William Blake traces the Body of Christ in the shape of the City, even though he finds it marred by the Satanic mills which grind in both industry and the rationalist mind. Another poet of the nineteenth century, Gerard Manley Hopkins, feels the spoiling even more acutely. Recoiling from the large industrial towns in which he was sent to work as a Jesuit priest, he discerns the Body of Christ primarily in the natural world. Such sounds as those of the sea and the skylark, reaching back into the dawn of the ages, 'shame this shallow and frail town' and 'ring right out our sordid turbid time.'[1] In a creative, even playful, use of the Christian tradition Hopkins finds an incarnation of Christ within nature, so that the poet can 'glean' Christ from the clouds, trace his 'world-wielding shoulder' in the hills and catch his masterful grace in the riding of a falcon on the steady air.

Thus, in Hopkins' view of the world, there is a striking contrast between the witness of nature to its creator, and the fallenness of humankind. His poem on 'The Sea and the Skylark' concludes by deploring that we who ought to be the crown of creation,

> Have lost that cheer and charm of earth's past prime:
> Our make and making break, are breaking, down
> To man's last dust, drain fast towards man's first slime.

Hopkins' imaginative use of the concept of incarnation, and his convictions about the fallen state of human beings, share a whole cluster of ideas which he develops about the human self and its relation to other distinct 'selves' in the world. He writes as a Christian poet, in continuity with the tradition of the Church and yet also with the tension that comes from any newness of vision. Reading his poetry can contribute, as we shall find, to the making of Christian theology today. But the dialogue also moves the other

116

way; strains emerge as Hopkins brings the themes of incarnation and fall together in his highly original vision of the cosmos, and theological insights from our own time can help to clarify where the problems lie.

'INSCAPE' AND 'INSTRESS'

Hopkins' version of the tension between freedom and limit in human existence belongs within an understanding of reality in which everything has a unique 'self' or its own characteristic form. He rejoices in the particularity of things, none exactly like another. While everything has its distinct identity, Hopkins gains particular pleasure from dappled and freckled things that combine shapes and colours in odd combinations:

> All things counter, original, spare, strange;
> Whatever is fickle, freckled (who knows how?)
> With swift, slow; sweet, sour; adazzle, dim. . . .[2]

Thus the universe is full of individual forms like notes in a musical scale or separate fractions in scales of light. Hopkins calls the form of these myriad selves their 'inscape', denoting that they have an outer shape (scape) which expresses an inner nature:

> Each mortal thing does one thing and the same:
> Deals out that being indoors each one dwells;
> Selves – goes itself; *myself* it speaks and spells,
> Crying *What I do is me: for that I came.*[3]

So creatures reflect sunlight in different ways – 'As kingfishers catch fire, dragonflies draw flame.' Each stone makes its own kind of splash when thrown into a well, each bell makes its own ring, 'finds tongue to fling out broad its name'. This last phrase makes clear that inscapes do not exist in isolation; there is contact and communion between the selves of all creatures, including human personalities. Hopkins finds inscapes to be sustained by a charge of energy which he calls 'stress', and this also makes a bridge of communication between them. One inscape delivers a surge of stress out of itself to another, and linked to the inscape this energy becomes 'instress'. In an early essay, Hopkins writes that 'I have often felt . . . the depth of an instress or how fast the inscape holds a thing.'[4] Stress, then, is the medium of sensation through which a human consciousness meets the world. When a person observes something in the natural world, he receives stress from it, accepting into his own inscape ('instressing') the intensity of feeling which the object emits. Thus stress upholds each individual thing and unifies the whole of nature. Some commentators on Hopkins' thought suggest, quite convincingly, that the inscape is actually nothing other than the form which the energy of stress takes in individual things.[5]

This is Hopkins' way of envisaging the human condition as suspended between freedom and limitations. A person is free to 'selve' himself, 'tasting' that inward self which is 'felt to be, to taste, more distinctive than the taste of clove or alum',[6] and then to express himself outwards in his own particular speech and action: so, for example, 'the just man justices'.[7] But his freedom of self must always be set in the context of other inscapes to which he is open and whose influence he is constantly absorbing through the circuits of stress. It is respect for the particularity of other things that motivates Hopkins' own astonishing use of language, stretching its capacities in a way that had not happened since Shakespeare. To grasp the uniqueness of the objects he observes, he creates compound words, shifts adjectives to surprising places,[8] chimes the sounds of words in the middle of lines and interrupts the expected syntax. Aptly, he himself speaks of poetry as 'the current language heightened . . . and *unlike* itself'.[9] His language reflects the pent-up energy within the inscapes of the world, observing of a candle-beam that 'to-fro tender trambeams truckle at the eye', in clouds a 'wilder, wilful-wavier/ Meal drift' and of bubbling water that 'a windpuff-bonnet of fawn-froth/ Turns and twindles.'[10] In the poem 'Henry Purcell', he hopes that God will forgive the composer his mistake of being a Protestant, because his music is able to penetrate to the very character of a human being, expressing the *self*:

It is the forged feature finds me; it is the rehearsal
Of own, of abrupt self there which so thrusts on, so throngs the
    ear.

Purcell concentrates not upon himself but the thought or emotion he is expressing; unawares, however, he therefore lets us catch a whiff of his own self, as we see the peculiar marks under the wings of a storm-bird as it raises them for flight. Open to the wider inscapes of the world, he thereby does not lose but enhances himself:

> Have an eye to the sakes of him, quaint moonmarks, to his
>   pelted plumage under
> Wings. . . .

The tragedy of human life, as we shall see, is that we lose this balance between freedom of self and the respecting of the created world that forms our limits.

But we have not reached the heart of the dialectic between the human self and the other inscapes of creation, until we realise that for Hopkins the 'stress' that holds everything together is nothing less than the grace of God. In the fellowship of the Trinity, 'the first outstress of God's power was Christ'.[11] So the triune God 'selves' himself,[12] moving beyond his being into his creation with the stress of love: 'He fathers-forth whose beauty is past change.'[13] He has made all things with their own self, in order that they may exist in communion with him, for when an inscape 'stresses itself' or speaks itself out, it is in fact responding to God. It is opening itself to God by riding upon the surge of energy that comes from his own presence in his world; the stress of grace unites it with the divine lovescape. As Hopkins explains in a meditation, quoting (without attribution) from the founder of his religious order, St Ignatius Loyola:

> God dwells in creatures: in the elements giving them being; in the plants giving them growth; in the animals giving them sensation; in men giving them understanding; and so in me. . . .[14]

Hopkins' idea of 'stress' therefore allows him to understand two movements going on at once as objects in creation 'selve' themselves, crying 'what I do is me': there is the response of the creatures to God, and the 'selving' or doing-be of the triune God through them:

> . . . . For Christ plays in ten thousand places,
> Lovely in limbs and lovely in eyes not his
>   To the Father through the features of men's faces.[15]

This is no simple identification of God and the world, no loss of freedom, but a *participation* of all created things in the life of God as they lean upon the movement (stress) of his love. Objects in the natural world give praise to God by simply being themselves, but human beings respond at the highest level of the will. We receive a stress from an object of beauty in the natural world, accept this into ourselves ('instress' it) and then respond in adoration and surrender to God, stressing or speaking out the grace which has come from him: 'his mystery must be instressed, stressed'.[16] So aesthetic experience becomes religious experience because the whole universe is a sacrament of the love of God. God by his will upholds all the inscapes of nature; from them we receive an impression of beauty, and respond to the Creator by an act of *our* will. Hopkins makes the classic statement of this sequence in his poem, 'The Wreck of the Deutschland':

> I kiss my hand
> To the stars, lovely-asunder
> Starlight, wafting him out of it; and
> Glow, glory in thunder;
> Kiss my hand to the dappled-with-damson west;
> Since, tho' he is under the world's splendour and wonder,
> His mystery must be instressed, stressed;
> For I greet him the days I meet him, and bless when I
> understand.

We meet the grace of God indwelling the beauty of nature ('wafting him out of it', 'under the world's splendour'), and respond ('kiss my hand to the stars'), stressing the mystery. So 'the world is charged with the grandeur of God',[17] and despite all human trampling on its inscapes, 'nature is never spent' since God the Holy Spirit continues to brood over it. Thus the freedom of the human self is set in the context not simply of other inscapes, but of the God who is present within them. Using Hopkins' terms, this is the 'freedom of pitch' or area in which we have 'freedom of play'.[18] The free choice of the soul for God recalls the moment of elective will in the colloquy which closes each of the Ignatian Exercises which Hopkins used in his spiritual retreats as a priest.[19] After contemplation, using the imagination to create scenes in which Christ is present to the mind (the composition of place), Ignatius requires an examination of conscience, and then a direct address to God, turning to him with the assent of love. So, in several of his 'nature sonnets', Hopkins first presents a vision of God (and Christ in particular) present in the stars, the drifting clouds, a soaring bird and human limbs, and then makes the response, 'I did say yes':[20] 'the heart rears wings bolder and bolder', 'Come you indoors, come home', 'I say more . . .', 'my heart in hiding/ Stirred . . . O my chevalier!'[21] Similar too is the belief of Duns Scotus, Hopkins' favourite medieval philosopher, that knowledge of God is not a matter of pure intellect as Aquinas supposed, but a matter of the intelligence's being directed by will and desire. The way to God is through the choosing self.

Thus the mind absorbs the stress of grace, and then stresses it with a deliberate act of will, saying yes. The result is an even more intense delivery of grace, raising the self to communion with God. The whole pattern of Hopkins' poem 'The Wreck of the Deutschland' is in fact based on these three moments of stress, tracing the weaving of them through two stories told in parallel – God's calling of a group of nuns to martyrdom in a shipwreck, and Hopkins' own call to the priesthood. With this poem (in 1875) Hopkins broke the seven years of virtual silence he had imposed upon his making of poetry after entering the Jesuit order. With it he seems to have resolved the acute tension he had earlier felt between a love of mortal beauty and devotion to the spiritual life, as he now finds nature to be a sacrament of the presence of God. At the heart of all wondering at the glory of God in the natural world is the experience that 'his mystery must be instressed, stressed'; the poem makes clear that this very same experience comes in an even more awe-inspiring way in time of spiritual conflict and crisis. It is these movements of stress that are disturbed in the fallen state of human beings, and which we shall find to be confused in Hopkins' own later dark night of the soul.

The first surge of stress touches the personality and creates desire for God; it is 'affective' grace. The 'stroke and a stress that stars and storms deliver' awakens us to search after God: 'Over again I feel thy finger and find thee.' Hopkins feels it not only in the natural 'glory of thunder' but in the 'lightning and lashed rod' of the moment when he knew himself called to the priesthood, 'the midriff astrain with leaning of, laced with fire of stress'. The nuns feel the awful finger of God, almost 'unmaking' them, in the literal storm at sea in which their ship is wrecked: 'they fought with

God's cold'. Then comes the second moment of stress, the 'elective' grace that enables the soul to make its choice for God. In everyday experience we can 'kiss [our] hand to the stars'; Hopkins recalls that in his crisis, when the sweep and the hurl of God's power trod him down, 'I did say yes' and 'fled with the fling of the heart to the heart of the host.' He reflects that the last thing fallen man ('thy rebel, dogged in den') often thinks of doing is hearing God's Word and speaking it back to him, whether it is in the best or worst experiences in life: 'Oh,/ We lash with the best or worst/ Word last.' But the nun in the shipwreck does 'lash' the Word to her desperate plight; she responds with her 'yes', crying in a loud voice 'O Christ, Christ, come quickly.' In speaking this word, in stressing the mystery, she is leaning upon the grace of Christ who *is* the Word of God and who is there in the storm. She reads the 'unshapeable shock night',

> Wording it how but by him that present and past,
> Heaven and earth are word of, worded by?

The selving of a personality, its 'doing-be' is also then a 'wording', the response to God that takes the form of the 'yes' of faith and the artefact of a poem.[22] After the stresses of affective and elective grace comes 'the grace of elevation', as the self receives a further charge of stress from God, bringing it into deeper union with himself. In observing the 'stars and storms' in nature, Hopkins says 'I bless when I understand'. In assenting to God in his spiritual crisis he finds his heart is enabled to 'tower from the grace to the grace', and that his self is sustained by the 'pressure' of grace, like water held steady in a well which is fed by streams trickling from a mountain. The result of lashing the Word to our 'shock night' is to find ourselves 'roped with . . . . Christ's gift'. These are pictorial accounts of what we can define in abstraction as the inscape upheld by instress. For the tall nun and her four companions the stress of elevating grace means entrance to heaven itself, and eternal fellowship with Christ, 'fetched in the storm of his strides'.

THE FALL: UNSELVING THE WORLD

Continuing the imagery of storm and sea in 'The Wreck of the Deutschland', Hopkins celebrates the sustaining grace of God as a wall which holds back or 'staunches' the flood, 'Stanching, quenching [the] ocean of a motionable mind'. In startling anticipation of a phrase which the theologian Paul Tillich was to make well-known many years later, Hopkins thus declares God to be 'Ground of being, and granite of it'.[23] His reference to the 'motionable' mind draws attention, moreover, to a further dimension of the limits that confront human freedom. Modern theologians, as we have already seen, find that the tensions of existence produce an anxiety which can only be dealt with authentically by trust in God. But instead we seek to quieten our anxiety in our own way, either by asserting our freedom and ignoring our limits, or by abandoning ourselves to the forces that condition us. Either way, we seek to find our security in making some object within the world our 'ultimate concern'. Hopkins also detects this latter trend towards idolatry, in an attempt to cope with the motion of the world. Nature is like a heaving ocean or a raging fire; its forms (inscapes) are in perpetual flux, colours shifting in the spectrum, melodies soaring and falling in wind and bird, the light sinking to sunset. At the heart of nature is death, as all beauty passes away. The human being shows his fallenness in seeking to grasp and possess the selves of the world. In 'The Leaden Echo and the Golden Echo' the temptation is to find 'some bow or brooch or braid or brace, lace, latch or catch or key to keep' beauty from vanishing away.

The result is not a lessening of anxiety, but despair. The golden echo urges the observer to 'Give beauty back . . . to God, beauty's self and beauty's giver.' Mortal beauty is to be met as 'heaven's sweet gift, then leave, leave that alone'.[24] According to Hopkins we meet the grace of God *through* the beauty of the world; we are not to confuse the Creator with creation, and in saying yes to God we find him to be the only final and permanent reality. Thus the stress is received and returned.

In idolatry we lose the balance between our freedom and the limits with which creation surrounds us. Seeking to make some finite thing ultimate may be to surrender to what conditions us, but it may also take the form of seeking to dominate the inscapes of the world. In Hopkins' view, the dialectic between self and others is out of balance because humanity has set out to assert its freedom, 'the heir/ To his own selfbent so bound, so tied to his turn',[25] and so to destroy the 'selves' of our 'rich round world'. Returning to the hamlet of Binsey, just outside Oxford, Hopkins finds the poplars have been felled. The particular character of the riverside scene had been the way that the 'airy cages' of the branches had caught the 'leaping sun' and the shadows of the bathers, bringing them into a special unity; now the self of the area had been destroyed, as one prick in an eyeball 'will make no eye at all'.

> After-comers cannot guess the beauty been.
> Ten or twelve, only ten or twelve
> Strokes of havoc unselve
> The sweet especial rural scene. . . .[26]

This inscape has been 'unselved' by subtraction; a little down the road Oxford itself has been unselved by addition. The particular nature of Oxford had been, according to Hopkins, the immediate 'encounter' of town with country, the dappled beauty of a 'towery city and branchy between towers', its swarms of bells and larks merging.[27] This was the outer shape of another encounter, an inner form where intellectual arguments met: 'here coped and poised powers'. But 'thou hast a base and brickish skirt there'; the encounter has been obscured, the character of Oxford has been soured, by the new red-brick suburban sprawl. Now, the result of unselving the world around us by asserting our own freedom, Hopkins perceives to be that we become locked or 'bound' in ourselves: we become 'selfwrung, selfstrung', and our thoughts 'grind' against each other in the confined space.[28] Hell is a prison, as Hopkins suggests in a meditation, because there the spirit 'instresses' nothing except 'acts of its own'.[29]

TRADITION AND NOVELTY: THE INCARNATION

The grace of God flowing through creation, upholding all its inscapes, can be understood as the brooding of the Holy Spirit or the grandeur of the Father. But usually, as we have seen, Hopkins identifies it as the presence of the divine Son who has become incarnate as Jesus Christ. In 'The Wreck of the Deutschland' he urges us to believe that the 'stroke and a stress that stars and storms deliver' does not come from the bliss of a God who remains in heaven, but from

> The dense and the driven Passion, and frightful sweat:
> Thence the discharge of it, there its swelling to be.

Though God's grace is in high flood already in creation, it breaks through to 'flush' all mortal beings when Christ is buried in the womb of Mary ('Warm-laid grave of a womb-life grey') and laid in the tomb after Calvary. The stress of grace 'rides time like riding a river'; it streams from the humility and passion of Jesus which happens within our history, and it is the influence of his suffering. Christ, 'Our passion-plunged giant risen' is thus incarnate throughout the inscapes of nature, and his features can be recognised in the individual forms of things. The universe is his playground, or the barn in which his eucharistic grain is stored. He can be 'gleaned' from the harvest fields of the clouds, and the stars are the 'piece-bright paling' which encloses his home.[30] Writing in his diary, Hopkins records the 'inscape [mixed of] strength and grace' in a bluebell, and remarks that 'I know the beauty of our Lord by it'.[31]

All this means that the stress we return to God ('his mystery must be instressed, stressed') will imitate the self-giving and sacrifice of Christ; the inner being of St Francis, for instance, is a 'lovescape crucified'.[32] In Hopkins' poem 'The Windhover: To Christ our Lord', the observer recognises first the majesty of Christ in the way that the 'dapple-dawn-drawn-falcon' masters the currents of air, swinging and gliding like the sweep of a skate's heel on a bend. But then comes a shift of thought in the highly ambiguous word 'buckle':

> Brute beauty and valour and act, oh, air, pride plumes here
> 　　Buckle! AND the fire that breaks from thee then, a billion
> Times told lovelier, more dangerous, O my chevalier!

The verb is indicative, continuing the majestic theme that Christ as divine Knight buckles on or arms himself with the elements of nature; it is also imperative, calling the 'heart in hiding' to respond ('I did say yes') by engaging itself in the spiritual battle. But 'buckle' is surely also a poignant play on words; the falcon drops down or collapses in the air as it plummets in a dive. So Christ has stooped low in humility, his life has buckled and crumpled, but from this passion there flashes the fire of sacrifice which is the energy in the world. Humble things can reveal beauty as they selve themselves; earth falls in front of a ploughblade but shines darkly as it is cut open, and half-burnt embers fall apart to 'gash gold-vermillion'. The response of the heart to the stress which flames from the bird is thus to follow the path of sacrifice.

To find Christ and his passion at the heart of the inscapes of the world is not, of course, altogether novel. The Apostle Paul identifies Christ with the same 'wisdom' which is portrayed in earlier Jewish poems as the pattern contemplated by God as he made the universe;[33] everything is intended to find its reality in Christ, so that 'all things hold together in him'.[34] The writer of the Fourth Gospel similarly identifies Christ as the Word which God had with him from the beginning and spoke forth as he created: 'all things were made through him' (John 1:3). Even closer to Hopkins is the thought of the philosopher Duns Scotus, whom Hopkins honours in the title of his poem on Oxford we have already considered – 'Duns Scotus' Oxford'.[35] Hopkins had arrived at his ideas of inscape and instress before reading Scotus, but when he did read him during his novitiate he was excited to find them confirmed and expanded. 'Just then', Hopkins wrote, 'when I took in any inscape of the sky or sea I thought of Scotus'.[36]

Like Hopkins, Scotus begins his account of reality not with general laws and principles, but with particular things. What distinguishes one individual from all others is simply its 'thisness' (*haecceitas*, or in Hopkins' curious spelling *ecceitas*), and this issues from the sheer will of God. Things are what they are because God wants them to be so. They are also united to each other in Christ, because according to Scotus God always intended his Son to become incarnate in the world, irrespective of the need to deal with the disaster of the fall. Creation was made with Jesus Christ in view, following from the primordial decision of God that the Son should become a human being and so bring finite creatures into the fellowship of the Godhead. As Hopkins expresses this belief in a meditation, 'The first intention of God outside himself . . . . the first outstress of God's power, was Christ.'[37] The consequent fall of humankind meant that incarnation would be the means of redemption from sin, but in some form it would have happened anyway. The consequence of this view is that the Word (*Logos*) of God at the centre of creation is not just a spiritual reality, but the Word made human flesh.

Standing within the tradition of the Catholic faith, faithful to belief in the incarnation of the eternal Word, Hopkins makes his own creative moves. He sets his own story of finding Christ in the selves of nature alongside the story of the Logos in the world. In doing so he draws upon such minority reports within the tradition as Scotist cosmology and Ignatian discipline of meditation, together with the Romantic view that imagination can unify the mind with the wholeness of reality; nevertheless he is still striking out into new territory of the spirit. The concept that the being of God can be grasped by intuition through the particular 'selves' of things is certainly already present in Scotus,[38] in what the philosopher calls a 'vision of existence'. But in Hopkins' vision of stress and inscape there is an astonishing fleshing-out of the idea, giving the encounter with God-in-Christ an immediacy and solidity. He is the 'energy-centre'[39] of the cosmos.

Hopkins, we notice, does not use the expanded form of the simile but the compression of metaphors. He does not say that the character of something in the world is 'like' Christ, because it is in his image; rather, it *is* Christ – in the sense that the energy (stress) that upholds it is the grace of Christ. They are the same, yet distinct. The bird is the divine Dauphin, the hills are his shoulders, the clouds are sacks of eucharistic grain.[40] Hopkins re-uses the Pauline ideas of being 'justified' and members of the Body of Christ with a simple immediacy; the just man 'acts in God's eye what in God's eye he is – Christ',[41] so that Christ is 'lovely in limbs not his' and to utter the word of response to God is to give birth to Christ in flesh again, making 'new Bethlehems' of us.[42] The idea of stress thus allows Hopkins to speak in a startling way of the identifying of Christ with the world, while not swamping the selves of either the natural objects or human persons.

Moreover, the compression of metaphor is much wider than the occasions when Christ is explicitly recognised in the world. In minting his images, Hopkins fuses objects with *each other* in an immediate way, usually without the link of 'as' and 'like'. Surprisingly unlike things are brought together, in compounds such as 'rope-over thigh', 'knee-nave', 'shadowtackle', 'rutpeel', 'beak-leaved', and 'fresh-firecoal chestnut-falls'. The underlying assumption is that they are linked by Christ; he is the hidden term of relation. Unique things can be compared, not because of any general laws of which they are part, but because the common element is Christ. Because the stress of Christ's presence upholds all things, because *he* is their neighbour, they can co-habit in concept and picture. They are all limbs of the one body. In 'The Windhover', for example, it is the relation to Christ that brings together the motley collection of bird, knight, skate, ploughshare and embers. In the provoking phrase of Daniel Harris, 'the incarnation has made metaphor superfluous'.[43]

IMAGINATION SHAPES THEOLOGY: THE FORM OF CHRIST IN THE WORLD

Now, Hopkins' vision of the incarnation at the heart of creation can, I believe, have an influence upon the theological question about 'the form that Christ takes in the world' (to use Dietrich Bonhoeffer's phrase). Theologians will ask what it can mean to speak of 'meeting' the risen Christ today, or being 'in Christ'. From the time of St Paul onwards, the Spirit or breath of God at work in the world has been brought into close connection with the Spirit of Christ; Paul himself tends to blur the 'edges' between the identities of the risen Christ and the Spirit of God.[44] But in what sense can we know Christ in or through the divine Spirit? Again, what can it mean to identify Christ with the wisdom upon which the world is patterned, or in modern jargon to call Christ 'the key to reality'?

One answer which a modern theologian can give to those questions would be to loosen the link between the human personality of Jesus of Nazareth and the divine Logos, Wisdom or Spirit. It is suggested that when we speak of encountering Christ we really mean that the same Spirit of God who was at work in the life of the human Jesus goes on being at work in the world and in human lives today. Because the Holy Spirit, or God immanent in the world, produces the same marks of true humanity in people here and now that he brought to birth in the ministry of Jesus, we naturally think of participation in the Spirit as meeting Jesus Christ.[45] Because Jesus evidenced the pattern of true humanity, open to God in obedience and to others in self-giving love, he can also be called the 'Wisdom' of God; there is embodied in him that purpose which God has for his creation, forming personalities out of the growth and flux of the natural world. But (it is said) what we experience now *is* God's purpose, not the human Jesus in whom that purpose was uniquely displayed.[46] Similarly, Jesus may be identified with the Logos or divine self-utterance because God has fully expressed himself through him. God has made himself one with Jesus, not in being but in function, acting through him so that the loving deeds of Jesus were isomorphous with those of the heavenly father. What we encounter now is therefore the eternal Logos or self-expression of God's nature, which can now be embodied in other people, communities and even things of beauty.[47] According to this view, we recognise the Logos and Wisdom of God here and now as the human Jesus of Nazareth (and so call him 'the Christ') inasmuch as the activity or Spirit of God was focused in him.

But another kind of theological answer would be this. God fully identified himself with the crucified man Jesus of Nazareth, not only in activity but also in *being*. As holy mystery, only God can reveal himself, and so if Jesus fully revealed God he must have been one with God essentially.[48] Moreover, human persons have their being in what they do and the relationships they make, so that if a man had been totally open to God in a relationship of obedience, and had been totally transparent to his activity, then he would be inseparable from the very being of God.[49] When we are concerned with personality there is a moving boundary between doing and being. So we cannot now think about, or experience, God's self-expression (Logos) and purpose for creation (Wisdom) without the human Jesus, and this is at least part of the meaning of the resurrection. It follows from this that God could only identify himself so fully with a human son because he has a mode of his own being which is eternally in the form of sonship, as well as a mode which is like a father; thus we arrive at the doctrine of the Trinity.[50] Finally, since God has united himself so fully with a human personality, the Holy Spirit who creates communion within God and fellowship between God and his creatures has taken on the characteristics of the human life of Jesus.[51]

Rough though these sketches are, they do represent two main approaches to Christology in present-day thinking. They are sometimes labelled as 'functional' and 'ontological' respectively. Both of them can fairly lay claim to be an interpretation of the Christian faith, and both recognise the mystery of the grace of God within the person of Christ. I do not here want to argue the case for each in detail, though I also have no wish to hide my preference for the second. Rather, my point is that theological talk, which is usually highly abstract and conceptual, ought not to be carried on without paying some attention to the very different kind of language used by a poet such as Hopkins. He is 'wording' the experience that the Christ who is present in the world seems to be the human Jesus who was crucified and not simply the eternal Logos. He expresses this in a playful and experimental way, in image that is frail under the demands of rational analysis, but which carries its own weight. He is witnessing to something that finally eludes theological concepts, but to which the concept has to try to do justice. In my opinion, the 'ontological' approach is more consistent with such experiences as Hopkins articulates, but the crucial point is that doctrinal formulation must come into dialogue with the poetry. Here, the direction of the dialogue is from literature to theology, in a deductive way. But the influence also flows the other way, inductively providing a hermeneutical tool for criticism of the poetry.

A CRITICAL PERSPECTIVE: THE GOD WHO HIDES HIMSELF

The theologian who affirms that God is free to reveal himself in the world will also want to warn that he is free to hide himself. Karl Barth, for instance, declares that God veils himself in the very act of unveiling himself; the God who opens himself to us is the hidden God, and we would never have known that he *is* Mystery unless he had made himself known to us.[52] Barth is a significant theologian to bring into dialogue with Hopkins, since like Scotus and Hopkins he believes that the whole of the physical creation is the setting (almost the by-product) of God's decision from all eternity that the divine Son should be identified with the man Jesus of Nazareth. In Christ, God eternally elects human beings for a covenant relationship with himself, and the creation follows as the stage for the covenant drama to take place.[53] Like Hopkins also, he speaks of our meeting the divine Word, who is Christ, through the medium of worldly objects; there is a 'secular form of the word of God'.[54] He does, of course, differ strongly from Hopkins in his rejection of any kind of natural theology; according to Barth, though God is free to reveal himself through many media,[55] the only worldly forms of the Word that Christian believers ought to interest themselves in are the humanity of Christ, the human word of scripture and the all-too-human word of preaching.

Even if, with Hopkins, we make our range of concern with natural things through which the divine Word can be met far wider than Barth allows, nevertheless he rightly draws our attention to the dynamics of the revelatory event. If Christ, as the Word of God, is encountered through worldly objects, then there will be a blend of revelation and hiddenness. Barth prompts us to see four reasons why this should be so.[56] First, God is unveiling himself in what is totally unlike himself, finite materiality, and so we are bound to see him 'through a glass darkly'. Yet he is humble enough to veil his glory in matter so that we can meet him and enter into fellowship with him. Second, the freedom of the Word of God means that it can never be possessed by human beings or stand under their control; God hides himself because he remains free to address and challenge the human self in new and unexpected ways. Third, God has revealed himself definitively in the cross of Jesus, and so has veiled his glory in suffering and death. Fourth, and perhaps most significantly for our study of Hopkins, the world through which God unveils his being is fallen. It has slipped away from his purpose at every level of creation, and so is bound to obscure the presence of the creator. Finally, the theologian Dietrich Bonhoeffer offers us a rather different reason; the world has 'come of age', and God deliberately veils himself in order to wean us away from a childish dependency upon what we imagine to be a dominating father-figure. He wants us to live 'as if there were no God' (*etsi non deus daretur*) and so 'allows himself to be pushed out of the world onto the cross'.[57] All these aspects of the hiddenness of God have something in common; they all, even the last, make clear that God is not actually absent from the world. As Bonhoeffer puts it, 'that is precisely the way . . . in which he is with us and helps us'. He withdraws, not altogether from the scene but from immediate availability.

Now, with the advantage of this theological perspective, we notice that in the central period of his poetry (1876–83), Hopkins takes little account of any negative swing into hiddenness. While the critic David Downes speaks rather incautiously of Hopkins' having developed a 'Romantic proof for the existence of God',[58] he does neglect the veiling of God in the world. We are therefore alerted to problems that may arise, not so much in Hopkins' own interior spiritual life (for any psychological account here must be speculative), as within the text itself, within the framework of a piece of imaginative writing in tension with tradition.

In the first place, we notice that Hopkins' sacramental vision of the world is sometimes in danger of suppressing nature through transubstantiation into the body of Christ. As we have seen, in theory the idea of inscape and instress preserves all selves in their distinct identity. In line with modern understanding of the sacraments among both Protestant and Catholic theologians, Hopkins finds the real presence of Christ to be a matter of his action in the elements of the world, and their transformation into places of encounter with him: 'I greet him the days I meet him.' John Robinson is therefore rather unfair on Hopkins when he remarks that his sacramentalism results in a failure to see things as they really are, in 'a collapse of perspectives which comes from seeing everything as actually or potentially holy'.[59] However, Robinson does acutely perceive that there are moments in Hopkins' poems when he sanctifies the cruelty and suffering of nature as the beauty of Christ. This, as Robinson suggests, is not just a moral failure in sensitivity to tragedy, but an aesthetic one; in exclamations like 'breathe, body of lovely Death', 'storm flakes were . . . lily showers' and 'is the shipwrack then a harvest?' Hopkins has lost sight of the fact that he is describing a wreck.[60] When he exults

Wring thy rebel, dogged in den,
   Man's malice, with wrecking and storm.
Beyond saying sweet, past telling of tongue,
Thou art lightning and love, I found it, a winter and warm . . .

he has ceased to see the physical destruction of storms except as a symbol of a spiritual 'wrecking'. The darkness in nature is to be admired as a shape of the hand of God. Even in 'The Windhover' he hovers on the verge of admiring the cross of Christ embodied in the world as a thing of beauty, as the embers 'fall, gall themselves and gash gold-vermillion'. The feeling of immediacy about the presence of Christ which can be so effective can also then jar upon the reader, as it does in Hopkins' incongruous remark on the actual eucharistic wafer: 'Forth Christ from cupboard fetched . . . .'.[61]

Such lapses are rare, but they are symptoms of a failure (at this point) to recognise that God is hidden as well as revealed in suffering. Associated with this, and perhaps more serious for Hopkins' relationship to the Christian tradition, is his tendency to view nature as unfallen. When Christ and nature are identified without any sense of hiddenness, the slipping of the cosmos away from the purpose of God cannot be taken seriously. This is exacerbated by Hopkins' conviction, under the lasting influence of his tutor at Balliol, Walter Pater, that beauty is linked to morality. 'Bodily beauty, even the beauty of blooming health, is from the soul', he wrote in a letter.[62] 'Self flashes off frame and face' –

especially the features of the face of children; the beautiful is the good. Now, since nature is beautiful, and the home of Christ, it must be immune from sin. Humankind leaves the world 'bare' and 'smeared with toil', but nature always has power of recovery, returning to its morning: 'For all this nature is never spent.'[63] In contrast, Hopkins finds a disappointed ideal in man; he loses his springtime as he grows to adulthood. Hopkins celebrates a primal innocence in young children, who share the 'dearest freshness deep down things' of nature; there is 'Innocent mind and Mayday in girl and boy',[64] and the bugler boy who comes to Hopkins for communion is 'fresh youth fretted in a bloomfall'.[65] Even in the later, more troubled period of his poetry, Hopkins celebrates the 'lovely lads' that St Gregory saw as 'wet-fresh windfalls'.[66] Yet Spring passes in human life and does not return; Hopkins, perhaps rather self-indulgently, wishes not to see the bugler boy as he grows older:

> Let me though see no more of him, and not disappointment
>   Those sweet hopes quell.

Hopkins is not captivated by the theme of a Christ *hidden* in the turmoil and complexities of adult human life; it is the open witness of childhood to Christ as the young hero which Hopkins appears to value. But his nostalgia for springtime, wishing that the oil of unction were a magical charm that 'locks love ever in a lad',[67] results in a collision between his convictions about the incarnation of Christ in nature and the fallen state of adult human beings. The two themes come into tension, and even some confusion, with each other and with the Christian tradition. In faithfulness to the Catholic tradition of a historical fall, a once-for-all cosmic decline, in one poem Hopkins interprets the beauty of spring in both childhood and nature as reflecting a lost Eden Garden, a Spring-time of the world:

> What is all this juice and all this joy?
>   A strain of the earth's sweet being in the beginning
> In Eden garden. – Have, get, before it cloy,
>
>   Before it cloud, Christ, lord, and sour with sinning . . .[68]

But elsewhere in his poetry at this time there is no recognition of the fall of nature into what the Apostle Paul calls a 'futility' and 'groaning' (Rom. 8: 20–22). The springtime of nature is ever re-newed despite human ravaging of it, its darkness turning to light each dawn, since the incarnate Christ inhabits its centre. In fact, Hopkins is far more interested, not in a past fall, but in the fall that takes place here and now in human life, the failure to keep the relationship open between self and other selves that we have explored. Using the conceptual models I have already discussed, we may say his picture of the fall follows less a U-shaped curve than a line of tension. In 'Spring and Fall: to a young child' the fall lies *ahead* for Margaret; it is when she 'knows why' she sorrows, and is cold to such sights as the falling of 'leafmeal', that she will have fallen. This is 'the blight man is born for'. In a late poem, 'On the Portrait of two beautiful young people', he knows that the two children will enter corruption; he acknowledges the view of the Church that 'corruption was the world's first woe', but he still protests against the havoc that the worm makes in the fruit of life. He refuses to accept it as a logical necessity:

> Oh but I bear my burning witness though
> Against the wild and wanton work of men . . .[69]

There, in that tension, the fragment breaks off. But why then is the fall inevitable? Either it is an inherited taint, deriving from a primeval cosmic collapse (the downward line of the U-shaped curve), or it arises from the tension in which human beings live, caught between their freedom and the limits of their finitude. Hopkins, one feels, inclines to the latter view (which I have been urging throughout this study), but in either understanding nature must be less perfect and more threatening in itself than Hopkins finds it to be at this period in his poetry. In the traditional account of the fall, the decline of the garden into thorns and thistles which frustrate human work is integral to the event; further, the story places a tempting serpent in creation *before* the moment of human choice. There is a persistent biblical portrayal of nature as a wilder-ness, where the effect of human sin is seen not so much as the spoiling of something perfect as a failure to bring an already existing chaos into order.[70] The story of the pre-cosmic fall of the angels that emerged in Jewish and Christian tradition seems to be a way of trying to cope with the evident disturbance of the environ-ment in which the human pair were placed. If, on the other hand, the Genesis story is understood as a mythological account of human existence, the fallenness of nature (whether located before or after the free choice of humankind) must be interpreted in terms of the pressure towards anxiety which our finite limits exert upon us; this is what Tillich calls 'tragic destiny', since the polarity of freedom and destiny ends inevitably (though not by a logical necessity) in sin.[71]

Whether fall is located in past event or present tensions, a Christian view of nature cannot lose a sense of its real distortions, despite the incarnational presence of the Logos. It is this that leads theologians to speak of the hiddenness of God. But in this period of Hopkins' poetry, the darkness at the heart of nature is minimised, as the smudge of humanity which will wear off, as winter which merges into spring, or as an instrument in the hands of God, who 'hast thy dark descending and most art merciful then'.

THE DARK NIGHT

Reading the poems of 1876–83 from a doctrinal perspective exposes an unresolved dilemma between incarnation and fall, and so it seems that they *must* in time deal in one way or another with the theme of the hiddenness of Christ. This actually occurs in the series of six sonnets, written between January and summer 1885, which express a terrible sense of being unable to find Christ within the inscapes of the world. When the poet 'words' himself, his cries seem like letters undelivered to 'dearest him that lives alas! away';[72] they are returned to the sender because the recipient has moved home and left no forwarding address.

We must, however, resist the temptation to find causes. Theology and experience certainly interact, but while it may be the case that the unresolved tensions of belief have led to an experience of the 'dark night of the soul', it may be (as one critic has maintained)[73] that Hopkins' theology was, conversely, always at the mercy of his temperament.[74] Such circumstances as his loneliness in Ireland, his 'grief of mind' over the handling of the Irish question in British politics,[75] and the stultifying routine of his academic duties at University College, Dublin ('It is killing work to examine a nation'),[76] all no doubt contributed something to the desolation into which he was plunged. Nor is this kind of purgation alien to the experience of many mystics on their spiritual ascent, and is even allowed for within the Ignatian Spiritual

Exercises. What we can, however, perceive most clearly from a doctrinal perspective is that the mood of these sonnets of desolation relates to the confusion between incarnation and fall. At the darkest point of the series, the uneasy juxtaposition has been resolved by fallenness overwhelming incarnation. They refer back constantly to themes and images of the earlier poetry, but reverse the confidence about being able to find the Body of Christ in the natural world. Instead, there comes upon the observer the hell that he had earlier ascribed to those who lack the ability to instress the glory of God, who are not open to other inscapes, and who are imprisoned in themselves. In aesthetic terms, all this amounts to a loss of creativity, under 'heaven's baffling ban'.

At the threshold to the desolate sonnets is one written in the last months of 1884, 'Spelt from Sibyl's leaves'. Following the pattern of the fifth Ignatian meditation, upon hell,[77] the poet envisages a rack on which the self endures the torment of being bound to itself, 'Where, selfwrung, selfstrung . . . thoughts against thoughts in groans grind'. While the daily experience of the falling of night is a symbol for the coming of the last judgement, we must not miss the point that it is a real scene that the poet is observing. The natural event of evening is no longer felt as testimony to the dawn that will come (*Poems*, 31), but as straining to be 'time's vast, womb-of-all, home-of-all, *hearse-of-all* night'. The stars are not homely 'firefolk', forming the close and bright fence of Christ's abode (*Poems*, 32), but so distant that they give only a 'wild hollow hoarlight' to the earth. In the twilight the 'dappled' beauty of the world (*Poems*, 37) is 'unbound', as things retreat into the stark outline of their isolated selves, 'self in self steeped and pashed'. The poet finds this prophetic of the apocalypse, when the 'veined variety' of human lives will be reduced to the black and white division of sheep and goats, but it is also the way he actually feels the impact of the night here and now, as something that 'whelms and will end us'. The Body of Christ, incarnate in nature, is being 'dismembered'. The boughs seem 'beakleaved . . . dragonish', an adjective that Hopkins uses elsewhere of the devil.[78]

In this sombre sonnet Hopkins is reflecting upon hell in general; in the following six he reports his own hell. 'I wake and feel the fell of dark, not day': the darkness that stifles and confines the self like an animal's pelt (fell) not only *has* fallen (fell) but *is* fallen, as part of lapsed nature. These sonnets continue to echo former poems, only to reverse their greeting of the incarnation. Instead of a sense of the Body of Christ in the whole cosmos, there are now images of a single human body in disintegration. Where once he heard all things cry out 'what I do is me', the poet now knows only his *own* bitter inscape: 'my taste was me'.[79] Once he gathered meal-drift from the silk-sacks of the clouds; now there is only a macabre eucharist of the self, as 'selfyeast of spirit a dull dough sours'.[80] Once he knew grace as a 'released shower, let flash to the shire', but now the only moisture is from the 'sweating self'.[81] Once he knew himself held steady by the pressure of instress, like being held by a rope 'all the way down from the tall/ Fells or flanks of the voel'; now he hangs unsupported over the void:[82]

> O the mind, mind has mountains; cliffs of fall
> Frightful, sheer, no-man-fathomed. Hold them cheap
> May who ne'er hung there.

A key element within this state of self-enclosure is the conflict between the affective and elective will. The arousing of the mind to desire of God through divine stress is now discordant with the act of choice. Thus, in 'Carrion Comfort' the moment when he 'kissed the rod' no longer has the clarity of a similar moment in the past, as described in 'The Wreck of the Deutschland' ('I did say yes/ O at lightning and lashed rod'). Though he has submitted, the poet does not know whom to cheer in the wrestling match, the 'hero whose heaven-handling flung me' or 'me that fought him'. The confusion is caught in the cry, 'O which one? Is it each one?' The loss of harmony in the will is further reflected in the report that 'we hear our hearts grate on themselves', and even when urging 'My own heart let me have more pity on' he distinguishes between his heart and 'me'.

In his study of these sonnets, Daniel Harris suggests that the image of the mountains of the mind, together with the very few other nature images in these poems (e.g. 'my chaff', 'heart's ivy') are not penetrations of inscapes in their own right but self-projections.[83] Nature is now so scarred by human sin that it simply images the human heart, and the distance between the observer and the observed has collapsed, into the pathetic fallacy and solipsism. The Christ whose presence required a real interchange between poet and nature is now absent. This critique does alert us to the caging[84] of the poet within himself, the failure to hold the tension between self and its outer limits, and the collision between fall and incarnation in nature. I am not convinced, however, that the critique of solipsism holds for the image of the 'skies/ Between-pie mountains' of the sonnet 'My own heart'; here the poet does seem to be actually looking at the dappled heavens. But this brings us to the question as to whether it is strictly accurate to talk about the disappearance or 'absence' of Christ as a consistent experience throughout the sonnet series.

HIDDENNESS OR ABSENCE?

We cannot know in what order Hopkins actually wrote the six 'terrible sonnets'. The fair copy he made of them ends with the two sonnets 'Patience' and 'My own heart let me have more pity on', thus apparently presenting a movement from deepening desolation into consolation. We cannot be sure, however, that the order of composition followed the pattern of the dark night of St John of the Cross, from death to resurrection. Some critics suggest that this arrangement leads the reader into a mistaken view of Hopkins' spiritual journey, which actually ended with 'the shattering experience of the disappearance of God'.[85] Looked at from this perspective, they urge that the two 'sonnets of consolation' do not in fact offer the sense of partial recovery that is often assumed, an argument which seems to be strengthened by the wintry tone of the last three sonnets Hopkins wrote in 1889. Other critics, on the contrary, maintain that the series 'follows too closely the classical descent and ascent of the Ignatian exercises to be fortuitous',[86] given the strong influence of the Ignatian pattern on Hopkins' other poetry. Bringing the sonnets into dialogue with theology will certainly not settle the question of order of composition, but it will offer critical tools for interpreting the mood of the poems written during 1885–89, and so make a contribution to answering the question of whether they present any signs of a recovery of Hopkins' vision of inscape and instress.

The theologian of today has been faced with the phenomenon of the apparent disappearance of God from human consciousness. We have already seen the appeal made to Blake's poetry by one member of the 'Death of God' movement, in order to support the view that we have no means at present of talking about the relationship of God to the world. However, the theologian will want to draw his own conclusions from the fact that the modern world is no longer conscious of God as an immediate, causative factor in daily life. He will want to ask whether this witnesses to the *absence* or the *hiddenness* of God. It may not be a sign of the withdrawal of God but his deliberate hiddenness for the sake of human freedom; God consents, as Dietrich Bonhoeffer put it, to be edged out of the world on to a cross. Bonhoeffer's fragmentary comments, written from a Nazi prison twenty years before the 'Death of God' movement, on the necessity of living *etsi deus non daretur* – as if there were no God – have rightly become a classical text:

> And we cannot be honest unless we recognise that we have to live in the world *etsi deus non daretur*. And this is just what we do recognise – before God! God himself compels us to recognise it. So our coming of age leads us to a recognition of our true situation before God. God would have us know that we must live as men who manage our lives without him. The God who is with us is the God who forsakes us (Mark 15:34). The God who lets us live in the world without the working hypothesis of God is the God before whom we stand continually. Before God and with God we live without God. God lets himself be pushed out of the world on to the cross. He is weak and powerless in the world, and that is precisely the way, the only way, in which he is with us and helps us.[87]

We notice that Bonhoeffer speaks, not of the absence of God (which was the way that 'death of God' theologians read him),[88] but of a God who 'is with us and helps us' because he shares our suffering. The world out of which he is 'edged' is a world in which things can be verified, and where objects are under our control and open to our analysis.

Now, if we read the 'terrible sonnets' of Hopkins from this perspective, we shall be alert to a distinction between absence and hiddenness. At the same time, the poems themselves will make a contribution to the theological exploration of the 'disappearance of God', giving the theologian cause to reflect upon a witness of great sensitivity to the character of the world. Reading with this alertness, we can certainly find an expression of the absence of God in the three darkest sonnets ('No worst', 'To seem the stranger' and 'I wake and feel the fell of dark'). The poet hoards his word 'unheard' by the one who 'lives alas! away', and cries 'Comforter, where, where is your comforting?' But the sonnet 'Carrion Comfort' interprets the experience of 'that night, that year/ Of now done darkness' as a wrestling of the soul with God. The very dislocation between affective and elective stress to which I have drawn attention requires the presence of God, even if he wears the veil of an enemy. The poet knows himself to be scanned by 'darksome devouring eyes', a phrase which hints at the look of a lover hidden in the stern gaze of the opponent. In remembering that 'I wretch lay wrestling with (my God!) my God', he blends the cry of forsakenness of the crucified Christ with a recognition that he is still after all dealing with *my* God. The whole poem reflects the Old Testament story of Jacob's wrestling with God, hidden beneath the guise of a strong man, and recalls Jacob's insistent cry that 'I will not let you go until you bless me (Genesis 32:26).'

With this key from Carrion Comfort, we can detect just a hint of the hidden-present one even in the most desolate sonnet of the series. In 'No worst' the poet is caught in a whirlwind, which recalls the whirlwind from which God spoke to Job, and perhaps even (as Mariani suggests)[89] the mighty rushing wind that preceded the coming of the Holy Spirit to the disciples in the upper room. The only comfort he can find is small and ironic enough – 'all/ life does does end' – but this does seem to point, not to annihilation, but to the grace of God hidden in death.

The two sonnets of consolation pick up quite clearly the theme of a hidden but not absent God, and show the poet coming to terms with this kind of grace. At the heart of both poems is an affirmation, though painful and reluctant, of the *unexpected* coming of Christ. In 'Patience' he asks 'where is he who more and more distills/ Delicious kindness?' and answers that he 'comes those ways we know'. The 'way' is to prepare the heart through the discipline of patient prayer, like making walls of a honeycomb firm and crisp, ready to be filled when the honey finally flows. Similarly, in 'My own heart' comfort is not to be found by becoming absorbed in our inner state of lack of comfort – 'by groping round my comfortless'. Rather the poet calls upon his heart to stop tormenting itself by probing its dark corners; he must simply wait for the unforeseen coming, leaving 'root-room' for comfort to be planted. Then the smiling consolation of God will unexpectedly break through, like the sudden appearing of dappled (pied) sky lighting the gap between mountain peaks:

                              let joy size

At God knows when to God knows what; whose smile
's not wrung, see you; unforseen times rather – as skies
Betweenpie mountains – lights a lovely mile.

The omnipotent grace of God drenches the world, but now
Hopkins perceives that a man cannot make it flow for him by
concentrating on his thirst: 'Thirst's all-in-all in all a world of wet.'
In another fragment of the time he suggests that we hold our
minds hopefully to Christ like a mirror to catch his reflection, but
the more we polish the mirror the more we see only ourselves:
'hold till hand aches and wonders what is there'.[90] Now, Daniel
Harris in his study of the 'terrible sonnets' protests that there is no
spiritual recovery in all this, but still a hanging over the abyss. The
'hypothetical coming' that the poet looks for is hardly the perpetual immanence of Christ in the world that he once knew. He
suggests that Hopkins has switched all his hope to an apocalyptic
vision, a waiting for the Second Coming or *parousia* (i.e. 'appearing') of Christ at the end of the age.[91] But to suggest that this was
Hopkins' *only* expectation is to miss the theological point that
hiddenness is not absence. A hidden God calls us to be open to
unexpected encounters with himself; as Hopkins' poems express a
waiting for Christ, so Bonhoeffer calls us to 'prepare the way' for
comings of the Christ who 'hides himself . . . goes incognito' in
the world.[92] In the New Testament, the *parousia* is the definitive
example of an unexpected divine coming, but the parables of Jesus
are also urging an attitude of alertness for many sudden comings
of the master of the house *within* history.[93]

   In line with this reconciliation to the hidden grace of God, we
now find descriptions of a natural world in which the glory of God
is veiled and more ambiguous. In 'Ashboughs', the way that the
boughs seem to touch the heavens can be described as 'new-
nestling' in them, and playing on them like an instrument, but
they also appear like 'talons' raking the sky. The earth can still
bring beauty to birth in the human mind, for those whose eyes can
see, but she is old and her trees hold out gnarled and groping
hands in praise to God:

            . . . it is old earth's groping towards the steep
         Heaven whom she childs us by.

In his tribute to St Alphonsus Rodriguez Hopkins celebrates the hidden work of God in human lives that seem quiet and uneventful, and yet are the location of a long inner spiritual struggle. Similarly, nature bears testimony not only to the dramatic work of the Creator, who 'hews mountain and continent/ Earth, all, out' but also to a 'trickling increment'; there is a secret inner pressure which is hardly discernible yet which slowly gives veins to violets and height to trees. Hopkins had detected the same 'lingering-out sweet skill' years before,[94] but now the truth comes to him with a new depth in the light of his own need for patience.

The glory of God is hidden in creation, because the incarnation of Christ is the veiling of divinity within the world. This perception lies at the heart of the poem 'That nature is a Heraclitean fire', which has been often criticised for introducing the resurrection suddenly and without connection with the flux of the world that precedes it. Hopkins describes all nature in movement, with clouds, light, earth and water all shifting and shadowing: 'Million-fuelled, nature's bonfire burns on.' In the midst of this, every 'manshape', each with a unique inscape ('disseveral, a star') is extinguished: 'Man, how fast his firedint, his mark on mind is gone . . .'. Abruptly then Hopkins declares, 'Enough! the resurrection . . .'. Critics[95] protest that this is simply an apocalyptic replacing of nature, 'in a flash', and only confirms the fact that here and now God is absent for Hopkins. But this exegesis neglects the force of the final words 'immortal diamond':

> In a flash, at a trumpet crash,
> I am all at once what Christ is, since he was what I am, and
> This Jack, joke, poor potsherd, patch, matchwood, immortal
>   diamond,
>   Is immortal diamond.

The reference to the incarnation is no mere artificial link between present and future as critics suggest. The human self is buried in the ash of nature's bonfire as 'mortal trash', just as diamond is buried in earth as dull carbon. But the Christian view of eternal life is not the automatic and inevitable emerging of diamond from ash as the liberation of the soul from within the prison of the body. That is the Greek view of immortality. The Christian understanding is that death puts an end to life, and is only conquered through the resurrection of Jesus in which human beings share. Thus the incarnation is the burying of Christ himself in the ash of the world. Again we return to an early perception of Hopkins, that the incarnation was 'Warm-laid grave of a womb-life grey',[96] but with new access of meaning; if Christ is no longer celebrated as shining out in the wildfire of nature, this is not because he is absent but because he is hidden in the ashes and clinkers.

A view of nature in which God-Christ is veiled ought also to have consequences for an understanding of human fallenness; there can be no absolute contrast between impure humanity and pure nature. Nature shares in the fallen state, and this in turn means that the human person can be neither expected to reach an unrealistic ideal nor regarded as the sole corrupting factor in the cosmos. Neither crown nor slime, he can be treated for what he is – a being with finite limitations and yet some potential of freedom. In his last poems Hopkins does still celebrate ideal manly power ('Churlsgrace, child of Amansstrength') and youthful beauty ('wet-fresh windfalls'), and recoils from the packs of 'Tom Navvies' who have been turned into manwolves by unemployment, whose 'packs infest the age'.[97] But there also emerges a rueful, gently self-mocking portrait of the human being as unpretentious 'Jack-self'. In his penultimate sonnet[98] he pictures the saint, like Moses the Shepherd of Israel 'fronting forked lightning' in his confrontation with God; he also pictures the Satan who falls like lightning from heaven, 'a story of just, majestical and giant groans'. But most of us are neither saint nor fallen angel, but simply human: 'Man Jack the man is, just; his mate a hussy.' Hopkins numbers himself among such; tragic emotions are out of place when the human visage is like an image reflected in a spoon – less Promethean than slightly grotesque. So Hopkins can direct an irony against himself for getting so worked up: 'tame/ My tempests there, my fire and fever fussy'. At this last moment of his poetry and life Hopkins finds a tolerance of human beings (though not a toleration of the human *condition*), which accepts both freedom and limit.

Reading the poetry of 1885–89 from a theological perspective, we thus detect a movement away from a sense of total withdrawal of God to a recognition of his hidden presence. This, conversely, must have an effect upon theological discussion about the modern sense of the 'death of God'; Hopkins' witness to the veiling of a God who is still not absent ought to be heard. There are, moreover, two other contributions that Hopkins' developed vision of mortal beauty can make to the theologian's task. Hopkins has a theology in which knowledge of God can be gained from nature, but at his best he understands this not as a matter of observation and deduction by the unaided use of human reason, but as encounter with a self-revealing God. His poetry is an aesthetic working-out of the theological idea of 'general revelation' that I outlined in the second chapter. Only such a theology can make sense of the darkness in nature, for while God cannot be *proved* from a cosmos where there is suffering and pain, he can be *encountered* within it. The poetry of Hopkins can prevent the theologian from being edged into the corner of thinking there are only two alternatives – that either the human mind can make its own way to God through reasoning from the witness of nature, or that God reveals himself in Christ and Bible alone.

There is one more significant element in a dialogue between poetry and theology where God is celebrated as the hidden-present One. Two of Hopkins' last poems contain the note of protest against a loss of creativity, explicit in 'Thou art indeed just, Lord' and implicit in the final 'To R.B.' Commentators either find this protest to be evidence for the fact that God has finally 'disappeared' for Hopkins, or they find it sublimated within a submission to God.[99] But, while protest is itself a witness that Hopkins is aware of the presence of God (or he would not be speaking to him), it cannot be underplayed. The poetry of Hopkins insists, if we had not learnt this from Jeremiah and Job, that protest is a genuine part of religious experience which theology must interpret without reducing it. In his poem based on Jeremiah's complaint, 'Why do the wicked prosper?'[100] Hopkins has indeed added the address 'O thou my friend' to the prophet's words, and his concluding plea places the pronoun 'mine' in a position to qualify 'Lord' with a lingering stress, as well as 'life':

> . . . birds build – but not I build; no, but strain,
> Time's eunuch, and not breed one work that wakes.
> Mine, O thou lord of life, send my roots rain.

But we must not undermine the protest against the deadening effect upon the poetic mind of the hiddenness of God in the world. Wind shakes the fretted leaves, but this does not breathe Spirit into the poet. In 'To R.B.' (i.e. Robert Bridges) inspiration is portrayed as a jet of breath, 'like the blowpipe flame' that impregnates the womb of the mind; but the poet's winter world fails to deliver that spurt of stress, and the very last line of the sonnet gives a vivid sound picture of small gasps of breath escaping, as from a collapsed pipe. If Bridges notices that his poetry lacks in truly creative music,

> My winter world, that scarcely breathes that bliss
> Now, yields you, with some sighs, our explanation.

The implication is clear; the world, or rather the Creator, is responsible, and must join with Hopkins in offering an ('our') explanation. Theology must grapple with this protest. It may justify the hiddenness of God as a concomitant of human freedom, partly as a divine strategy which makes room for this freedom and partly as a situation that arises from the results of human freedom (that is, sin). In the latter case we may say that God himself protests against the veiling of his glory in fallen nature, contradicting the present reality of the world by the promise of the resurrection. The only way past 'protest atheism', as Jürgen Moltmann suggests, is to affirm 'a protesting God involved in human sorrow'.[101] But no justification can be complete. God remains responsible for initiating the project of freedom in his creation, desiring to bring free personalities into fellowship with himself. Whether the risk was worth it is left for us to judge, and God is humble enough to leave us the verdict. What we can say, theologically, is that in the cross God himself has shared the consequences of that risk, and so can offer us the fellowship of a 'fellow-sufferer who understands'. Critically, we can also observe that the poems in which Hopkins laments his loss of creativity show no loss of 'the rise, the carol, the creation' and are among his finest poetry.

7

D.H. Lawrence: *Agape* and *Eros*

Like William Blake a century before him, D.H. Lawrence is aware of the disintegrating of the human personality under the stress of life, and is in search of the wholeness or 'integrity' of the self.[1] His characters do not inhabit myths as Blake's do, yet they form the cast of legends rather than documentaries; though they can be placed on the English social scene, Lawrence depicts their inner states of mind with an intensity that readers often protest is not 'realistic'. Just as Blake's figures whirl between death and life in bewildering metamorphoses, Lawrence's whirl between hate and love for each other with a shocking suddenness. But like Blake, Lawrence is not describing feelings with a clinical precision; he is evoking moods of the conscious and unconscious mind that cannot be captured in words, but which can be hinted at by a disturbing use of language.

Like Blake also, Lawrence finds that our concentration upon the mental consciousness has suppressed the springs of creative impulse within us. Where Blake lamented the suppressing of the imagination, Lawrence asks us to rediscover the 'spontaneous motion' of the self, or the 'creative quick': 'the quick of the self is *there*. You needn't try to get behind it. As leave try to get behind the sun.'[2] While he sometimes calls this deep centre of life the unconscious, and at other times the 'primal consciousness', he is clear that its 'primary impulses, desires, motives'[3] are a kind of knowledge which is more radical than mental reasoning; as Birkin accuses Hermione, in the novel *Women in Love*:[4]

> Passion and the instincts – you want them hard enough, but through your head, in your consciousness. It all takes place in the head, under that skull of yours.

In an echo of Blake's *Zoas*, Lawrence locates the various kinds of life-force in different parts of the body, placing the primal or passional consciousness in the abdomen. For Lawrence, however, the basic tension between freedom and limit is less at root a conflict between internal faculties, than a 'polarized flux'[5] between the spontaneous self and other realities outside it. It is through the mental consciousness that we have 'a recognition of abysmal otherness' and so Lawrence detects a 'twofold passional circuit of the lower vital self-realization, and the upper, intense realization of the other'.[6] The knowledge of the beloved, 'that which I myself am not', is 'knowledge of the *limits* of the self'.[7] The vital self can only develop by coming up against resistances to its impulsiveness and spontaneity, whether those boundaries are in the natural world, society or other individual selves. This has already become a familiar theme in this study, but Lawrence makes a distinctive contribution; he sees that the way this balance becomes disturbed, and the path to its recovery, is bound up with modes of love.

Since modern Christian theology has also been greatly concerned with the meaning of love, often coming into conflict with more classical theological ideas about love as *agape*, there is obvious scope here for the Christian critic to set up an illuminating dialogue between literature and doctrine. In fact, Lawrence himself is already in constant dialogue with the Christian tradition in this matter, accusing Jesus of imposing a spiritual ideal and overlooking the human boundaries:

> To be able to live at all, mankind must be loved more tolerantly and contemptuously than Jesus loved it, loved, for all that, more truly, since it is loved for itself, for what it is, not for what it ought to be. Jesus loved mankind for what it might be, free and limitless.[8]

This quotation makes clear that Lawrence, unlike Blake, is not a Christian writer in the sense I have already defined this character. He is not committed to a certain tradition of symbols, doing new things with them from *within* the community that lives by them. But he does draw upon the story and images of the Christian faith, and is certainly a 'religious' writer in the sense that he is alert to a mystery of being that transcends the material world. As Paul protests to Miriam, in *Sons and Lovers*,[9]

> I reckon a crow is religious when it sails across the sky. But it only does it because it feels itself carried to where it's going, not because it thinks it is being eternal.

THE LOVE WHICH FULFILS THE SELF

Lawrence's novels depict two major dimensions of love between human persons, which, as we shall see, also happen to be the aspects of love which interest the theologian. In an essay, Lawrence names them as 'sacred' and 'profane' love, and portrays them respectively as a 'coming together' and a 'going apart'.[10] How much he believes the first to be dependent upon the second is shown in a conversation between Rupert Birkin and Ursula Brangwen in *Women in Love*:

> 'What I want is a strange conjunction with you –' he said quietly; '– not meeting and mingling; – you are quite right: – but an equilibrium, a pure balance of two single beings: – as the stars balance each other.' She looked at him. He was very earnest, and earnestness was always rather ridiculous, commonplace, to her. It made her feel unfree and uncomfortable. Yet she liked him so much. But why drag in the stars (p.165).

Birkin, who is a thinly disguised self-portrait of Lawrence himself, is proposing an ideal love union to be one in which love affirms and completes the individual self. Lawrence is opposed to what he calls here 'mingling' and in other places 'merging', or a losing of each person in the other. When two people are in love, there should be no 'absorbing', or 'sucking' of one partner's being into the other. Rather, Lawrence (through Birkin here) is looking for 'singleness' or integrity of the self. Through the communion of love, each lover should fulfil his or her own being, becoming more truly what he or she is. 'In each', thinks Birkin, 'the individual is primal, sex is subordinate, but perfectly polarised. The man has his pure freedom, the woman hers. Each admits the different nature in the other'. (p.225)

But how can the harmony between self and another be maintained? How can each free self remain 'in gem-like singleness, proud as a lion, isolated as a star'[11] while limited by its orbit with another? Lawrence's first answer is through the exercise of the will, which he describes as 'a great balancing faculty'.[12] When Birkin's male cat cuffs a wandering female stray with 'sudden little blows of his magic white paws', Birkin denies that he is acting as a bully:

With the Mino it is the desire to bring the female cat into a pure stable equilibrium, a transcendent and abiding rapport with the single male. Whereas without him, you see, she is a mere stray, a fluffy sporadic bit of chaos (p.166).

His theory is that Mino is not exercising a Nietzschian 'will to power' but a 'will to ability', enabling the female cat to become more truly herself, finding her own identity in a stable relationship with the other. But Lawrence recognises that this exertion of the will can easily slide into a dominating of one partner by another, a fall into possessiveness. So, when he affirms that 'Adam kept Eve in the indestructible paradise, when he kept her single with himself, like a star in its orbit', Ursula bursts in with the objection, 'a satellite of Mars – that's what she's to be! . . . You want a satellite!' (p.167) Though Birkin replies indignantly that he 'neither implied nor indicated nor mentioned a satellite', she refuses to let the objection go. The image of two stars, balanced by their gravitational fields in one orbit, easily slips into the image of the one as a moon in the orbit of the other; thus we feel the inevitability with which the will becomes distorted, and the tension falls into disorder.

The will, then, should be holding each spontaneous self separate in a self-fulfilling love. But it can capitulate to the mental consciousness and fail to draw upon the vital force of the primary impulses. As a result, the dark reservoir of spontaneous feeling can burst open in an uncontrolled fashion. Like the flaming boy 'Orc' in Blake's mythology, passion repressed by the mind breaks out in unhealthy ways. When the intellectual society hostess of *Women in Love*, Hermione, brings a paperweight crashing down on Birkin's head and nearly kills him, 'she was purely unconscious in her ecstasy' (p.117). She is normally stiff and intense in a 'tight conscious world' (p.44), always wanting 'to know', to possess with her mind whatever she observes. While Birkin actually praises her for her one moment of spontaneity with the paperweight, her dark self of 'animal instinct' has erupted destructively because she has not 'got any real body, any dark sensual body of life.' (p.46) In another symbol, we find that Gerald is confident in mastering the water when he swims on the surface, but when he has to dive deep down 'there seems a whole universe under there; and as cold as hell, you're as helpless as if your head was cut off.' (p.206)

The mental consciousness, towards which the will can

overbalance, is not simply the power of reasoning; it has the wider scope of providing awareness of others, 'the adding of another self to the own self, through the mode of apprehension.'[13] The equilibrium between the self and other reality can, as we have already seen in other contexts, be upset by over-assertion of either freedom or limit. On the one hand, then, Lawrence depicts the free will as attempting to control the world around. When Gerald Crich by force of will holds his frightened horse forward towards a passing train, Ursula diagnoses the act as 'a lust for bullying, a real *Wille Zur Macht*' (p.167). Lawrence's particular insight is that this mental 'will to power' over others is actually a *loss* of selfhood and freedom, since it neglects the deep, impulsive life which makes the individual distinct. On the other hand, the balance can also be disturbed by a surrender to the reality of others, an abandonment to what limits us; in terms of love, this is a sentiment and a sympathy which is 'all merging into the other'. Lawrence maintains that this selfless love is in fact another kind of 'bullying', an imposing upon the other because it does not enable the other to be 'burnt apart into separate clarity of being'.[14] When Gudrun dances before the fierce Highland cattle, holding them spell-bound, the symbol has many echoes, evoking both will-to-power, and a selfless 'fusing into one':

> . . . her feet pulsing as if in some little frenzy of unconscious sensation, her arms, her wrists, her hands stretching and heaving and falling and reaching and falling, her breasts lifted and shaken towards the cattle, her throat exposed as if in some voluptuous ecstasy towards them. . . . Soon she would touch them, actually touch them (p.187).

The sexual undertones here are evident and, as we shall see later, the urge to touch someone can be a sign of wanting to impose upon him. Gudrun and Gerald are going to destroy each other through attempting to absorb each other, though they experience hints of a different kind of love; in a canoe one day Gudrun is aware of 'their being balanced in separation, in the boat' so that her reply 'but I'm very near' is as true as his remark 'there is a space between us.' (p.198)

Ironically, Lawrence himself perhaps shows his own failure to keep the balance in that his male characters are often obsessed by the fear that it is the females who always try to absorb them; it is the female desire for 'merging' that must be resisted by the will of the male.[15] In Birkin's view of the matter,

> He wanted to be with Ursula as free as with himself, single and clear and cool, yet balanced, polarised with her. The merging, the clutching, the mingling of love was become madly abhorrent to him. But it seemed to him, woman was always so horrible and clutching, she had such a lust for possession, a greed of self-importance in love. She wanted to have, to own, to control, to be dominant. Everything must be referred back to her, to Woman, to the Great Mother of everything, out of whom proceeded everything and to whom everything must finally be rendered up (p.224).

We must question whether this is actually recognising the reality of the female as truly other; Lawrence, indeed, is an artist and not a dogmatician and undercuts Birkin's assertions by the sly remark that he meditated like this when he was ill, and that 'he liked sometimes to be ill'.

THE IMAGE OF THE FALL

As Birkin's earlier remark about Adam's keeping Eve 'single with himself' illustrates, Lawrence finds the story of Eden before the fall to be an effective symbol for the wholeness of the self in relationships.[16] Similarly, he does not treat the account of the coupling between 'the Sons of God and the daughters of men' in Genesis 6 as a fall-story, but as a symbol of true passion and of the 'power to enable' in relationships.[17] However, though he is acutely aware of the fallen state of human life in modern industrial society, he does not make the stories part of a myth of the eternal return. There is to be no return to a past Eden; in the terms we have been discussing the matter, there is no U-shaped curve of history.

The self must go on developing in the direction of singleness, in the context of successive societies and cultures. This is made clear when Birkin meditates further on his model of the stars in equilibrium: 'Why should we consider ourselves, men and women, as broken fragments of one whole? It is not true. . . . Rather we are the singling away into purity and clear being, of things that were mixed.'[18] The implicit reference here is to Plato's fall-myth in his

Symposium, describing an original state, when human beings were a mixture of both sexes.[19] According to the myth, the gods punished humankind for its pride by splitting each being apart, so that (in Birkin's words) 'the process of singling into individuality resulted in the great polarization of sex.' Lying behind Lawrence's use of the myth is also the Genesis account of the creation of woman from the rib of Adam, and the biblical ideal of sexual relationship as becoming 'one flesh' again. But Birkin's commentary upon these myths is to protest that sexual relationships do not make two one again, as if 'the still aching scar of laceration' were to be healed. Rather, he sees the point of the myths as showing that the process of separation of the sexes is not complete, and that the process is to go on being completed through passion:

> Rather the sex is that which remains in us of the mixed, the unresolved. And passion is the further separating of this mixture, that which is manly being taken into the being of the man, that which is womanly passing to the man, till the two are clear and whole as angels, the admixture of sex being in the highest sense surpassed, leaving two single beings constellated together like two stars.[20]

We recall that Blake had also appealed to a myth of the original androgyny of human beings, as a means of depicting the fragmentation of the self in its present fallen state. But Lawrence takes a slightly different angle on the myth. In 'the old age' of Adam and Eve, 'the separation was imperfect, even then. And so our world cycle passes.' There is to come a new day, when each lover 'is fulfilled in difference'. The novels and stories of Lawrence picture the coming of that day, as people attain the freedom of their own separate being through passion, without 'any of the horrible merging, mingling self-abnegation of love'.[21] True love maintains and completes the self. The paradisial image of Adam and Eve is a useful symbol of balanced relationships, but there can be no return to a past golden age since the process of separation was not complete in any past age.

The process is one of continual tension between the impulsive self, which arises from dark regions in the unconscious, and the other realities which are grasped by the mind. We have already seen how the spontaneous self needs to find balance with other selves, in what one critic has called 'a dialectic between impulse and resistance'.[22] In a persistent image, the 'hardness' or gem-like nature of others must be recognised and enabled, so that 'hard' identity can be developed in the self. Yvette, in *The Virgin and the Gipsy*, only finds that hardness in the gipsy: 'something hard inside her met his stare. . . . something hard in her registered . . . a purity like a living sneer'.[23] The self can meet the same quality in a natural landscape, as in the 'hard, silent abidingness of rock, the surging resistance of a tree . . .'.[24]

Society also can supply this necessary 'resistance' against which the self defines itself. In Lawrence's novels it is usually the man who needs the wider perspective of the 'far off world of cities and governments', since he is playing the enabling role in the male–female relationship, but this is not always the case. In *The Rainbow*, the farming community of Brangwens lives in a 'blood intimacy' with the soil and each other, in a paradisial intercourse between 'blood, earth and sky and beast and green plants'. But the women 'looked out from the heated, blind intercourse of farm life to the spoken world beyond'.[25] The account in this novel of the earlier life of the Ursula of *Women in Love* shows her trying to find herself in the context of work in a wider society, though she has not achieved her aim by the end of the book. She is well-placed to mock at Birkin's pretentious description of an ideal self as being like a 'hare, sitting up' alone on a landscape totally empty of human beings.[26] She, and the other women of the Marsh, know that the personality needs a larger context to become truly itself. Society and culture are a necessary limit and defining boundary for freedom.

Lawrence is in rebellion against the destructive influence of modern society upon the self; but the dialectic between the free self and the limits of society is a subtle one. Raymond Williams justly comments that, 'He attacked the industrial society of England, not because it offered community to the individual but because it frustrated it.'[27] As Birkin shows by purchasing an antique chair for his new home, he values the culture a society produces, as long as it does not become an idol, stifling the spontaneity of the self here and now. The point is getting the right balance between freedom and limit.

SELF-FULFILLING LOVE AND SPIRITUALITY

In *The Rainbow*, there is just a hint that the Christian tradition of spirituality might be of positive value in awakening us to the unconscious self of passion and instinct, and in combatting the tyranny of the intellect. In her growing years, Ursula finds that the images of the Bible open up an awareness of a visionary world that transcends mental argument, if they are used with a 'non-literal application'.[28] Like the sex urge, Christian images can prompt a sense of wonder and 'protect the dark forest'[29] of the primal self against the invasion of scientific calculation, as symbolised in the laboratory of Tom Brangwen. Though Ursula is presented as luxuriating in her dream world at the expense of her outer life in society, Lawrence himself uses the images in the same way, especially the one which attracted Ursula herself, where the 'Sons of God came in unto the daughters of men'. But in the earlier novel, *Sons and Lovers*, Lawrence presents Christian spirituality in a more negative way, as being another form of possessive love, which Birkin's theory of the 'constellated stars' will oppose.

Sons and Lovers is an extended study of the 'horrible merging and absorbing' tendency in love which so revolts Lawrence. In the first place, the possessive love of his mother blocks Paul's full development within a relationship with another woman, Miriam. But it is in the Paul–Miriam affair that Lawrence works out the irony that sympathy and self-giving (love as 'coming together') can result not only in the loss of the self that gives, but the self on whom the giving is imposed. In his immensely subtle description, things are not always what they seem. As Paul, for instance, becomes more sexually awakened, he believes that Miriam is simply suppressing the desires of the physical body. She has a mystical, spiritual disposition, which is always seeking communion:

> To Miriam, Christ and God made one great figure which she loved tremblingly and passionately when a tremendous sunset burned out the Western sky . . . (p.176).[30]

She even trembles in spiritual awe before the algebra Paul teaches her, making him protest, 'Why do you tremble your soul before it. You don't learn Algebra with your blessed soul. Can't you look at it with your clear simple wits?' (p.194) Following the example of her mother, who exalts even the humble task of boiling potatoes to the plane of a religious trust, she makes a communion service out of smelling the wild roses: 'she went forward and touched them in worship'. (p.198) Actually their difference in temperament is helping both of them; she teaches him a sensitivity to living things, and he gives a mental form and clarity to her vague perceptions. But Paul believes that this spirituality blocks her engagement in physical passion, and looking back later on the way their affair has gone, he tells her 'You are a nun':

> You are a nun. . . . The words went deeply into her heart again and again. Nothing he had ever said had gone into her so deeply, fixedly, like a mortal wound (p.308).

At first sight it does seem that Miriam simply lives by a religious dualism, repressing the 'dark body of sensual life' from the 'lofty' position of spiritual ideals, as Hermione had exalted the intellectual ideal. But the distortion of the will by mental consciousness goes deeper than this. Lawrence makes clear that Miriam does not resist physical passion; the unhealthy thing is that she wants it *in a certain way*. What Paul recoils from is not simply that she wants him as a spiritual partner, but that she wants to use physical love for what she understands to be spiritual ends. She recognises the urge to passion, but will not allow this urge to have its own free creativity. So he feels the love of Miriam as a kind of bullying, or interfering with his soul. An early incident, which Lawrence calls an 'Annunciation' makes clear that Miriam is actually sexually awakened before Paul; as she comes upon him suddenly in a lane, she has a 'revelation' that 'she must love him' (p.205), and she longs for physical contact with him before he is even aware of his feelings (p.214). But she wants physical love as a religious act, a kind of prayer. So she waits for the moments when Paul is in a state of 'fine abstraction', reflecting upon spiritual and moral issues, and only then offers to touch and kiss him. 'She wanted to run her hands down his sides. She always wanted to embrace him, so long as he did not want her.' (p.233) Miriam certainly helps Paul to reflect upon the spiritual issues that his commonsense mother scorns; she encourages him 'to wrestle with his own soul, frowning, passionate in his desire for understanding. And in this passion for understanding her soul lay close to his.' But this is the moment she chooses to touch him physically, as a means of touching his soul: 'Then, if she put her arm in his, it caused him almost torture. His consciousness seemed to split.' (p.214)

In his view, she does not want him in bodily, but only in spiritual love; he complains that 'I'm so damned spiritual with you always!' But this is a partial misunderstanding; 'She remained silent thinking. "Then why don't you be otherwise?"'. The truth is barely conscious for either of them; she wants a real kiss, but in the service of spiritual experience and ideals, and so she wants it when he himself is not physically aroused:

> He saw her crouching, brooding figure, and it seemed to tear him in two . . . 'You make me so spiritual!' he lamented. 'And I don't want to be spiritual.' She took her finger from her mouth with a little pop, and looked up at him almost challenging. . . . If he could have kissed her in abstract purity he would have done so. But he could not kiss her thus – and she seemed to leave no other way. And she yearned to him (p.232).

So he turns back to doing a French translation with her. Later, when he accuses her of never wanting him, but only what he could 'reel off for her', she protests, 'Why, when would you let me take you!' (p.239)[31] Lying in the grass in spring, we read that he could not bear to look at Miriam; 'she seemed to want him, and he resisted. He resisted all the time.' But he cannot give her tenderness because

> . . . he felt that she wanted the soul out of his body, and not him. She did not want to meet him so that there were the two of them, man and woman together. She wanted to draw all of him into her (p.239).

These are scenes which summon up the deep criss-cross currents of emotion in a masterly way. They cannot be completely analysed, and Lawrence himself could not have fully answered Paul's question to Miriam, 'If you put red berries in your hair, why do you always look like some . . . priestess, and never like a reveller?' (p.231) But they point to the fragmenting of the personality, and in particular to a possessive kind of love that tries to absorb the other person. Paul says that it tries to 'wheedle the soul out of things' rather than 'going straight'. Miriam's kind of love does recognise the 'dark self', and as with Ursula's use of the Bible, her spirituality awakens her to the wonder of life. She does not repress the body as the intellectual will does, but Miriam is still not a 'reveller' in life because she tries to make the dark self a mere vehicle for spiritual ideals and moral values. She will not allow it to be spontaneous, forming her into 'the single self, inviolable and unique'.[32] Her love is possessive because it puts the other at a disadvantage by offering physical passion only at times when the other does not want it and cannot return it. It is possessive because it is imposed upon the other; under the guise of total self-giving, it is really domination.

So we come to the very foundation of Lawrence's quarrel with Christianity. He felt that the Christian conception of the love of God meant an absorbing of human beings. Like his devotee, Miriam, God wants to suck the soul out of us, to bully us, not to allow us to be ourselves in our individuality. His love is not of Birkin's kind, a love which maintains and fulfils the self, but is a 'horrible merging and mingling' in which the self is lost. This, then, is also the love which Christians are supposedly to have for each other. But the necessity for 'gem-like singleness, proud as a lion, isolated as a star' within us cannot be finally suppressed; if we repress it, we shall hate both what we have become and then hate our neighbours as ourselves.[33] If the Christian protests that he understands from the cross of Jesus that so far from dominating us God's love is self-sacrificing, Lawrence replies that this is precisely the problem. A person is imposing and interfering if he wants, like Miriam, to give love in a way that prevents the other from being essentially him- or herself in giving something also. Early on, Miriam conceives of her love as a sacrifice, and models herself upon the crucified Christ:

> 'Lord, if it is Thy will that I should love him, make me love him – as Christ would, who died for the souls of men.' . . . Then she fell into that rapture of self-sacrifice, identifying herself with a God who was sacrificed, which gives to so many souls their deepest bliss (p.212).

Finally she submits to Paul's urging for sexual intercourse in the same mood of sacrifice; Paul finds it not bliss but a cold offering, which makes clear that their relationship has died.

EROS AND AGAPE

As we place the Lawrentian and the Christian love stories side by side, we can now give a theological name to Birkin's definition of love. The love which affirms the personality of the lover as a single star is *eros*. *Eros* is desire, but not just sexual desire; it is the quest to be satisfied at the deepest levels of being, a search for the beautiful and the good that will maintain and fulfil the self. Lawrence in fact disagrees with the Freudian analysis of the unconscious; the primary motivation for the dark 'passional consciousness' (or unconscious, or 'blood consciousness') is not the sexual urge, but the urge for creativity, for 'building something wonderful'.[34] Now, Christian theologians have usually distinguished *eros* from a second kind of love, an *agape* which is defined as a totally self-giving and self-spending love, sacrificing the self without expectation of receiving anything in return. Christian theology has, of course, been in accord with Lawrence in rejecting possessiveness in love as thoroughly unhealthy, but it has often tried to counter this distortion by commending a love which is *agape* unmixed with any *eros*.[35]

Now, we have seen that Lawrence is issuing a warning through his novels that an excessive *agape* kind of love is a dangerous thing. Living in our polar tension between the freedom of the self and the limits of other reality, we can lose our balance if we deny self-fulfilment in the interests of promoting self-sacrifice. It is not only an intellectual self-will that makes love possessive and dominating, suggests Lawrence, but an extreme spirituality of self-denial. Lawrence therefore throws down a challenge to the Christian theologian to think carefully about the relationship between *agape* and *eros*. Through our incarnation in the relationships and moods of Lawrence's characters, we feel the truth that love must include *eros*, and that it must not (as much classical theology has suggested) be totally replaced by *agape*. The implications of this for theology I shall sketch out shortly.

Lawrence has two interwoven criticisms of Christian spirituality. In the first place, he sees it as affirming only one of the two great life-urges; attempting to live from the love-urge alone, it fails to cultivate the power-urge.[36] While preaching the altruistic love of all humanity, Christianity dismisses the true 'will to power' that Birkin calls the 'will to ability', the motivation for fostering one's own integrity of being and enabling others to have it too. So Christian love appears as a form of bullying, imposing a state of life upon others. In commenting upon the images of judgement in the New Testament *Apocalypse*, Lawrence concludes that 'Bullying is the negative form of power. The modern Christian state is a soul-destroying force, for it is made up of fragments which have no organic whole, only a collective whole.'[37] Lawrence also, however, shapes this criticism in terms of two kinds of love-urge rather than two-life urges; Christian spirituality, in his view, ignores the urge towards self-fulfilment in love which is a proper power in personal life. In his short novel, *The Man Who Died*, Lawrence finally sums up in a brief compass his whole dialogue with the Christian understanding of love.

In this novella, Lawrence retells the story of the resurrection of Jesus, under the thinly-veiled disguise of a story about the survival of a 'prophet' after being crucified. In part one of the story, originally called 'The Escaped Cock', the prophet in his new-born existence sets free a proud and strutting cock which had been tied by the leg. This symbolises his new freedom. His sensuous faculties, subordinated during the years of his mission, can now be released. True freedom can only come from recognising that there is supreme value in fostering one's own self, however little it may seem in the context of the vastness of nature and the breadth of society; the prophet reflects that 'I wanted to be greater than the limits of my own hands and feet, so I brought betrayal on myself.'[38] He realises that his whole ministry of teaching has been a 'laying the compulsion of love upon all men', imposing ideals upon them (such as turning the other cheek as faithfully observed by Miriam),[39] and thus ignoring their need to be themselves in their bodily reality. 'I was wrong to try to interfere', he thinks, having tried to embrace whole multitudes with a self-giving love (*agape*) without ever satisfying the demands of his own being (*eros*). 'In my mission I ran to excess. I gave more than I took, and that also is woe and vanity'.[40] Risen back into a world which seems new and strange to him, he is now in quest of a new kind of contact with others, a touch which will not destroy the 'single life' and the 'intrinsic solitude' which he now understands to be essential for himself and for others:

> Risen from the dead, he had realised at last that the body, too, has its little life, and beyond that, the greater life. . . . the body rises again to give and to take, to take and to give, ungreedily.[41]

The prophet in his new life meets two women, who are possessive in the different ways of excessive giving and excessive taking. The first, a peasant woman who gives him sanctuary, desires greedily only to take from him, to possess him as an object of sexual desire. Though he does not respond, this encounter does help to reawaken his sexual feelings. The second woman is more dangerous, for like

Miriam she wants to possess by giving. Madeleine (the Magdalen), wants him to return to his old ministry of teaching because she needs someone to serve. 'She wanted to give without taking',[42] but this is the love which compels others, which once he preached and which now he dreads. At this critical point Lawrence draws upon a major phrase of the Christian tradition about the resurrection, the words spoken by Jesus to Mary in the garden: 'do not touch me'. But the word 'touch' is full of Lawrence's revulsion against the contact which absorbs and interferes, the touch of a Miriam or a Gudrun. The explanation 'because I am not yet ascended to my Father' is also recast as 'I am not yet healed . . . and in touch with the flesh'.[43] The first part of the story ends with the prophet setting off to walk through the world alone, as Paul walks towards the town at the end of his relationship with Miriam, in search of the human touch which does not compel.

But is it true that Christian love 'gives without taking', and must never involve self-fulfilment or self-affirmation? A major reason why Christian thinkers have wanted to take the exclusive view of an *agape* uncontaminated by *eros* is that love for humankind is understood as a reflection of God's own love for the world, and traditionally it has been thought inconceivable that God should gain anything from his creation. But in recent theology, there has been a greater willingness to conceive of God as fulfilling his own being through the world. There are valid elements in both views, and in the end the experience with which Lawrence confronts us vicariously in his novels is a valuable criterion in weighing them up.

The traditional assertion of God's love as pure *agape* has often been based upon the metaphysical idea of God's 'aseity' or self-sufficiency. The argument runs that the only explanation for a contingent world must be a totally 'necessary' Being, a divine Being who has the cause of his existence entirely in himself, who is not affected by the world in any way, and who moves all things without being moved by them. In short, a changing world can only be caused by an unchanging God. This means God cannot be enriched in his being through relationship with his creation. In the precise terminology of E.L. Mascall, God can only be glorified 'accidentally' by his creatures, in so far as his glory is manifested in and through them; he cannot be glorified 'essentially', in the sense that they would add anything to the depth of his eternal bliss.[44] Now, such a metaphysical concept of God is considered to harmonise well with a view of love as pure self-giving. If, it is argued,

God were also fulfilling himself through fellowship with his world, 'then creation, while it might be an act of love, would certainly not be an act of purely unselfish love'.[45] This view implies, however, that the love of God cannot strictly be conceived as 'sympathetic', or a suffering-with his creatures, since this would mean that he was vulnerable to change.[46] Immutability and impassibility are logically bound together. In this classical conception, the 'love' of God is understood as beneficence, a doing-good to others, and not as an emotion.

An assault has been made upon this tight argument by a good deal of modern theology, which has affirmed a strong element of *eros* in the life of God. Since human beings are the objects of the searching love of God, fellowship with them must satisfy the desire of God and complete his joy. The gospel text that 'he who loses his life. . . . shall gain it' has been taken to describe the effects of both human and divine love. Theologians have increasingly come to affirm that we become more truly ourselves when we give ourselves away, and that we sacrifice ourselves only to find that we receive ourselves back; *agape* and *eros* are bound up together, for self-giving love is in the end a self-realisation. Support for the truth of this mysterious interchange has been found in two strands of the human experience of love.

First, in the mutuality of love the lover allows the other to be fully himself and so to make his own contribution to the relationship.[47] Thus the person who opens himself in love is bound to gain something for himself from the response of the other. By analogy, if God allows his creatures freely to contribute to his project of creation, then he will gain something from their creativity.[48] Love as a one-sided 'doing good' is cold charity. Second, love means a sharing of experience and hence a participation in the suffering of another.[49] The link between love and empathy is clear, for example, in the power of suffering to communicate love when other forms of communication have broken down.[50] By analogy, if God knows the lives of his creatures fully and is known by them, he is bound to suffer sympathetically with them, and in this way to be changed by them. But since God cannot be degraded by change, and can only change to become more fully himself, it follows that his being must be enhanced and fulfilled through suffering. Relying upon such observations from human experience, the theologian Eberhard Jüngel concludes that, 'In coming close to each other, lovers come close to themselves in a new way.' Similarly, the being of

God can be defined as 'an event of a still greater selflessness within a very great self-relatedness'.[51]

Human experience of love may convince us that love of God is also a matter of 'giving and taking' (in Lawrence's own phrase). But we must still address the metaphysical questions raised by classical theology. How can a God who takes something from the world to complete his being be truly God? One kind of answer is that given by Process Theology; the principle of creativity *requires* God to be influenced by the world as well as to influence it, because everything is in a process of becoming.[52] Within a cosmic network of persuasion, God's sovereignty is modified and yet still affirmed since he is the most powerful influence among many. While learning from the Process emphasis upon activity of God as persuasive influence rather than irresistible force, other theologians have offered a more traditional view of the sovereignty of God. Jürgen Moltmann, for example, insists that it is the desire of God to be completed and glorified by his creation;[53] this process is not a matter of necessity thrust upon God, but springs from his own resolve of love. As Barth proposed earlier, God is free enough to be conditioned as well as unconditioned by his world.[54] Grappling more directly with classical theology, Keith Ward makes the useful distinction here between self-existence and self-sufficiency;[55] the first concept does not have to be equated with the second. A God who is necessarily the sole cause of his own existence can choose to allow others to contribute to the *way* he exists.

Here is an answer to Lawrence's objection that the Christian idea of the love of God is of an absorbing, bullying kind. Far from that, God seeks us in a love that wants true fellowship, so that as we give ourselves away to God we become full personalities, with our own integrity of being. In this kind of theology, *agape* and *eros*, self-realising and self-giving love, are integrated in God himself. Through his creating and redeeming acts, God sacrificially (*agape*) allows us to enrich his own life and satisfy his desire for relationship (*eros*). In completing himself through a quest for humankind (*eros*), God gives himself to the uttermost, allowing himself to be constrained and hurt by his own world (*agape*). The quest of *eros* is in fact a journey of sacrificial love.

But, having said this, the objections of a more classical theology have not been silenced. Is a God who is helpless before the response of his creatures, whose eternal bliss is disturbed by suffering, and who can only fulfil his purposes through persuasion and not by coercion, worthy of worship? By placing the Christian story and the novelist's story side by side, illumination is thrown upon faith. When we ask perplexing questions about the meaning of love, and are confronted by various theological options, the novelist can help to edge the theologian towards a decision. Theories about love can be tested by living vicariously in the experience of a whole range of characters who love, and who can extend our experience. Through Lawrence's novels, I suggest, we feel the truth that love must include *eros* as well as *agape*.

But then illumination is thrown the other way as well. From the theological perspective of the love of God, we notice something about the way Lawrence depicts his characters. We are given a criterion for criticism. Love should indeed include the dimension of self-fulfilment, but we notice that there is a dangerous overlap between the 'will to enable' and the 'will to power'; we agree with Ursula that stars in orbit can become satellites. An ambiguity, for example, hangs over the scene of parting between Paul and Miriam; he refuses marriage with her because he fears 'you want to put me in your pocket', but he still wanted her to exercise a firm will, 'to hold him, and say, with joy and authority . . . "You are mine for a mate"'[56] At the end of a later novel, *Aaron's Rod*, we are left in similar uncertainty about whether Aaron should submit to the leadership of Lilly. '"And whom shall I submit to?" he said. "Your soul will tell you," replied the other.' Lilly believes that people should yield to the greater 'will to power' in a strong leader, as long as it is 'dark, fructifying power', springing from the impulsive soul rather than the mind; but he also believes that 'every man is a sacred and holy individual, never to be violated'.[57] Aaron's flute (one meaning of his 'rod'), his means of livelihood and so of self-determination since leaving his possessive wife and home, is smashed. Does this mean the way forward is to submit to one who has a greater power-urge?

Lawrence places his characters in this dilemma because he can apparently only see self-completion as coming about through a deliberate maintaining of the self, and a never-ending conflict with those (especially women) who want to absorb it. His characters often seem to lose their freedom in obsessive fear of being possessed. Christian theology suggests that we achieve self-realisation not by making it our direct goal, but as a by-product of self-giving love. This mystery of interchange happens because we are involved in fellowship with a God whose own life integrates self-giving and self-fulfilment. Indeed, we are invited into a community where this is already happening, in the inner relationships of Father, Son and Spirit. In this communion, as the theologian Heribert Mühlen suggests, we can see an analogy to the experience of human relationships that we only become really close to another person when we experience him or her as different from us. Only from our awareness of 'difference' from ourselves (this phrase constantly occurs in Lawrence too), can the relationship take on a new depth of nearness. So in God,

> The distinction of the divine persons, in so far as they are distinct modes of being, is so great that it could not be conceived of as greater, while their unity is so intensive that it could not be conceived of as more intensive.[58]

Lawrence too, as we shall see, is in search of a community where singleness of self does not mean either isolation or an imposing of self on others, but he does not seem to have found it.

THE LOVE THAT ABANDONS THE SELF

In attempting to keep an equilibrium between the freedom of the self and the limit formed by other realities, we have seen that the will inevitably overbalances. What Lawrence clearly abhors in this collapse is the loss of the self with its spontaneity and impulses. While he affirms that the profane love which 'seeks its own' (*eros*) should be inseparable from the sacred love which 'seeks perfect communion of oneness'[59] (*agape*), it is clear that Lawrence envisages the first dimension as the key; it is not surprising that one critic considers that this amounts to an 'erotic solipsism', even at the very moment of consummation.[60] The *eros* completes the self, and enables others to be fulfilled in their singleness as well. But Lawrence also suggests another way that the two loves can be held together, and so the freedom and limit of the self be held in balance. He alerts us to another kind of selfless love, which seems at first to be a curious affirmation that the self should after all be abandoned. For example, a further deficiency of Miriam's love for Paul in *Sons and Lovers* is her inability to 'lose' herself in 'the great passion'. This is portrayed symbolically early on when she fears to let herself go on a swing; when Paul swings there was 'not a particle of him that did not swing' (p.188), but as he thrusts her forward she grips the rope, stiff with intensity. Her will which makes her want to possess Paul also inhibits her from letting herself go into a greater flow of life. Much later, Paul thinks about his experience of love with her:

> Never any relaxing, never any leaving himself to the great hunger and impersonality of passion; he must be brought back to a deliberate, reflective creature. As if from a swoon of passion she called him back to the littleness, to the personal relationship. He could not bear it. 'Leave me alone – leave me alone!' he wanted to cry; but she wanted him to look at her with eyes full of love. (p.347)

It seems that a careful distinction has to be made between two kinds of loss of the self. Lawrence rejects the kind of loss of self which is a being absorbed into the self of another; but he desires the loss of the self in an impersonal force 'in which love is encompassed and surpassed'.[61] It is love beyond love, the difference between 'swooning' (which is good) and 'merging' (which is bad). A little further on he speaks of this self-abandonment as a sleep:

> To be rid of our individuality, which is our will, which is our effort – to live effortless, a kind of conscious sleep – that is very beautiful I think . . . (p.351).

Lovers must not lose their individuality by being sucked into each other, but they must let go the stiff individuality of the will and abandon themselves to – what? There is something here which Lawrence cannot define, but which transcends even the 'dark forest' and the 'blood consciousness'. He may use a word like passion, or the image of 'one surpassing heaven of a rose blossom',[62] but in the end he is hinting at a mystery of being which is not only present in the individual dark forest of the self, but in the universal dark forest of nature. Rupert Birkin later finds it in a 'subtlety of vegetation travelling into one's blood', as he lies naked 'in a sort of darkness' in the grass under the fir-trees. It is a living which is 'smeared away into the beyond' (p.350). While Paul is uneasy about Miriam's mystical spirituality, when he comes to speak of his 'relaxing', he thinks in a mystical way himself: 'The highest of all was to melt out into the darkness and sway there, identified with the great Being' (p.350). When he speaks of the death of self as 'sleeping in wonder', we read that Miriam 'had been afraid before of the brute in him: now of the mystic'. (p.351)

Lawrence is, then, commending an abandonment of self to this 'force of life' (p.347), as the stars in orbit are surrendered not to each other, but to the field of force between them. The two kinds of loss of the individual ego, one lifegiving and the other destructive, are taken up fully in *Women in Love*. Alongside the loathing of a 'merging and mingling' in love there runs the urging towards the other kind of self-abandonment. In wrestling naked with his friend Gerald, Birkin achieves a 'lapsing out', for which the snow with its cold, even brilliance becomes a symbol. It is fitting that Gerald should finally perish in the snow, reaching in literal death the 'death to self' which had eluded him all the while. At one point earlier, rocking in a boat on the lake, there had come the promise that such a relaxation of the will could happen in his love for Gudrun:

> Now he had let go, imperceptibly he was melting into oneness with the whole. It was like pure, perfect sleep, his first great sleep of life. He had been so insistent, so guarded, all his life. But here was sleep, and peace, and perfect lapsing out. (p.199)

But the promise is thwarted, and he sleeps only in the snow at last. It is clear that Lawrence finds the positive self-loss of 'swooning' or 'swinging out into the dark' to be a kind of religious experience. We may name this 'melting into oneness' as a version of *agape*, though it should not be simply confused with the 'sacred love' which Lawrence calls melting into communion with another individual self. The greater life and deeper dark is a kind of meta-*agape*, and Lawrence himself seems to find it most appropriate to reuse the Christian symbol, 'Holy Ghost'. Individual spontaneity is thus a 'little Ghost', as part of the greater and incomprehensible flow in which one individual is bound to another. Echoing Blake's images, Lawrence depicts the separateness of the self as a tiger and its selflessness as a lamb; the 'little ghost inside you which sees both ways'[63] will, believes Lawrence, bring harmony in the dialogue between tiger and lamb, between dark and light. Even in the seed of a dandelion, 'as it floats with its little umbrella of hairs, sits the Holy Ghost in tiny compass. The Holy Ghost is that which holds the light and dark. . . . united in one little clue.' To surrender to this flood of life will even, Lawrence believes, harmonise the self with the final limit of death; in *The Woman Who Rode Away*, the heroine finds as she anticipates her ritual death at the hands of the Indians, that 'womanhood was to be cast once more into the great stream of impersonal sex and impersonal passion' and this gives her the 'exquisite sense of bleeding out into the higher beauty and harmony of things'.[64]

Surrender to this dark force is the experience of being 'carried' by a power of life as a bird is carried on the wind. Here again we can find a reciprocal relationship between the Lawrentian love story and the Christian one. Recent Christian theology has found a sense of spontaneity and risk in love that is strongly present in Lawrence's account of 'lapsing out'. *Agape* is understood, not merely as benevolence, but as a venture into the unknown, a swinging out into strange and hidden territory in a journey of hope and trust. The process theologian Daniel Day Williams draws attention to what he calls a 'pilgrimage of love':

> We cannot know fully the meaning of love until it has done all its work . . . what love may do and will do, what creative and redemptive work lies ahead, can only be known partially in the history of love until the 'end'.[65]

Love does not insist on knowing the end of the journey; it does not calculate the benefits before loving and it takes the risks of suffering. The images with which Lawrence evokes the unknown region into which love ventures should help the theologian to express the risk.

But this observation also leads us to a critique upon the Lawrentian love-story from the viewpoint of Christian theology. We must not rush too quickly into claiming, with one critic, that this surrender to the Spirit is 'almost Christian';[66] T.S. Eliot rightly warns us of the dark and alien gods of nature.[67] From the Christian perspective, *agape* is never a pilgrimage into an impersonal area, but always into the lives of others, and ultimately into the life of God himself. The dark unknown is the depth of personal being, human and divine. When we love we make a hazardous journey into the feelings of another, and Christian theology does not fear, as Lawrence apparently does, that to take this kind of risk would be to lose our individuality in a terrible 'merging'. In Walt Whitman, for instance, Lawrence diagnosed and regretted a sympathy which was 'a passionate feeling *for* the negro slave, or the prostitute, or the syphilitic – which is merging. A sinking of Walt Whitman's soul in the souls of these others.'[68] Instead, Whitman should have simply felt *with* them, keeping his own soul 'in integrity' and helping them to keep their own souls free.

By contrast, we have already seen that Christian theology conceives of the personality as being enriched by self-giving, and not disintegrated. It is when we make a pilgrimage into the strange land of others' lives that we find who we really are. But even more than this, we may say (with some modern Christian theology) that God himself is embarked upon such a pilgrimage of love; in his humility, and by his own desire, he is on a journey to his own future glory.[69] If, as I have suggested, God takes the risks of allowing his creatures to contribute to his creation, then he must leave some things open in the future. Recent theology has suggested that it is still coherent to talk of a 'God' who does not fully know the future; omniscience can be redefined in term of God's perfect knowledge of all the reality there *is* to be known at any moment. God then knows the possibilities there are for the world, but he does not know them as actualities until potentials are realised.[70] We may say that it is God's desire to make a community of persons, and not just puppets, that makes him take this limitation upon himself. He journeys then into the personal lives of others, and so comes to fulfilment of creative joy.

These reflections from modern Christian theology are not merely a critique of Lawrence in the sense of offering an alternative. Rather, they provide a perspective from which the critic can detect an unease in Lawrence's own account of the different dimension of love. The theologian is interested in asking what the results of self-abandonment to an impersonal force of life, the Lawrentian Holy Ghost, would be. Can *this* kind of meta-*agape* unite the two dimensions of *eros* and *agape* in relationships, the 'being apart' and the 'coming together'? When we ask this question, we notice that Lawrence's self-abandoning is really an extension of *eros*, a further throw of the impulsive self that shapes our singleness. This is hardly likely to keep the equilibrium between freedom and limit, and Lawrence uneasily recognises that surrender to the dark current of life still needs to be balanced by the mind, which is conscious of others. Birkin defends an African statuette of a nude woman, which is 'mindless and utterly sensual' as an example of high culture, but he knows that 'this isn't everything'.[71] In reply to

Hermione's accusation that the children in the classroom are being 'burdened to death' by the mind (an uncharacteristic comment by Hermione, which is actually only another of her postures) Birkin cries that what is wrong is 'not too much mind, but too little'.[72] The mind has been 'imprisoned within a limited, a false set of concepts' which it has gleaned from its surrounding society and culture. This is why Mellors, in *Lady Chatterley's Lover,* insists on using the 'shocking words' about sex, and on speaking in broad dialect; he is cleansing himself of verbal idols.

In Lawrence's view, these idols appear when the mental consciousness ignores the dark self of body and passion; then it finds itself enslaved to the limits of society and its institutions, rather than exercising its freedom within them. Gerald Crich, in *Women in Love,* is shaped by the industrial idol of efficiency and production in all his relationships, and Hermione simply lives through a range of masks which are culturally acceptable. The ego is not free at all, but is bound by 'papier-mâché realized selves'.[73] There is a striking parallel here to the theological idea that the ideals and tools of our environment can become idols, and in the end acquire a demonic force over us. According to theologians, this happens when we try to quieten our anxieties over the tensions of existence by putting our trust in what is less than ultimate.[74] But for Lawrence, the ultimate is not God, but an undefined depth of 'Being'. Can an openness to this 'great rose of space' break the idols?

Some contemporary theologians also certainly speak of our ultimate concern as 'the ground of our Being', and as 'not less than personal' rather than as a strictly personal God, but they do envisage Being Itself as representing a contradiction to all merely human values. Being Itself is not in the same scale of reality as beings. For Lawrence, however, like Nietzsche, the 'revaluation of all values' seems to end with an exaltation of one particular human value, the urge to life; Lawrence equates the depth of Being rather too closely with the spontaneous (erotic) self of passion and instinct. It is questionable whether this will represent sufficient challenge to the mental will in its attempts to make its own securities.

Lawrence, as we have seen, does not deny the need to integrate the free, impulsive self with the society that forms its boundaries. Otherwise, 'lapsing out' becomes mere indulgence. In *The Man Who Died,* the prophet is driven away from the priestess by her slaves, because she has lost control over her external world. 'And he thought, "Why did the woman of Isis relinquish her portion in the daily world?"'.[75] At the end of *Lady Chatterley's Lover*, Mellors expresses the need for a society which has learned 'to come into tender touch', where the men 'learn to be naked and handsome, and to sing in a mass and dance the old group dances, and carve the stools they sit on . . .'.[76] But where is such a community to be found, and is the desire for such a community coherent with Lawrence's view of *eros* and singleness? The only hint he seems to give is that artists and novelists like himself might make a suitable group who dance and sing, and 'wear coloured trousers'.[77] We notice that in *Lady Chatterley's Lover*, society is finally rejected for the phallic consciousness which makes the peace for which Mellors seeks.

The difficulty which we perceive Lawrence as having in bringing together his versions of *eros* and *agape* is brought out vividly in *The Man Who Died*. The second part of the story expresses Lawrence's version of true self-loss, as the first expounds his view of self-fulfilling *eros*. The prophet who sets out into the world at the end of the first part of the story, in quest of the 'touch' which does not compel, meets a priestess of Isis in the second. The priestess, like the prophet, is a virgin; as he has now begun to do, she has splendidly realised her own personality, and her inner integrity impresses the prophet with its 'life so different' from him (p.39). She clearly has 'another consciousness' (p.42), and yet she is Isis in search of her dead Osiris. They abandon themselves to a reality which Lawrence describes in the often-repeated words 'stillness', 'darkness' and 'the being in touch': 'Now the world is one flower of many-petalled darkness, and I am in its perfume as in a touch.' (p.44) The traditional phrase from the Easter garden story 'touch me not' has been transformed into a universal deity called 'the living Touch' which must not be 'profaned'.

> This is the great atonement, the being in touch. The grey sea and the rain, the wet narcissus and the woman I wait for, the invisible Isis and the unseen sun are all in touch, and at one.

The stranger and the priestess are making a spiritual pilgrimage, swinging out together into an unknown territory, symbolised in the world of the Mediterranean sea and sky. The Temple of their love is neither in her Egypt or his Palestine, neither West nor East, but in that utopian 'Between' which has always haunted the European memory. As E.M. Forster celebrates it, 'The Mediterranean is the human norm.'[78]

So Lawrence completes his story of a man who has died, and who can finally claim 'I am risen' through the love of a woman.[79] The trouble is, as the critic Graham Hough puts it, 'it is hard to accept the stranger of the second part of the book as identical with the prophet of the first. . . . The stranger in the second part is not so much a different person as a person out of a different story; the change is a change in the mode of perception.'[80] Hough attributes this dislocation to the abrupt change between mythologies, from the Christian symbols to the Egyptian mysteries. But we notice that the shift is also between the two dimensions of love we have been analysing, and which are not properly integrated here. We move from a man who has simply recovered his own inner desire to be himself, to a man who 'comes together' with another. But how are the two modes of love, profane and sacred, actually reconciled? Lawrence hopes to convince us of the unity of *eros* and *agape* by surrender to the greater life which is semi-hypostasised here as the 'Touch', and also by the setting in the Mediterranean Between. But all that can be said of a life in which the two kinds of love are apparently harmonised is, 'He would go alone with his destiny. Yet not alone, for the touch would be upon him, even as he left his touch on her.' (p.45) This is putting a great deal of weight upon the objective reality of this 'touch', as a re-mythologising of the personal 'Father' God whom the stranger constantly invokes.

The novels of Lawrence thus prompt the theologian to ask how the modes of *agape* and *eros* are united in his own concept of God, and in the human life which is an imitation of God's life. The novels help the theologian to make theological decisions, and I suggest that they point us firmly towards a God whose being is personal relationship and community, the Trinitarian God who cannot be reduced to an Absolute Individual. In both God and humankind, eros fulfils the personality while *agape* makes a sacrificial journey into the personalness of others, and the fact that fulfilment comes through sacrifice makes clear that personal reality is always in relationship.

The 'inbetween', the spiritual Mediterranean, is the personal life of God in whom human relationships are included. They are 'in touch' because they are 'in God'. Lawrence is actually in search of a community where the different dimensions of love will be unified; he is in quest of Blake's holy City. But he fears that to take the path of self-abandonment into the lives of others is to lose himself. Christian theology affirms that he who loses his life finds it.

8

Iris Murdoch and Love of the Truth

'Good art is truthful.'[1] On this text Iris Murdoch has based (so far) twenty-four novels and three books of philosophy, aiming to show in her technique of writing that the artist is a truth-teller, and to show in her themes that all people should be no less lovers of the truth if they are to be truly human. In fact, Murdoch believes (following her great mentor, Plato) that the quest for the truth is the search for the Good, and to love the one is to love the other. Even a passing experience of falling in love can make someone more keenly aware of what is true in the surrounding world. In Murdoch's vision of reality, there is thus an indissoluble bond between truth, love and goodness, and the reader of her novels becomes a traveller through regions of moral value as well as intense passion. Murdoch does not profess to believe in an objectively existing and personal God, but the interest of her work for a Christian theologian is summed up in a remark of one of her characters: "That's what God is for, to make our lies truth.'[2]

THE FALL INTO LACK OF TRUTH

The characters in Iris Murdoch's novels learn, or fail to learn, to be truthful, which means giving attention to what is real around them. At one level of reality (we shall see that there is another, more transcendent level) this means noticing people as they actually are, rather than as we want them to be for our convenience. It means delighting in all the contingent details of the world, recognising the 'otherness' of people and things, and living with all the hazards of accident. At the very least the disciples of goodness accept the 'muddle' of the world, and at the best they experience its amazing variety as being the Sublime. Jenkin[3] has learned to look upon the world like this, so that walking the streets of London

173

was to walk through 'a great collection or exhibition of little events or encounters'.

A prominent symbol for the 'hardness'[4] and separateness of objects in their own right is the stones with which Murdoch strews her landscapes. Characters marvel at the myriad of pebbles upon the beach, each different from the other; Sinclair has made a notable collection of these, and 'had known each individual stone personally and given some of them names'.[5] When Anne Cavidge meets Jesus Christ in a vision he shows her a small stone, reminiscent of the Lady Julian's account in her mystical treatise of how she was shown 'a little thing the size of a hazel-nut'.[6] Ann is in the agonising predicament of loving a man who has loved her friend Gertrude devotedly (and without reward) for many years; should she tell him her own love? By showing her a stone, Christ makes clear that there is no easy answer, no instant salvation. She must find the truth of her situation, which is there like the integrity of the stone, existing in its own truth.

Like other modern writers, then, Murdoch is presenting the need for a balance between our freedom and the limits that confront us. As in Hopkins' vision of the world, where

> Each mortal thing does one thing and the same:
> . . . *myself* it speaks and spells,

the limitations lie in respecting the otherness of things. The characters who search for the Good imitate the creative Demiurge in Plato's myth, who 'realises his limits' when faced by the 'jumble' of the world.[7] The 'very small area of freedom' in human life does not consist in the mere exercise of willpower, but is 'that in us which attends to the real and is attracted by the good'.[8] Living in the tension between freedom and limit is frequently pictured as the skill of swimming; the sea is an apt symbol for the multiplicity and vastness of worldly phenomena, and to succeed in swimming is to keep one's balance amid the 'ocean of accident'[9] in daily life. Murdoch's good characters are strong swimmers, or like Dora at the end of *The Bell*, they learn to swim, 'buoyant and fearless in the water'.[10] Those who are not in quest of the Good frequently drown, not only in metaphor but in fact.[11]

As in the vision of William Blake, Murdoch emphasises that keeping a balance between freedom and limit means the death of the self. To give attention to other things and people is to love goodness as well as truth because it means 'unselving'[12] or 'de-centring' from oneself. In a moment of revelation, facing death by drowning in a bog, Effingham Cooper discovers 'the passion of a lover' for 'all that was not himself':

> This then was love, to look and look until one exists no more, *this* was the love that was the same as death. He looked, and knew with a clarity which was one with the increasing light, that with the death of the self the world becomes quite automatically the object of a perfect love.[13]

There are three aspects of Murdoch's treatment of the theme of freedom and limit which, I suggest, are peculiarly her own. They all concern the love of truth, and they appear in her own work in constant dialogue with the Christian tradition, as well as providing matter for our own dialogue in this study. First, she concentrates upon the link between 'attention' to the contingent facts of the world and the death of the self. From this perspective she fleshes out in her novels an experience which can be aptly called sin, fallenness and hell. Second, she links this moral theme with a theory of art, in which such religious concepts as revelation, grace, salvation and images of God are brought into play. Third, she reflects upon the relationship between the death of the self and human suffering, where she has some critical things to say about the failures of Christianity in its attempt at the 'long task of unselving'.[14]

In her storytelling, then, Murdoch vividly depicts the feelings of characters who fail to give attention to others, and build a self-enclosed world around themselves. Jake, in her very first novel, sets the tone for a long list of successors when he exclaims, 'I hate contingency' and remarks of his companion, 'I count Finn as an inhabitant of my universe, and cannot conceive that he has one containing me. . . .'[15] Murdoch exposes the tragic fact that we all manufacture worlds for ourselves; our minds are the 'sacred and profane love-machines' which she explores in her novel of that title.[16] Other images for the cosmic artefacts that we build and imprison ourselves within are boxes, dark cupboards, cages and eggs.[17] This self-centring takes the social form of intimate circles or 'courts' of relatives and friends, usually middle-class, professional and university-educated; in the plots of the novels there are contin-ual reminiscences of the inbred social groups of Shakespeare's comedies which need to be broken open by comic tricks.[18] The mythical form in which this human condition is presented is the fable of the 'imprisoned princess'. In some novels women are literally imprisoned, as for example Charles Arrowby shuts up his former childhood sweetheart, now an elderly woman, in a dark room in order to protect her from her husband and recapture her love.[19] In others, characters fantasise about finding an imprisoned damsel or keeping her safe from others.[20]

Behind all these images of confinement there lies the Platonic myth of the cave, and the inhabitants of a world of shadows. In Murdoch's synthesis of Freud and Plato, the fire in the cave is the ego, aping the sun outside and producing illusions in which the cave-dwellers are content to live.[21] So perpetual and ingrained is this tendency of her characters to construct worlds according to their own patterns that we are not surprised to find Murdoch pronouncing judgement upon modern philosophy in these terms: 'we have lost the vision of a reality separate from ourselves, and we have no adequate concept of *original sin*'.[22] As we have noted, the Christian theologian may be uneasy about speaking of a paradox of fallenness, in which sin is not logically necessary but inevitable in practice. Yet the theologian may find that the characters portrayed in Murdoch's novels give substance to the theory; we know, through living their lives vicariously that they are morally responsible beings, and yet we know also that they cannot help falling – though at different depths – into a self-made universe.

For some, who wilfully cultivate their own world and ignore the 'separate reality' of others, the fall is very deep. When Duncan sins against the truth by spying on his wife rather than confronting her openly about her love-affair with his former friend Crimond, he finds himself in hell: 'We are all a vile lot of rotten, stinking sinners, black as hell';[23] his fall down the stairs after a fight with Crimond is symbolic of a moral fall, and the partial loss of sight that results is also a spiritual blindness. When Edward plays the magician and tricks Mark into taking a drug against his wish, he is failing to recognise his friend as a person in his own right. After Mark's consequent fatal accident, Edward is plunged into a state of hopelessness: 'This is hell, where there is no time.'[24]

Now, it is characteristic of hell to find that the contingent details of the world, the 'jumble' of life, are not a delight but a horror. The experience of the sublime has been reversed into vertigo, a negative vision. As Duncan stares at the fragments of a broken teapot, he experiences 'as in a mystical vision . . . the pointlessness of life'.[25] Morgan, in *A Fairly Honourable Defeat* descends into the Underground as into the underworld, and emerging finds the shabby details of the streets unbearable: 'The horror, the horror of the world'. This anti-vision is triggered, it seems, by the memory of an abortion in which she had felt no regret for the unborn child, no respect for it as a unique object in its own right: 'She had killed it so casually and drunk half a bottle of bourbon afterwards.'[26]

The myriad stones upon the beach that can symbolise joy in the variety of the world can also be the occasion for nausea at sheer contingency. Theo, in *The Nice and the Good*, has some sense of the demands of the Good, but has not been strong enough to pursue it; he finds the stones on the Dorset coast to be terrible in their factuality.[27] Anne Cavidge, in *Nuns and Soldiers*, is more determined upon the quest for the Good, yet she too is appalled by the stones:

> What do their details matter, what does it matter whether Christ redeemed the world or not, it doesn't matter, our minds can't grasp such things. . . . Look at these stones, My Lord and My God. . . . there they are.[28]

Shortly after these reflections she plunges into the sea and nearly drowns, unable to clamber out on to the slope of stones, all her strength strangely gone. When Christ appears to her in a vision later, it is a little chipped stone from this beach that he holds out to her, inviting her to accept its 'thereness'.

The theological paradox of fallenness, the human predicament where the sin of self-centredness is not necessary but inevitable, is fleshed out by such experiences. Even characters who want to be disciples of the Good, and know that only love is necessary, find that they easily slip from vision to anti-vision. The sufferings of people and the inhumanity of their torturers is naturally one of the pressures that makes us turn inward, away from facing the world as it is, to construct our own fantasy one. Stuart, the 'apprentice' of the Good, sums up the horror of the Jewish Holocaust in a single contingent fact; a girl who plaited her hair one morning was dead by the evening, and her hair recycled for other uses: 'Oh it was the details, the details that were so unendurable.'[29] Yet such intolerable details must not be forgotten; suffering must be confronted and the truth must be told about it, not (as we shall see) in order to indulge ourselves by lamenting our own sinfulness and abasing ourselves, but to lead us to *death* of the self.

THE BREAKING OF FALSE WORLDS

To escape from the box, or to smash the shell of the egg in which we are sheltering cannot be achieved simply by an act of our will. Christian theologians speak of 'grace' as a gift from beyond us which enables us to turn from the security of idols and to live courageously in the tensions of life. Grace must be understood, not as an impersonal supernatural substance, but as God's own gracious encounter with human persons, inviting and eliciting trust in place of anxiety. Now, Murdoch believes that the defeat of egoism requires moral effort, but she also discerns the need for something analogous to 'grace', something to enable 'the. . . . reorientation of an energy which is naturally selfish'.[30]

The first form which these ministers of grace assume in Murdoch's novels is the shock of an unexpected event or unlikely relationship. The contingent, accidental events of the world which her characters try to shut out can break in suddenly to disturb their neat, self-enclosed worlds. They are shocked into noticing others, jolted towards the truth.[31] At the same time, of course, the shock operates upon the reader. For instance, the love-affairs which develop are 'odd', challenging our tidy ideas of how people behave. They cut across the usual barriers – old and young fall in love together, brothers and sisters love each other incestuously or in a manner that borders on it, people move from heterosexual to homosexual relationships and back again, class divisions are crossed, one member of a long-established circle of intimates falls in love with an outsider, and someone who is hated at one moment becomes the object of passionate love at another. Critics protest, 'But people don't behave like this!', yet Murdoch *is* unveiling the unpredictability of human nature to which we are often blind. At the same time, of course, she has made the relationships and passions she describes even more erratic because she wants to startle us out of our self-created worlds. As we shall see, she allows that literature must resort to tricks and 'magic' in order to reveal what is real; good art can lie its way into the truth.

As with unlikely relationships, random and haphazard events

can shock Murdoch's characters – and the reader – into awareness of the truth. In *The Sacred and Profane Love Machine*, for example, she uses an ingenious 'magical' device which enables us to share in the main character's experience of having his machine-made worlds blown open by the accidental. The novel begins with a small boy of eight or nine standing outside a garden and staring in. The house belongs to Blaise Gavender, a successful psychiatrist, and for the first 60 pages of the novel we explore the life of his family, residing in a fashionable area of South London. Then the narrator switches the scene to a rather squalid flat in a very unfashionable area of London, where lives an unsuccessful school-teacher called Emily McHugh. We learn that her small son Luca is difficult to handle, awkward and introverted. So we explore in turn two very different worlds. Suddenly, even casually, halfway through a sentence we read that 'For some time now Emily had been trying to persuade Blaise to go to see Luca's form master.'[32] With a shock we discover that the two worlds connect. Blaise has two families; unknown to his wife Harriet, Emily is his mistress and Luca his son. Blaise thinks he has constructed two separate, carefully sealed worlds around himself, and that he alone crosses between them as he crosses Putney Bridge. His own ego is the centre of them both, with Harriet as his sacred love and Emily his profane love.[33] But now the boy, Luca, has crossed between; he was the boy looking into the garden as the novel opened. He has done the unthinkable thing of finding his own way across London, and Blaise finds that a life he thought he had got neatly ordered is in chaos. His two cosmic eggs are broken.

The casual explosion halfway through a sentence thus enables us to experience the same sensation as Blaise, discovering that the occupants of his two worlds have lives of their own and are going to make demands on him. Our accidental movement in reading reflects the contingent nature of the boy's journey, dethroning Blaise from the centre of his solar systems. His feeble attempts at making a moral choice are finally ended by another random happening; his wife Harriet is gunned down in a terrorist attack at Hanover airport, while attempting to make a new life for herself with Luca. Her death is brutally accidental, seemingly unconnected to the rest of the action which is not in the style of an international thriller but a social tragi-comedy. Yet, as Emily reminds Blaise earlier in a row about her domestic miseries, life is full of such contingencies: 'God, sometimes I feel like people who go to an airport with a machine gun and just shoot everyone within sight. You simply have no idea how much I suffer.'[34]

Murdoch thus designs an accidental event or unlikely relationship to disturb her characters and her readers into *noticing* the truth. This is the proper craft of an artist, who can only reflect what is real through some artifice. Here we are already considering the second of Murdoch's means of grace, which is the art-object itself and especially literature. In her essays on philosophy and art, as well as through the conversations in her novels, Murdoch makes clear that 'good art reveals the minute. . . . random details of the world'.[35] Murdoch believes that art should be mimetic of reality, and she vigorously attacks those who write mere 'fantasy', fulfilling their own wishes through their characters, indulging themselves with a purely private consolation. Yet she insists that good art does nevertheless console us, 'cheering us up' by giving form to what often seems a formless life. Imagination uses image and story to impose a pattern on what is otherwise chaotic, as I argued in the first chapter of this study. Murdoch is well aware of these 'magical tricks' of art, and is contriving a pattern of unlikely relationships and accidental events in order to break our fantasies and bring us to truth. As she expresses it in a gnomic sentence: 'Philosophy is clarification, but literature is mystification.'[36]

Art thus achieves liberation from self and an awakening to truth through its patterns and consoling forms. This is because a work of art is, in Murdoch's definition, 'a quasi-sensuous *self-contained* entity'.[37] Because it is an attempt (though always a failed one, as it recognises itself) at making a complete statement in an incomplete world, it is an object which clearly exists over against us with a reality all its own. It is 'thingy'[38] (and, in philosophical terms, contingent) and by its intense 'otherness' it diverts our attention from ourselves, and prompts a quest for the truth. Indeed, if it is good art the artist has already been attending to what is particular, other than himself, in the making of the artefact. Dora, in *The Bell*, looks at her favourite pictures in the National Gallery, and sees them as 'something real outside herself, which spoke to her kindly and yet in sovereign tones', destroying 'dreary, trance-like solipsisms'.[39]

Even a book of political theory can create the liberating effect of a work of art, if (unlike philosophy proper) it makes the ambitious attempt at a complete vision of reality. In her novel, the *Book and the Brotherhood*, the book of the title is said to be 'about everything. . . . an attempt to think the whole thing through' and so has an 'inert separateness, [an] authoritative thereness'.[40] The brotherhood of friends who had years before commissioned one of their number, Crimond, to write the book have since drifted away from sympathy with his Marxist outlook. Gerard, for example, passionately disagrees with the message of the book when he finally reads it, but believes it to be a wonderful work because 'it will force its opponents to think'.[41] Art loosens us from ourselves, and so attention to it is analogous to 'respect' for morals (what Kant calls *Achtung*); art is not itself exactly morality but should lead to moral action as the self is turned outwards.[42] Indeed, Murdoch suggests that reflection upon art is a kind of religious experience, since it

> perhaps provides for many people, in an unreligious age without prayer or sacraments, their clearest *experience* of something grasped as separate and precious and beneficial and held quietly and unpossessively in the attention. Good art which we love can seem holy and attending to it can be like praying.[43]

This effect is intensified when the work of art is already a religious symbol, whether in visual art or story. In *The Bell* two visitors to the religious community at Imber, Dora and Toby, find the old Abbey bell at the bottom of the lake where it has lain hidden for centuries, and they raise it secretly at night. Gazing on it, Dora feels reverence for it as she had for the portraits in the gallery: 'it was a thing from another world'. The gospel story of the life of Christ, as graven by the medieval artist on the bell, has power to arouse the attention of the observer to reality:

> The squat figures faced her from the sloping surface of the bronze, solid, simple, beautiful, absurd, full to the brim with something which was to the artist not an object of speculation or imagination. These scenes had been more real to him than his childhood and more familiar. He reported them faithfully.[44]

The members of the community at Imber certainly need to have their attention drawn to the truth of the world and other people. Though they are a lay religious community, living in the grounds of an active abbey, they fail to exercise their spiritual impulses in a way that makes for truth. Both their leaders, in their different ways, fail to notice others as they really are; James is blinded by legalism, and Michael by guilt over a homosexual incident in the past. The inscription on the bell is apt for them, and also leads us to consider a third means of grace which Murdoch finds for the egocentric self: the bell announces, *Vox ego sum Amoris. Gabriel vocor* – 'I am the voice of love. I am called Gabriel.'

Falling in love can be an annunciation, the message of an angel shocking the ego into awareness of someone else's distinct being. Through the energy of the dark *eros* 'the centre of significance is suddenly ripped out of the self'.[45] The lover's attention is turned to the beloved, and thence outwards to live in 'the dangerous, real, contingent world'.[46] Thus *eros* can also be an inspiration for art, as in the experience of Bradley Pearson in *The Black Prince*. Bradley has the potential to be a good writer, but his creativity is blocked by an exaggerated restraint, a failure to open himself to the life of the world which is the material of his art. Through his passionate affair with Julia Baffin, nearly forty years younger than himself and the daughter of a rival novelist, Bradley is 'saved as an artist'. Ironically, however, he destroys the relationship by his failure at a critical moment to tell Julia the truth. From that point events gather pace, beyond Bradley's control, and he dies in prison wrongfully convicted of murdering Arnold Baffin.

The pain of 'unselving', whether through art or Eros, is symbolised in the Greek myth of Marsyas, which has long intrigued Iris Murdoch.[47] As the loser in a musical competition with the god Apollo, the mortal Marsyas suffers the punishment of being flayed alive. In Neo-Platonism this myth was used to express the ordeal of purifying the self through divine illumination, and Murdoch combines this with the function of Apollo as God of art. Thus in Bradley's own exegesis of Shakespeare, Hamlet represents 'the empty, tormented sinful consciousness of man seared by the bright light of art, the god's flayed victim'.[48] But since Eros, or Dionysius, can also be identified as one aspect of Apollo, both art *and* love can 'flay' the self, stripping off the egocentric shell we grow around ourselves. This composite figure of Apollo-Eros is the Black Prince of the novel's title, and he takes form in the mysterious figure of P. Loxias who befriends and comforts Bradley in his last years:

> I felt as if he had suffered the lack of me throughout his life; and at the end I suffered with him and suffered, at last, his mortality. I needed him too. He added a dimension to my being.[49]

Bradley's ordeal also thus affirms that the higher Eros, or love of the Good, can be reached through the lower Eros, or sexual desire. Through great passion, lovers can arrive at an 'impersonal' state in which they are no longer absorbed in each other but simply exposed to what is real. To Bradley, after their love-making, Julia had 'the dazed, empty look of a great statue', and she confesses to feeling 'quite impersonal. . . . I'm in a place where I've never been before'.[50] In such moments there is what Murdoch has called a revelation, a 'flash from a higher level'.[51] Art can act like this, 'revealing the really real',[52] and Murdoch's characters, like Dora in *The Bell*, sometimes have such experiences looking at pictures in galleries. Beyond the good of accepting the reality of others, beyond loving the contingent details of the world, there is an ultimate Good. There is a supreme moral value, which Murdoch calls (after Plato) 'the sovereignty of Good'. Goodness is there, transcending all the particularities of life; it is not a subjective illusion or a merely pragmatic motivation for good acts. Yet this sovereign good is strictly unreachable; it is the 'unnameable good' of Plato, or the 'imageless God' of St John of the Cross. As the priest, Brendan, explains in *Henry and Cato*:

> It's the greatest pain and the greatest paradox of all that personal love has to break at some point, the ego has to break, something absolutely natural and seemingly good, perhaps the only good, has to be given up. After that there's darkness and silence and space. And God is there. Remember St. John of the Cross. Where the images end you fall into the abyss, but it is the abyss of faith. When you have nothing left you have nothing left but hope.[53]

We cannot possess the Ultimate Good. Revelations can be deceptive because they are only *intuitions* of the whole of reality; we cannot build too much upon them, for they do not put the transcendent Good into our hands. Rather, we can only undertake the discipline of striving towards it, doing good for no reward. We are to be 'good for nothing',[54] always questing towards and obedient to the Supreme Good, while knowing it is unattainable in itself. Here Murdoch disagrees with Plato in the final part of his myth of the cave, where he pictures the good man as finally able to look at the sun. Nevertheless, Murdoch believes that the Good itself can be loved, and meditated upon; it can be 'a central point of reflection' even though it is invisible and cannot be represented. Talk of

'God' can be an apt symbol for this transcendent Good, since God provides, for believers, a 'non-degradable love-object'.[55] This, then, is a fourth means of grace for human beings caught in a box of their own making; we can attend to and serve the Good itself. As the critic Elizabeth Dipple neatly puts it, we are to reach towards 'reality' through love of 'realism'.[56] To attend to the 'goods' that *are* visible, to the many contingent things that are 'lovely, pure and of good report', will lead to 'an increasing awareness of the unity . . . of the moral world',[57] even though that One Good cannot be directly experienced.

In religious terms, the one Spirit is scattered into the many particulars of the world. As Rose looks at her brother's collection of stones, with 'so much individuality, so much to notice' in each one, she muses, 'How accidental everything was, and how spirit was scattered everywhere, beautiful, and awful'.[58] In mythical terms, as expounded by Carel Fisher in *The Time of the Angels*, 'the death of God has set the angels free':

> Angels are the thoughts of God. Now he has been dissolved into his thoughts which are beyond our conception in their nature and their multiplicity and their power.[59]

In this novel, Murdoch is responding to the 'Death of God' movement in the Church of the 1960s, to which I have already referred in my exegesis of William Blake.[60] In the face of the modern consciousness of loss and absence of God, the question is whether it is possible to go on striving for the Good. Carel is an Anglican rector who has come to the conviction that there is no God; aptly he has been moved to a parish in the middle of London which is nothing more than a demolition site, the rectory standing in the middle of a waste area of mud with neither church nor houses to serve. Carel's reaction to the loss of God is to surrender to evil; he knows that the single Good has been scattered into the many, but these he regards as forces of chance which are inevitably hostile to human life.

> 'The death of God has set the angels free. And they are terrible. . . . God was at least the name of something which we thought was good. Now even the name has gone and the spiritual world is scattered.'[61]

He realises that 'good is only good if one is good for nothing',[62] but he believes such a stance to be totally impossible. If there is no single, universal Good to be grasped, then there is no goodness at all. This conclusion is not, of course, a necessary one; it is a choice he makes, as other characters in Murdoch's novels adopt her own stance of serving the good. Thus Carel creates his own universe around himself, and the contingent becomes a horror to him as to all who do so. In his own language, the angels become terrors and he is their 'prey'. He is in a hellish underworld, of which the underground railway that rumbles away beneath the rectory is a constant reminder.

Carel replaces God with himself, playing God-games such as throwing paper darts as his own angelic messengers to signify his approval or disapproval of those who receive them. He exercises a destructive willpower over the inhabitants of the rectory, holding them prisoner by their mingled fear and love of him. In his solipsism he constructs his own mythologies, with two objects of his desire: 'Lucky the man who has the sugar plum fairy and the swan princess.'[63] Pattie, the negro maid, is his sugar plum fairy – 'my black goddess, my counter-Virgin, my anti-Maria' – and from her ample body he believes he gets love incarnate in the flesh. His swan princess is his supposed niece, Elizabeth, who is an invalid with a back ailment; he also calls her his 'sleeping beauty', keeping her confined to her room in a prison of apathy or a contented daze. From her he imagines he gets a more spiritual love. He is in fact secretly having sexual relationships with both of them, even though he knows that Elizabeth is his illegitimate younger daughter. He is perhaps making a parody of the Trinity, with himself as the Father, Pattie as the Son (love in the flesh) and Elizabeth as the Holy Spirit.[64] In other novels Murdoch explores the way that religious belief can become a means of reinforcing our cosmic shells; here she demonstrates that loss of belief can lead to the same kind of deistic solipsism. By creative fantasy of every kind we try to fit others into our world.

THE DANGERS OF MAGIC

Murdoch shows herself acutely aware that all the means of grace she presents can be corrupted into a means of self-interest. What ought to be instruments of truth can be bent into tools of fantasy and manipulation, and the word 'magic' resounds continually through the pages of her novels as a cipher for this corruption. Instead of being pulled out of themselves, her characters fall into a deeper prison of the self. It is not only the conflict between truth and magic, but also (as we shall see) the *ambiguity* that her work displays about the status of such 'magic', that provides the most fertile ground for dialogue with Christian doctrine. From this perspective we must now explore again the means of grace that I have already outlined.

While accidental events and unlikely relationships can shock people into noticing the truth, it is a mark of self-centredness to want to *procure* shocks for others. This is to don the robe of the magician,[65] to wield a magical power over others' lives. It is not an acceptance of contingency and limits, but a false attempt at freedom over them, by sheer act of will. In *The Time of the Angels* the Rector's daughter, Muriel, seeks to arrange an accidental event to dispel what she believes to be the stifling atmosphere of the rectory, and in particular the unhealthy sleep of apathy into which her cousin Elizabeth has sunk. Muriel has come to know the son of the caretaker, a young man who has fantasies about livening up his sexual experience by finding a sleeping beauty, a virgin princess who needs to be awakened by his kiss. Muriel plans to loose Leo on her cousin:

Leo was noisy, unexpected, unpredictable and new. . . . A shake, a shock would do them all good. . . . With Leo she would procure Elizabeth an experience. She would procure herself an experience.[66]

But instead of their being shaken out of themselves, this plot results in a deeper fall into self, symbolised by Muriel's falling out of the linen cupboard with Leo, after spying on Elizabeth through a crack in the wall. She has seen what Carel and Elizabeth are doing together in secret, and it is the decisive point of moral decline for her. To look into the world of others from a spy-hole of one's own, as well as to 'procure' an experience for another, is to deny that they have a world of their own at all. Real freedom is understanding that other people exist. The ambiguity, which we shall need to probe further, is that the novel-writer seems herself to be working the magic of procuring experiences, and giving us a spy-hole upon other worlds.

The grace of art can certainly be corrupted. An art object can be used for the black magic of self-indulgence.[67] The things that should disturb us can be woven into a net for trapping reality. In *The Bell*, for example, Dora plans a 'miracle' which she hopes will shake the community out of its self-righteousness, with its patronising view of her as 'the penitent wife'. She is going to use the bell to make an accidental thing happen. A new bell is to be installed at the Abbey, led there in a procession, veiled in white. She plans to substitute the medieval bell for the modern one:

> Think of the sensation . . . it would be like a real miracle, the sort of thing that makes people go on pilgrimages! . . . I should like to shake everybody up a bit. . . . She felt as if by the sheer force of her will she could make the great bell rise. After all, and after her own fashion, she would fight. In this holy community she would play the witch.[68]

In the end, although she does raise the bell successfully with the aid of a young visitor to the community, Toby, she does not carry her plot through. Gazing upon the bell, she knows that to use it for a trick would be to betray its truth; 'she had thought to be its master and make it her plaything, but now it was mastering her and having its will'.[69] She remembers a phrase, that 'the truth-telling voice . . . must not be silenced'. So she gives voice to the truth, by throwing herself against the bell and making its mighty tongue ring out, calling people to the barn where the bell had been hidden. We recall Hopkins' bell in 'As Kingfishers catch fire':

> . . . each hung bell's
> Bow swung finds tongue to fling out broad its name;
> . . . *myself* it speaks and spells;
> Crying *What I do is me: for that I came.*

The bell speaks what it is, and alerts us to what we are. Toby, however, also wants to use it as a magical charm, thinking that he will impress Dora and win her love by the enormous undertaking of raising the bell from the lake. When it is safely stored in the barn, he falls upon Dora and they roll in passion into the mouth of the bell. This makes it ring – a slight, muffled ring, unlike the mighty roar which Dora is later to draw from it, but still a ring of truth.

A third attempt to manipulate the bell is made by Catherine Fawley, who uses it to reinforce her own image of herself which she wants to project to others. Neglecting the truth of her own inner feelings of passion, Catherine has vowed to enter the enclosed part of the Abbey as a nun, and is to be received as a novice on the same day that the new bell is to be installed. Both are dressed in white, both dedicated to God, both go in procession. For her and the whole lay community, spirituality is much a matter of certain external behaviour, and this pride is given a severe jolt as the bridge over the lake collapses and the new bell is tipped into the water.

Art-objects are abused when they are used as magical charms, and yet Murdoch admits that there is an inevitable component of 'magic' within them. As we have seen, a novel offers a completeness that is in the end illusory; it has a neatness of structure and pattern that is not true of life, and it can play the kind of tricks of accident that we have seen Murdoch delights in. In an address in 1972, Murdoch declared that 'Tyrants fear art because tyrants want to mystify while art tends to clarify',[70] and yet in an interview broadcast in 1978 she states that 'Philosophy aims to clarify. . . . Literature is full of tricks and magic and deliberate mystification.'[71] In both cases Murdoch is in fact making a consistent case for literature as a vehicle of truth, which calls for a 'purification' of thought,[72] but her wavering over the suitability of the word 'mystification' reveals the necessary ambiguity that remains. A philosopher in one of her novels rejects art (in the spirit of Plato), as 'magic that joins good and evil together',[73] but in her own philosophical work she has a more balanced view:

> Sophistry and magic break down at intervals, but they never go away and there is no end to their collusion with art and to the consolations which, perhaps fortunately for the human race, they can provide. . . .[74]

The dangerously thin line between a consolation that is healthy and promotes unselving, and one that is mere fantasy, becomes even thinner for Murdoch when she portrays the effect of religious symbolism. I have already mentioned her belief that talk about God *may be* a way of directing the attention to the 'undegradable love-object' that is the Good. On the other hand, religion becomes fantasy if we expect a personal God to intervene and supply us with 'instant salvation', or as her philosopher John Robert describes it, 'salvation by magic, being totally changed'.[75] In *The Time of the Angels* Carel's brother Marcus has no such belief in a personal God, and yet he also wants to use the old Christian images as magic talismans. He hopes that the faith of others, in a magical way, will act as charms against the threats of evil in our world:

> He did not believe in the Father, the Son and the Holy Ghost, but he wanted others to believe. He wanted the old structure to continue there beside him, near by, something he could occasionally reach out and touch with his hand.[76]

So he is horrified when he meets a modern (and well-fed) bishop who also thinks that God is dead, that 'those who have come nearest to God have spoken of blackness, even emptiness', so that 'Obedience to God must be an obedience without trimmings, an obedience, in a sense, for nothing.'[77] When Marcus protests that this takes away all the guarantees, the Bishop laughs and remarks, 'That's where faith comes in.'

Yet in the world of Murdoch's novels, the use of religious symbols as 'magic' is not unreservedly bad. After all, there is a legitimate magic in all art-objects, and Murdoch tends to treat the images of Christian belief – whether verbal or pictorial – as an intense form of the 'mystification' that art employs generally, even though they have an even greater capacity for unhealthy illusion. The girl Tamar in *The Book and the Brotherhood*, for example, finds that the Christian symbols of Christ and divine forgiveness release her from the hell of self-loathing in which she has become trapped after an abortion. Like the previous character, Morgan, she has neglected the 'miraculous *other* being'[78] of a child, and she is now obsessed by a daemon of otherness, believing that the dead child is persecuting her, and that it finally even kills her friend Jenkin. Announcing that she has become a Christian, she explains she must be saved from destruction:

> . . . I can't do it myself, and you can't do it either. I need supernatural help. Not that I believe it's supernatural or that there is any supernatural. But perhaps there is help somewhere, some force, some power. . . . When you're drowning you don't care what you hold onto. I just don't care whether God exists or

who Christ was. Perhaps I just believe in magic. Who cares? It's up to me, it's my salvation.[79]

Like Father Brendan in *Henry and Cato*, her spiritual adviser Father McAlister has no real belief in the objective existence of God or the resurrection of Christ either. But 'he believed in prayer, in Christ as a mystical Saviour, and in the *magical power* which had been entrusted to him when he was ordained a priest, a power to save souls and raise the fallen'.[80] Like other characters in Murdoch's novels,[81] he finds that he can know a 'mystical Christ' who is the way of truth for *him*, a Christ who is not literally resurrected but who faced the fact of death in all its terrible contingency and thus enables us to love God/the Good. So he takes Tamar through a process of 'getting to know her Christ', and tells her that 'If Christ saves, Christ lives. . . . *That* is the resurrection and the life.'[82] The reality of this 'mystical Christ', of whom one can say 'I know that my Redeemer lives' in a way that cannot be rationally analysed, is vividly hinted at in the experience of Anne Cavidge. As a result of her visionary 'meeting' with Christ she is convinced there is no personal God. Yet the finger with which she tried, like Mary Magdalen in the Gospel narrative (and D.H. Lawrence's mythical version of it), to grasp him and keep him with her will not heal up:

> It came to her that he was real, that he was unique. She was an atom of the universe and he was her own Christ, the Christ that belonged to her, laserbeamed to her alone from infinitely far away.[83]

Father McAlister knows that to use the symbols of God, the divinity of Christ, eternal life, salvation and forgiveness without a basis in an objectively existing God is a kind of magic. Though he rejoices in his 'magical power' as a priest, guarding and wielding these weapons, he is also uneasy; contemplating a children's nativity play, with the crib 'a glowing radiant object, so holy . . .', he reflects that:

> The power which I derive from my Christ is debased by its passage through me. It reaches me as love, it leaves me as magic. That is why I make *serious mistakes*.[84]

He has good reason to be uneasy: we notice danger-signs in Murdoch's narrative, such as his rejoicing in 'the fire of instant salvation'[85] and the final effect of his ministry on Tamar; though she does recover from her personal hell, she develops a kind of self-preserving calculation that falls short of true love. The question put by 'The Good Apprentice', Stuart, persists: 'Is magic bad?'[86] 'All the magic's gone' cries Beautiful Joe, the street urchin and petty criminal of *Henry and Cato*, when he sees Cato without his cassock;[87] he no longer wants to go away with a man who now looks like a middle-aged pervert in a corduroy jacket. Cato protests that 'a priest is just a symbol' and affirms his love for Joe, but we know that a symbol is not 'just' anything; his failure to grasp its power sets a series of events in train that finally ends in his humiliating kidnap by Joe and Joe's death at his hands.

The ambiguity about the magic of religious symbols is an acute form of the ambiguity attaching to any work of art. When a religious symbol is captured in an art-object the danger is most intense, since 'art materialises God', and tempts us to take the image 'for real'.[88] Yet all art inclines to make us content with images.[89] The ambivalence Murdoch displays over this is well illustrated in the incident of the loss of the icon in *The Time of the Angels*. For the caretaker, Eugene, the icon of the Trinity which he has preserved from his childhood home in St Petersburg, is the only fixed point in a shifting existence. Having endured many years in a refugee settlement, he has found the whole world since then to be a kind of transit camp, affording no permanent home. He has lost his faith in the 'bearded Russian God [who] had listened in the darkness to his supplications', yet in the darkness he loves the icon 'as a blank image of goodness from which all personality had been withdrawn.'[90] Like the bell at Imber, the icon can draw attention to the good, and Eugene has a basic respect for truth and goodness that gives him a dignity in his basement quarters, and makes him an attractive and comforting figure to several of the distressed souls who inhabit the novel. Significantly the icon depicts the Trinity in the only permissible way in Orthodox tradition, as three identical angels; we recall that the dispersion of goodness from One Absolute into the Many particulars of the world is mythologised by Murdoch as 'the time of the angels'.[91] 'How can those three be one?' demands Carel when he confronts the icon.[92] Seen through the eyes of Pattie, the West Indian-Irish maid, the angels have the particularity of everyday things:

it glows as if it were on fire. . . . It shows three angels confabulating round a table. The angels have rather small heads and very large pink haloes and anxious thoughtful expressions.[93]

When Eugene's feckless son, Leo, steals the icon and sells it to an antique shop, Eugene is at first devastated. But he begins to see that he has been treating it as a talisman of his lost childhood, a magical charm shielding him from the reality of the present: 'Let it go, let it go. Now he was a stripped man and better for it; so he told himself; *but he could not really think in this way.*'[94] There is the sharp ambivalence. If God is dead, must images of God also be lost in the cause of truth? Images of the Good cannot be totally evacuated of magic, and they will always be manipulated for the sake of fantasy; yet they have a place in the devotion of disciples of the Good. Muriel, into whose hands the icon comes, wants to misuse it to make a miracle, as Dora wants to use the Bell; by returning it to Eugene she will win his gratitude and his love – 'the miraculous return of the icon would open the gates of communication between them.'[95] We feel it right that the icon in fact gets back to Eugene by the black hand of Pattie; symbols of reality must not be exploited to buttress the self.

When we place Murdoch's stories alongside the Christian story, as she herself frequently does,[96] then makers of Christian doctrine should take account of her portrayal of characters who use and misuse religious images. Living through these stories should alert the theologian to the way that images of God and Christ have been used to dominate others and to bolster the will-to-power of the self. For instance, recent political theology has shown how images of God as sole ruler of the universe have been used to legitimate sole human rule in the state. The lordship of Christ has been used to sanction the lordship of bishop and king as Christ's representatives on earth.[97] But an empathetic entrance into the experience of Murdoch's characters should also enable the theologian to be imaginative about the many ways in which we appeal to images of God in order to impose our world upon others and increase our own security.

At the same time, the theologian who lives these lives vicariously cannot avoid grappling with the modern sense of 'loss of God' from the world. The fact that there is a widespread consciousness of the 'death of God' will no longer seem peripheral to the making of doctrine, if it did before; the need to interpret this consciousness will become central and urgent. There is a connection here with the misuse of images for the sake of human power; if God were present in the world as a *deus ex machina*, as an irresistible cause of events, then he would coerce the world into submission and feed a religion of domination. The secular feeling that cause and effect in the world can be explained perfectly well without God's being behind it goes with a sense of human autonomy, of a 'coming of age' in which human beings want no longer to be mere children in the Father's house but to take the adult responsibility of running the estate.[98]

In my comments on Blake's 'Noboddady' I have already drawn attention to recent theological response to the sense of 'death of God'; the theologian gladly admits that the image of a dictatorial cosmic ruler is indeed dead, but affirms that God is present in the world in a mode of weakness and suffering. It is because God really participates in the human experience of pain and death that he is not dead – i.e. irrelevant – to the world. As the theologian Eberhard Jüngel expresses it, we can only think and talk about God in a perishable world because he is 'related to perishability', as the cross of Jesus makes clear.[99] We may now add in the light of our study of Gerard Manley Hopkins and his sense of the veiling of God, that such a humble presence of God in the world must mean that he is hidden. The theologian can therefore interpret the modern lack of consciousness of God not as evidence for the absence of God, but as a sign of his deliberate hiddenness for the sake of human freedom.

Iris Murdoch objects that when Bonhoeffer says that God wants us to live 'as if there were no God',[100] he is no longer talking about God in any meaningful sense and so is 'misusing words'.[101] But Murdoch here seems to be confusing absence with hiddenness. As I have already observed, Bonhoeffer speaks, not of an absent God (and so no God at all), but of a God who 'is with us and helps us' precisely because he shares our suffering. The world out of which he is 'edged' is one where things are the object of our analysis and so under our control. By contrast, as Bultmann explains in commenting on Bonhoeffer's words, we must be in a constant state of readiness for unexpected encounters with the God who 'does not leave the I alone, the I that is encapsulated in its purposes and plans, but whose encounter transforms us, permits us to become new selves again and again'.[102] Such unexpected meetings happen in the midst of the world we know and can explain without God, not in the gaps of the unknown. God is not necessary to explain the world, but 'he is more than necessary', as Eberhard Jüngel puts it. A world which is already self-evident and interesting without God becomes even more interesting when lit up by revelation.[103]

There are obvious and striking parallels here with Murdoch's portrayal of characters who are surprised by unexpected incursions of the Good, and shocked out of the orbit of their own self. Murdoch has in fact commended a 'waiting' upon the Good, and acknowledges the influence of Simone Weil's notion of 'Waiting On God'. Like the God who is hidden in the midst of the world, the Good is scattered into the Many, and though her characters have their own moral responsibility they still need help from this hidden but not absent Good. But Murdoch has something further to say which is of importance for the shaping of a theology which waits upon the hidden God. How shall we recognise his presence, veiled in the midst of the world? How shall we know what it is to serve this serving God? That is a moral as well as devotional question, and for Christians who find God incarnate in Christ it takes the particular form of how to know the Christ who is present in the world. In her moral vision of what is real, Murdoch depicts characters who pay (or fail to pay) attention to contingent details of the world, to the facts. If the theologian finds their experience authentic, then he will be the more likely to follow Bonhoeffer again when he declares that 'God is in the facts themselves'.[104]

For Bonhoeffer, the reality of the world is permeated by Christ, since it is in Christ that God has taken human nature to himself. Christ then 'takes form' in every time and place in human history, and the Christian makes ethical decisions by conforming himself to the Christ who so takes form. 'The form of the Christ in the present' can only be found by a careful analysis of the situation itself, for Christ is there in the truth of the concrete facts and the contingent details. Bonhoeffer is 'situational' in his ethics in so far as he refuses to base them upon any moral laws which enshrine what is good once and for all; rather, the question is 'how Christ takes form among us *here and now*, or how we are conformed with His form.'[105] He is, however, more than situational in that what is good transcends the particular situation; it is actually the demand of the Christ who is present there. We are not just finding what our minds judge to be 'the loving thing to do'; we are being conformed to a Christ who is objectively present, and through whom we encounter God who has a purpose for his creation.

Now, from this perspective, the dialogue of the theologian with Murdoch's thought takes the reverse direction and becomes a critical comment upon her work. We have already noted her ambiguous stance towards the 'magic' of art and religious symbol – and now the theologian can proffer a critical perception into what is happening. For Murdoch the Many into which the Good is scattered, the many good things in art and nature upon which we meditate, are *impersonal* fragments of spiritual reality and sources of 'good energy' like sacraments.[106] Though she claims that 'anything can be a sacrament – transformed – like the bread and wine',[107] these fragments are not really analogous to the Christian sacraments, since they are not places of *encounter* with a personal God. For Bonhoeffer, the God who is hidden in the many 'facts' of the world unveils himself to the one who waits and watches. Truth is in meeting. Revelation, as we saw in the opening chapter, is not the communication of a proposition or message but a transforming encounter with the being of a self-disclosing God. In revelation, as Barth puts it, God takes a worldly object and uses it to objectify himself to us. Thus objects in the world, including words, are 'sacramental' in that God 'gives himself to be known' in them.[108] We do not make him an object of our knowing, and although he never speaks his Word except through human symbols, we must never confuse the two. This freedom of God to unveil or veil himself in worldly objects demythologises nature, and always resists the 'magic' of manipulating objects as things of power in themselves.

Murdoch, similarly, does not confuse the Good itself with the many goods that symbolise it. The Good in itself is unattainable, and we are to serve it 'for nothing'. Yet because the Good is scattered *into* its visible signs, and there is no objectively existing, personal God to be met in and through them, the signs necessarily become things of power in themselves. The danger of magic becomes most acute with religious symbols but, as we have seen, it is an incipient problem with all art and natural things of beauty. The theologian observes the uncertainties about 'magic' that appear in the novels, proffers an explanation for the phenomenon, and is probably more sensitive to its appearance than another reader might be. He may make the literary judgement that there are inconsistencies that arise from it, but of course he does not presume to suggest that this proves Murdoch to be wrong in her view of 'Good without God'. To find a personal God amid the contingencies of life is after all, an unverifiable leap of faith.

FALSE SAVIOURS

In reviewing the false shapes into which the instruments of the good can be warped by the self, we have not yet considered the distortions of love. While falling in love can de-centre the self, shaking it into noticing the existence of another and, together with the beloved, the reality of the contingent world, yet the experience can end in a deeper fall into self. Among several different ways this may happen to Murdoch's characters is the making of a saviour. Characters may impose the role upon another, seeking salvation from their love, or they may assume it voluntarily themselves. Either way, the result is an evasion of the truth that must be faced, a turning away from the hard details of the world, and a loss of moral responsibility.

Murdoch's characters often seek a saviour by confessing some misdeed, and then believing themselves to be 'saved' if the beloved goes on loving them despite it. They think they have told the truth and been forgiven, but they have shrugged off the proper quest for truth and the good. When Blaise, in *The Sacred and Profane Love Machine*, tells Harriet about his mistress Emily he carefully shapes the account in a letter to her (which he finds very moving), stating that the relationship lasted only briefly, that he long ago ceased to find Emily attractive, and that he visits her only 'at intervals' for the sake of the child. When Harriet forgives him, he believes himself to be saved:

> In now confessing this [I] can only cast myself on your love as a religious person casts himself onto God. . . . I ask you, madly perhaps, for your love as the only instrument of salvation. . . . The extra power which can save the world can only come from your perfect love, my angel and my wife.[109]

Blaise, however, is using her forgiveness to avoid dealing with the situation of Emily, which is becoming more and more intolerable to Emily herself. Having confessed, in an edited version, to his wife, he thinks he has done everything needful, but Emily protests, 'I wanted you to tell her because I thought this meant honesty and truth and a square deal for me. . . . The fact remains that I love you (yes, I must be stupid), and I want you to be my husband, my real husband, and live with me in a real house and look after your son . . .'. This is the 'real' situation, Blaise's real dilemma in which he fails to make a responsible choice.

This false salvation is a kind of magic, as Edward partly realises in *The Good Apprentice*. He has sought out his father, the once god-like and now senile Jesse Baltram, in order to confess his responsibility for the death of his friend Mark and ask his forgiveness. 'I love you so much', he tells him, 'You could do everything for me, you could make me all over again'.[110] But now that Mark's sister Brownie has spoken her own forgiveness, his father's vague words pale into nothing: 'What he had taken for redemption had all been illusions, effects of magic.'[111] The irony is that he is about to make a similar saviour out of Brownie. The novel begins with the words from the parable of the prodigal son, 'I will arise and go to my father, and will say unto him, father I have sinned . . .', but the true father is not Jesse but the 'Father and Maker of all' whom Plato identifies as the supreme form of the Good.

Part of the salvation-syndrome is the consent of the saviour, and this is no less an evasion of the real world. Tamar's plight in *The Book and the Brotherhood*, made pregnant by Duncan, has arisen from her desire to redeem him from despair by her love. 'You're saving me by pity' whimpers Duncan in her arms.[112] Similarly Henry, in *Henry and Cato*, tells his unsuitable fiancée that 'I love you because I've taken you on'.[113] Harriet casts herself in the same role of saviour with Blaise; now that the world in which she was once so placidly content has been broken up, and 'she sees the world as terrible', she constructs a number of redemption myths to try and deal with it. Having failed to save Blaise by forgiveness she attempts to apply saving love to her friends Monty and Edgar, and finally spins a fantasy in which her love will save Blaise's most difficult and frequently suicidal patient, Magnus Bowles. Unfortunately he turns out to be a fiction, invented for Blaise by Monty (the author of mediocre detective novels) in weekly instalments in order to cover up for his frequent absences with Emily. Magnus is the very epitome of everyone's failure to face reality; he has the most interesting dreams of all the characters, and these are Monty's only real works of art. Dreams, like art, have both the power to draw our attention to what is real, but can also be used to manipulate the truth.

In these examples we can already see the parallel Murdoch is drawing between false salvation in human love, and the dangerous desire for instant salvation from God. The two types of magic begin to fuse in the parody-religion of Carel in *The Time of the Angels*. The black Pattie is to be for Carel 'his dark angel', saving him by her love: 'Do you understand the doctrine of redemption? . . . Will you be crucified for me, Pattie? . . . You might make a miracle for me.'[114] He plans for her to be crucified by learning that he is having sexual relationships with his daughter Elizabeth; she will save him by remaining faithful in her love for him. Actually, she finds she cannot save him as he wants: 'She loved him but could do nothing with her love. It was for her own torment only and not for his salvation.'[115] This portrayal, with its linking of salvation and suffering, hints at a defect Murdoch finds at the heart of the Christian doctrine of redemption; in the words of another of her characters, 'The West studies suffering, the East studies death.'[116]

Murdoch's critique of redemptive suffering is of great interest for the theologian, alerting him to problems within his tradition. For Murdoch, the false magic that lies in confession to a saviour God is not just that this can divert the believer from his own moral effort, though we have seen from human examples of evading the truth that this can be a real danger. Even more subtly, Murdoch perceives that abasement before a personal God can lead to 'sadomasochism', and several of her characters find this typified in the scene which they read as the grovelling of Job before a thundering Jehovah (Job, Chapters 38–41). The tirade of Leonard Browne (in *A Fairly Honourable Defeat*), for instance, clearly refers to the narrative of Job's repentance for his complaints to the Almighty:

> after the damned irrelevant rubbish about the elephants and the whales and the morning stars and so on, there they are still whining and grovelling and enjoying being booted in the face. . . .[117]

I shall shortly want to question this exegesis of Job, but this does not affect Murdoch's main point, that confession and a seeking for salvation from God can mask the fact that we find our sins an interesting and absorbing subject. Suffering the torments of remorse about them can be a self-indulgence, which is simply another form of creating our own world around us. 'The sado-masochism of

Job'[118] substitutes suffering for death, that is the *true death of the self*. As Father Brendan expounds it (in *Henry and Cato*),

> Death is the great destroyer of all images and all stories, and human beings will do anything rather than envisage it. Their last resource is to rely on suffering, to try to cheat death by suffering instead. And suffering we know breeds images, it breeds the most beautiful images of all.[119]

Christ, however, did not cheat death by suffering instead. Like other priests in Murdoch's tales, Brendan believes in a Christ who is not resurrected but has really faced death. Christianity has gone wrong by replacing death by suffering, degrading the cross by the resurrection, where Christ was obedient to the Good unto a death whose horror he fully comprehended; as Nolan puts it in *The Unicorn*, 'true obedience is without illusion. A common soldier will die in silence, but Christ cried out.'[120] This is being good for nothing, without reward of resurrection. So the mystical Christ can turn us to the Good, and in this sense only he is alive: 'if Christ saves, he lives'[121] and conversely, in an anti-Pauline text, 'if Christ be risen our faith is vain'.[122] The failed man of letters and poet, Lucius, dies in making his best Haiku, a miniature work of art celebrating death as 'the great teacher'. The myth of Marsyas expresses the same truth, as a pagan version of the cross.

All this is exquisitely summed up in the visionary appearing of Christ to Anne Cavidge.[123] In response to her plea that she wants to be saved, 'to be made good', and 'to be washed whiter than snow', he gently insists that 'you must do it all yourself' and 'I am not a magician.' She cannot push away her responsibilities on to him, for he bids her (as he did Mary) 'Love me if you must my dear, but don't touch me.' She cannot cling to an easy Saviour, but must find the way of truth for herself through the tangles of her love, though Christ can be followed and even loved as one who took the path of truth himself. Christ has certainly suffered wounds on the cross and on the way to it, but they themselves cannot save; when she looks at his unscarred hands he says paradoxically, 'my wounds are imaginary'. That is, the suffering is 'not the point . . . though it has proved so interesting to you all!' Suffering has passed like a shadow: what remains is the challenge of facing death, which 'is one of my names'.

Living through the experience of Murdoch's characters should thus prompt the systematic theologian to rethink what he means when speaking of salvation as 'sharing in the suffering of Christ'. The Christian tradition in the West has indeed focused thought upon the sufferings of Christ, and the story Murdoch tells can exert a shaping influence at a point of theological decision about their redemptive significance. On the one hand, atonement through the cross of Jesus may be understood as achieved through suffering *inflicted* upon Christ by God the Father. The idea may take the older, Calvinistic form that the justice of God is satisfied by the imposing of a vicarious penalty upon Christ as a substitute for guilty sinners; so we 'have a share' in the benefits of the cross. But it may also take the very different form proposed by the modern theologian Jürgen Moltmann, who speaks of the Father as 'rejecting' or 'casting out' the Son in order that the rejected and outcast of the world may identify with him and so share fellowship in the divine life.[124] On the other hand, the suffering of Christ may be understood not as inflicted by the Father at all, but as the form which participation in the predicament of a fallen world must inevitably take. On this view, the suffering of Christ is his complete identification with our estranged and broken lives, undertaken in order to create a change in our response to God and each other. In a phrase of Tillich's, 'Not substitution, but free participation, is the character of the divine suffering.'[125]

In considering these doctrinal options, novels which test out feelings about the nature of salvation, dependence and suffering are relevant witness. They cannot, of course, prove that one theological path is correct, but stories and images have their own kind of truth that can affect a theological judgement. In my opinion they will add weight to the conclusion of one theologian, Dorothee Soelle, that worship of a God who inflicts suffering is 'Christian masochism' and 'theological sadism'.[126] They will also incline us, I believe, towards the view of a liberation theologian, Leonardo Boff, that the concept of such a God 'sacramentalizes' and 'legitimates' the exercise of violence by human authorities.[127] This question, as Murdoch shows so well, has wide implications for the image of God which we hold. A God who inflicts suffering, and who offers or witholds salvation as an instant boon, is a dominating figure whose favour we hope to gain at the expense of facing up to the reality of our own selves.

This is not actually the God whom Job encounters. When God appears and speaks from the whirlwind, the description he offers of a vast and complex creation (Chapters 38–41) is not, as Leonard supposes, 'irrelevant rubbish about the elephants and the whales and the morning stars'; nor is it simply a heavy underscoring of the power of a thundering Jehovah before whom Job has to tremble. It opens out the mysteries of a creation which eludes Job's grasp, and prompts him to gaze on the *particularity* of things, so that he sees the futility of demanding that God should act in one way or another. He repents, not of failing to submit to God, but of insisting that God should intervene to give him the rewards that he feels he deserves. In fact Job himself comes to see, like Murdoch's characters, that there is no magical solution. Murdoch's concern that we should be 'good for nothing' comes surprisingly close to the question posed about Job: 'does Job serve God for nought?' (Job 1:9) Perhaps Murdoch herself perceives this in making a passing reference to Job 41, that 'One must be good for nothing. . . . in the world of Jehovah and Leviathan.'[128]

The bidding of Murdoch's Christ that 'you must do it all your-self' and 'the work is yours'[129] awakens echoes of the classic debate between Augustine and Pelagius, with their respective successors. When we consider the ministers of grace Murdoch recognises and which I have already outlined, it would be crude, however, simply to dub her as a Pelagian. It is hard to be satisfied with either account of the relationship between human freedom and divine grace, when faced by the complex experience of such characters as Anne and Tamar. Living through their lives should shape the work of the theologian in creating new ways to understand the balance between human and divine freedom. It might well lead the theologian to explore a cooperative venture between the world and God, in which God freely and humbly chooses to allow his creatures to contribute something genuinely their own to his creative project.

Such a God would accept self-limitation, risk and consequent suffering. In such an image of God the theologian would begin to take seriously Murdoch's challenge about facing the reality of death. The resurrection of Jesus need not be seen as a mere cancelling-out of the cross, avoiding the impact of death. In the cross God has exposed his very being to the onslaught of death and nothingness; the resurrection shows that he has overcome death by taking it into his own being and making it his own. As the theologian Eberhard Jüngel puts it, henceforth death can only be understood as 'a phenomenon of God', or the 'death of the living

God'.[130] By identifying himself with the dead Jesus, God has used death to define his own being, absorbing death into life. To such reflections we may well be led by Murdoch's placing the phrase 'death is one of my names', on the lips of Christ, though she herself thinks this is undercut by resurrection or the objective existence of a personal God. At the same time, the reading of Murdoch's novels will confirm the view of Tillich that we never entirely escape the ambiguities of existence, and in particular the polarity of our freedom and our limits. We only remain human if we continue to face death as a shock, a threat to our being; through justification, which is the gift of knowing ourselves to be accepted, the ambiguities of life become healed, but still only in a fragmentary way.

JUSTIFICATION AND OPENNESS TO THE WORLD: A CRITICAL PERSPECTIVE

As we live through Murdoch's stories of true and false salvation, and place alongside them the Christian story of 'justification', the dialogue also moves the other way and gives us a critical insight upon her work. The theological term 'justification' expresses the experience of 'being put in the right' from beyond ourselves. There is support, resource – or grace – which transcends the tensions of freedom and limit within which we exist and which we encounter as sheer gift. As Jüngel puts it, hearing the Word which comes from beyond us 'interrupts' us,[131] disturbing all self-justification or the attempts to establish our own identity through (for example) our race, culture, money, health or sex. That is, looking to God for our identity strikes a blow at all attempts to build a world around ourselves and live within our self-enclosed horizons. The promise of a Saviour should not divert us from the search for reality, but exactly breaks into the machine-made worlds that Murdoch wants to disturb. As one who looks to the unnameable good (content to be called a 'Christian Buddhist'), Murdoch does not present characters who are summoned in this way. Having accepted her critique of relying upon a saviour and avoiding the death of the self, the question we may ask is how well her own ministers of salvation – including the shock of death which she stresses, like the philosopher Heidegger[132] – open her characters beyond themselves. When we ask that question, we notice that her 'good' characters tend to be isolated. The way of truth, 'doing it all yourself', turns out to be a stoical discipline which can appear privatised, and only meaningful from within the perspective of the sole participant. Anne does not tell her love to the 'Count', and Gertrude draws him into her own circle of love and warmth by granting him an intimate affection without their actually becoming lovers. Gertrude structures the world around herself, and wants to keep Anne as part of it, demanding 'you call it little to be loved by me?' But Anne goes to America to work with a lay religious order among deprived young people, alone and misunderstood, serving the God who does not exist. It is hard for us to see why Anne's decision should be the way of integrity for her; is it serving the truth to let Gertrude's circle have the 'soldier' they want, even if she denies them the 'nun'? As Gertrude's husband, a philosopher, is dying he reaches beyond the 'dance of bloodless categories' in an intensified quest for truth, and is reduced to a few fragments of speech that encapsulate meaning for him: 'hey hey the white swan', 'she shouldn't have sold the ring', 'logical space'; in his disciplined search for reality he is alone in a cage of his own language-game. But is Anne any less enclosed in her private space? She is presented as making her great sacrifice, not to save her friends but to remain in the truth of herself; yet we simply have to believe this is so. Other characters in quest of the Good appear similarly cut off from communication with others and from their sympathy; Stuart appears to be 'a corpse, a dead man', Kathleen seems to her husband to possess 'unlife', Tallis is regarded as an 'unperson', and his friends 'made nothing of Jenkin'.[133]

While some who quest for the good (and notably the 'saints' of religious traditions) are going to appear as outsiders to society,[134] if they are always marginalised they may cease to be the disturbers they need to be. Moreover, despite breaking the shells of their worlds, they may still appear to be trapped within their own self-enclosed space; in terms of the novel, this raises the question as to whether the portrayal of character is consistent with the underlying idea. In fact, the perplexing character of Crimond (in *The Book and the Brotherhood*) appears to embody Murdoch's own questioning about this, and seems to me to be her most radical testing of her own ideas. Early on he denies the ability of the ego to break its self-made world: 'the individual cannot overcome egoism, only society can aspire to do that.'[135] But the value of this thesis is thrown into doubt by Gerard's comment that Crimond's

Marxism shows the same masochism and desire for instant salvation as Calvinism,[136] and by Jean's judgement that anyway he enjoys 'being an incarnate individual'. Nevertheless, through Crimond, Murdoch has raised a questioning note, and this also extends to the value of facing death as a means of encountering reality. Crimond, aptly named after a popular tune for the setting of Psalm 23, twice passes through 'the valley of the shadow of death'. But the suicide pact with Jean and the duel with Duncan seem less a facing of reality than an imposing of his own will upon others, and so a reinforcing of his own world.

Iris Murdoch's novels call the reader to give 'attention' to the truth, living within the tensions between the free self and the particularities of the world. If the perspective of the Christian story of a hidden God and a justifying Saviour alerts us to possible strains within her presentation of plot, character and idea, it would surely be the kind of testing that she herself would welcome as a disciple of the Truth and the Good.

9

William Golding and the Human Darkness

THE ISLAND AND THE SEA

At the beginning of William Golding's first novel, *Lord of the Flies*,[1] we are presented with a small boy who has just become a castaway on an island in the South Seas. He stands on his head in 'the delight of a realized ambition. . . . No grown-ups!' The island on which Ralph, as one of a group of schoolboys, has been dropped represents freedom from the restrictions of an adult society; they have the gift of freedom to shape their own world, to control their own environment. Ralph exults, spreading his arms, that the island is 'all ours'. Yet there are also limitations pressing in upon their freedom. Most evidently the boundary of the sea which makes possible their freedom from other worlds also conditions it and puts a final question mark against it: 'faced by the brute obtuseness of the ocean, the miles of division, one was clamped down, one was helpless. . . .' (p.122). Moreover, the endless rhythm of the sea, its rise and fall like the breathing and sucking of a great Leviathan (p.115), has its counterpart in the ancient pulse of instinct within the children. When expressed in the rhythm of the dance with its refrain 'Kill the beast! Cut his throat! Spill its blood!', even Ralph finds that 'the desire to squeeze and hurt was over-mastering' (p.126). The age-long rhythm of nature fences the children in with outer and inner boundaries.

The boys on the island are a fable of humankind in its wider world. The island surrounded by the sea is a master-image for the human situation, in the tension between freedom and limit. In his novels Golding keeps presenting us with this image, though never simply repetitiously, through the varying and connected forms of island, rock, boat and cathedral. The island in *Lord of the Flies* is 'roughly boat-shaped', and at the end a 'trim cruiser' arrives in the nick of time to rescue Ralph from death at the hands of a howling

205

mob of children, reduced to primitive bloodlust and already the murderers of two of their number. In a shift of perspective, characteristic of the final pages of all Golding's novels, we suddenly see these threatening warriors and their spears through the eyes of a British naval officer, as 'a semi-circle of little boys, their bodies streaked with coloured clay, sharp sticks in their hands'. But even as the officer remarks rebukingly that 'I should have thought that a pack of British boys. . . . would have been able to put up a better show than that', our perspective shifts again to see the cruiser on the horizon. The ship which is to give them freedom also has its limits; the world around it is in the middle of a nuclear war – that is the 'better show' their elders have put up. The ship is an island, as the island is a ship. In the larger world there is the same tension.

In the prehistoric setting of *The Inheritors*, the vehicle of freedom is once again a boat, as the new race of Cro-magnon man asserts its mastery over a waterfall by dug-out canoes, ascending up the river to a higher lake. On the way they exterminate the few remaining survivors of Neanderthal man, whose gentle and innocent consciousness we inhabit for most of the story. At the end of the novel the perspective shifts so that we see through the eyes of the 'new people': 'A fair wind, steerage-way and plenty of water all around – what more could a man want?' Actually, their portage of the boat over the fall had 'taken them on to a new level not only of the land but of experience and emotion' (p.225); the real limit for them is not so much the water but the land which surrounds it, containing the dark forest and the terror of the unknown.

In *Pincher Martin* the island is a small rock in the middle of the North Atlantic, on which the protagonist apparently fights for his survival against the elements. In fact we discover that this decaying rock, 'one tooth set in the ancient jaw of a sunken world', is not only a base for the exercise of Martin's free-will; it has actually been created *by* sheer willpower from his memory of a once aching and now missing tooth. In the shift of perspective at the end we discover that the seven days of struggle have been an after-death experience, and the apparently heroic endurance is now clearly seen as a last fling of self-centred greed.

With *The Spire*, the island/rock/boat becomes a medieval cathedral to which the Dean, Jocelyn, is attempting to add a lofty spire in fulfilment of a vision. The 'four hundred foot of dare' rises from the jet of his will, asserting a freedom over all the known limits of the environment and elements. He asserts his will over 'the weight of the wind' (p.116), the shaky foundations of the building, the religious objections of his clergy, the conservatism of tradition represented by his aged verger, and the pagan superstition of the society around. The Cathedral is portrayed like a 'stone ship'; it floats like an ark on the 'raft' of the foundations, its windows are the sails and its new spire the mast; it is lashed by storm and swayed by the wind.[2] The limits which confine Jocelyn are, like those of the boys on the island-ship, not only outer but inner. There are not only the boundaries of external nature to contend with but his own, barely acknowledged, sexual impulses, taking form in the thrust of the spire from the body of the building.

The most recent trilogy of novels by Golding, *Rites of Passage*, *Close Quarters* and *Fire Down Below*, is set directly on a sailing ship of the early nineteenth century. The ship is a microcosm of society with all its conventions of class formally maintained; but, while seas and storms can magnify the function of the ship as a cramping limit upon the human spirit, the ship and its voyage also offer new opportunities of freedom in social relationship and spiritual development. Other novels of Golding are not quite so obviously controlled by the image of the island-ship, but (as we shall see) they exhibit the same sense of tension between freedom and limit in the human condition. For instance, the predicament of being suspended between two worlds, the cause–effect world of materialism and the world of the free spirit, runs throughout the novel *Free Fall*: the main character, Sammy Mountjoy, concludes that 'both are real. There is no bridge.' Taking another image from *Pincher Martin*, the human being is like a Cartesian diver, a small glass figure in a jar of water, 'delicately balanced between opposing forces' (p.9). Pincher, in the desperate raving of the sixth day, sees the situation in a more exaggerated light: 'Man . . . is a freak, an ejected foetus robbed of his natural development, thrown out in the world with a naked covering of parchment. . . . But nature stirs a pudding there . . .'. How can the stirred pudding, he asks, 'keep constant'? It is 'terror-unbalanced' and finally 'boils over' (p.190). As a creature, the human being is caught between the freedom of his consciousness and the 'tug' of his mute environment, and the poor 'hybrid' cannot keep his balance.

This is the context in which Golding, like the modern theologians we have previously reviewed, understands human fallenness. Golding, in reflecting on his fables, speaks of man 'in theological terms' as 'a fallen being. . . . He is gripped by original sin. His nature is sinful and his state perilous.'[3] This disease in creation, the novels make clear, is not a taint inherited from an Edenic event in the remote past, but the inevitability of failure to maintain one's balance amid the tensions of existence. Now in exploring these tensions, and the consequent fall, Golding constantly employs the image of darkness. Ralph, at the end of a fable in which the boys have fallen from civilisation to savagery, weeps 'for the end of innocence, the darkness of man's heart, and the fall through the air of the true, wise friend called Piggy'. A symbol that recurs several times in the novels is a descent into a dark cellar, reminiscent of a childhood experience of Golding's; in his autobiographical essay 'The Ladder and the Tree' he recalls the church graveyard that lay at the foot of his garden, the cellar whose old flint walls abutted the edge of the burial ground, 'rooted in darkness under the earth', and his imagining of an enemy that lay in wait for him there, coming with the darkness and reducing him to a 'shuddering terror that was incurable because it was indescribable'.[4]

But there are shades of darkness in the human experience. We have seen that a theological understanding of the human predicament will distinguish the anxiety that arises within the polarity of freedom and finitude from the sin which is an inauthentic way of dealing with anxiety. Since Golding is employing the image of darkness to explore the tensions of human nature and the tragedy of the fall, the theologian will have a critical perspective in reading the novels. He will be alert to the shifting shades of the dark, and be interested in the way that Golding distinguishes or fails to distinguish them. While literary critics have often centred upon the image of darkness in Golding's work, the theologian notices that they tend to treat it in an undifferentiated way as the night 'in which all cats are grey' (to use a metaphor from Hegel). At the same time, the movement of shadows on the landscape of Golding's fables, the sliding from one modality of dark to another and their overlap, should make a contribution to a theological approach to the ambiguities of human life.

THREE LEVELS OF DARKNESS

There is, in the first place, a darkness experienced by Golding's characters that corresponds to the basic anxiety a theologian detects in human life. Sammy, in *Free Fall*, enquires 'How did I come to be so frightened of the dark?' (p.154) He knew this 'generalized and irrational fear', lying awake in the dark rectory, long before he took that step which he traces in retrospect as being the decisive moment of fall. After reviewing his early life, he can only say that 'Once upon a time I was not frightened of the dark and later on I was' (p.164) Such a fear cannot be traced to a specific cause, such as the gloomy rectory or the dubious sexual proclivities of his guardian; it is 'generalized and mindless', a symptom of the human condition as children grow into an awareness of the world.[5] So, in *Lord of the Flies*, when Ralph falls asleep exhausted from escaping his hunters, 'sleep hurled him down a dark interior slope', and when he wakes he knows that 'the age-long nightmares of falling and death were past and that the morning was come . . .' (p.211).

In *The Inheritors* Golding does offer a diagnosis of the way that this basic darkness of anxiety arises in human life as a whole. The gentle Neanderthals, who cannot analyse the world around them by logical concepts but only receive picture-like intuitions of it through their senses, know no fear of the unknown in the dark forest. With their pre-rational minds they have attained no real transcendence over their environment, but bathe in it as their dead are wrapped in the womb of Oa, the earth-goddess. The 'new people', however, have an intelligence that can make deductions and manipulate the world around them; in consequence they are afraid because they know the limits to their power and knowledge. Lok, a Neanderthal, 'felt himself secure in the darkness, but understood the impervious power of the people in the light' (p.186). They keep their backs to the fire and face 'outwards at the darkness of the forest'. With their freedom to conquer the forest slope and waterfall, using a technology of rollers and levers, comes a new anxiety as they also feel their limitations. Lok watches with astonishment as:

> There was a hysterical speed in the efforts of Tuami and in the screaming voice of the old man. They were retreating up the slope as though cats with their evil teeth were after them, as though the river itself were flowing uphill (p.209).

Lok senses that 'they are frightened of the air'. They are also, and this he does not realise, frightened of him as a dweller among the dark trees. The new people are, as the theologian W. Pannenberg expresses it, 'open to the world';[6] Lok feels of the Stag-dancer that 'the world was not wide enough for him', and of all the new people that 'Oa did not bring them out of her belly.' But with this openness to their surroundings comes a new sense of limit, so an anxiety falls like darkness upon them. Similarly, the children in *Lord of the Flies* are frightened of a beast that comes in the dark, and are able to locate its home in the limitlessness of the sea: 'Daddy says they haven't found all the animals in the sea yet.' The children's eyes turn to 'the vast stretches of water, the high sea beyond, unknown indigo of infinite possibility . . .' (p.96).

But in each of these cases a basic fear of the dark, which is *not* sin in itself, is merging into a deeper kind of dark. The neutral darkness that accompanies the tension between freedom and limit, is always shading into the dark with which evil shrouds itself. For example, the fear of the dark which falls upon the adult Sammy when the Gestapo torturer locks him into a cupboard, is a deeper blackness because of his past sinful actions. His terrors over what he thinks to be a piece of human flesh on the floor of the cupboard, something wet, slimy and slug-like to the touch – probably (he thinks) a penis – are largely due to the way he has exploited the body of his former lover, Beatrice. Indeed, in his delivering of himself over to sensuality and hedonism, Sammy has adopted one of the two classic inauthentic responses to anxiety. He has over-balanced in the direction of abandoning freedom and embracing what conditions him. Similarly Sebastian Pedigree in *Darkness Visible* confesses that he has surrendered to 'a rhythm . . . a wave motion' which ends in the inevitable climax, 'the catastrophe moving and moving' to the moment when he'll be 'fumbling at their flies' (p.260). The age-old 'pedigree' of humanity takes the form of pederasty in his case, but all are shaped by some kind of inherited pressures.

Most of the boys on the island of *Lord of the Flies* also try to cope with their anxiety by taking the way of relapse into the dark tides of their natures. They abandon themselves to the instincts of self-survival, aggression and bloodlust, all summed up in the 'familiar rhythm' of the dance of killing the pig, performed in the darkness (p.205). Three of the boys, however, take the opposite path – of asserting their freedom, seeking to master their surroundings. Ralph uses his gift of administrative ability and organisation; he is the keeper of the conch shell by which he summons and tries to keep order in the boys' assembly. Piggy exercises freedom through his intelligence; he is the keeper of the glasses, which both enable him (like Prometheus) to be the bringer of fire, and symbolise his attempt to overcome limits by rationality:

> 'Life,' said Piggy expansively, is 'scientific, that's what it is. In a year or two when the war's over they'll be travelling to Mars and back. I know there isn't no beast – not with claws and all that, I mean. . . .' (p.92).

Simon asserts his freedom through imagination and intuition; he is the mystic, and his symbol is the little hide he builds for himself to contemplate in alone. Yet Golding dubs these three the 'three blind mice'; they are to be victims, but this is because they are also in the dark. For all their admirable attempts to transcend their environment through morality, intellect and spirituality, they ignore the limits of the flesh at their peril. Piggy, for instance, with his talk of 'science' tries to rationalise away not only the beast but the fear itself; his intellectual head is destined to be split open by the reactions against that fear. Both he and Ralph refuse to admit to themselves that they were implicated in the ritual murder of Simon; they were 'on the outside' of the terrible dance and 'left early' (pp.174–5). Thus the freedom of the blind mice is a detachment from reality: 'we never saw nothing'. Even Simon fails to reckon with the intoxicating rhythms of the body. Freed from his own fear by recognising that the beast is really within themselves, he is encouraged to climb the high rock and discovers that the swaying monster there is actually the trapped body of a dead parachutist. Perhaps too naively he expects the frantic dancers to understand his good news; Piggy has a grain of truth when he says that 'he hadn't no business crawling like that out of the dark'. (p.173)

Among others of Golding's characters who over-stress their freedom in an attempt to control their world are Chris ('Pincher') Martin, 'born with his mouth and his flies open and both hands open to grab' (p.120), and Sophy in *Darkness Visible* who uses apparently psychic powers ('being weird') to make things fall together 'as if the whole world was cooperating' (p.126). But the central symbol of *The Spire* enables Golding to offer a more sustained study of the distortion of the human movement of self-transcendence. Jocelyn loses his balance in the tensions of his vocation, asserting his free-will with a massive pride and neglecting both his own proper limits and those of others. According to Jocelyn, he has been given a vision of the new spire as the ultimate angle in the diagram of prayer which he perceives the Cathedral to be. In fact it is mainly the thrust of his own 'devouring Will, my master' (p.121), and to serve this will he sees others as 'his instruments, people he had to use' (p.55). When a pit is opened up to inspect the foundations, it appears that the building rests on an underbed of mud; the earth begins to move and the whole structure to ring with vibration:

> Now I know what I must do, he thought, this is what I am for. . . . The singing of the stones pierced him, and he fought it with jaws and fists clenched. His will began to burn fiercely and he thrust it into the four pillars, tamped it in with the pain of his neck and his head and his back. . . . It is a kind of prayer! So he knelt, stiff, painful and enduring; and all the time the singing of the stones operated on the inside of his head. At last, when he understood nothing else at all, he knew that the whole weight of the building was resting on his back. (pp.80–81)

In this assertion of the will over all the limits that confront him, Jocelyn is not only scorning the laws of physics but failing to recognise the unconscious urges within him that limit and condition his actions. He is encouraged by a warmth at his back that he interprets as the presence of his guardian angel; it is the holy fire which gives energy to the upward thrust of will and spire. Actually it appears to be a combination of the spinal tuberculosis that finally kills him, and suppressed sexual desire for his ward, Goody. He does not understand why his prayers are disturbed by an image of blazing red hair, nor why he has made a safe match of her with the aged Verger Pangall; consciously it has not crossed his mind that Pangall was impotent, but 'the cellerage knew about him. . . . and arranged the marriage' (p.213).

Jocelyn's 'cellar', symbolised by the pit beneath the spire, corresponds to the children's beast and Sammy's cupboard. The darkness it hoards is not simply the distortion of sexual desire, though of course the spire is (at least partly)[7] a phallic image, erect from the body of the building. Jocelyn's cellar also, for example, contains the sacrifice of Pangall to his project, since he has been ritually killed with a lance of mistletoe by the superstitious workmen, and been buried in the pit to avert evil. Pangall, like Simon on the boy's island, has been made a scapegoat, as the human heart projects its darkness outwards and tries to deal with it by embodying it in some victim. The New People in *The Inheritors* fasten their own inner darkness upon the Neanderthals, whom they regard as devils who 'live in the darkness under the trees'; even the baby they take away with them and foster appears for a moment to Tuami as a monstrous spider with six hairy legs (p.227).

Whether overbalancing to the side of limit or freedom, Golding's characters thus move from dark to dark, from the basic dark of anxiety to the deeper dark of evil. But they can also find a third kind of darkness. If they take the courage to go down the steps into the pit or cellar of their innermost being and face the darkness of evil there, they will notice another dimension to the dark, which is simply the irreducible mystery of the individual personality. There is a hidden self, incommunicable to others, unique in its own 'isness', existing like a 'dark, calm sea'.[8] This is the true dark, and Golding's characters can break through to its 'lighted centre'[9] if they will only open themselves in trust, rather than seeking securities to preserve their self-centre and evade the tensions of existence. Thus Sammy, crouching in his cupboard, has nowhere else to go except down into the inner chamber of his being, shot forward over 'unimaginable steps that were. . . . destructive of the centre', and crying 'help me, help me'. Then

> The thing that screamed left all living behind and came to the entry where death is close as darkness against eyeballs.
> And burst that door (p.185).

When Jocelyn also cries 'help me', the words are a 'key', opening up an entrance first to 'an infinite sea of grief', then to the asking of forgiveness from those whom he has injured, and finally to his vision of the spire as a thing of wonder as well as of bitter regret. Pedigree too, in his extremity, cries 'help me!' (*Darkness Visible*, p.265). The cry for help corresponds closely to the insight of Christian theologians who suggest that the authentic way of dealing with anxiety is trust; Reinhold Niebuhr, for example, affirms that 'freedom from anxiety' is possible only by 'trust in divine security'[10] and Pannenberg affirms that control over the world is only accessible through 'unconditioned trust in the infinite God'.[11] In a religious perspective, the polarity between freedom and limit is not witness to the absurdity of human existence, but prompts us to look beyond ourselves to support from another dimension. Sin, then, is unbelief – a refusal to trust in the resources that are offered to us in the midst of the anxiety of existence.[12] As Paul Tillich expresses it, sin is a 'turning away from the infinite ground of our being'.[13] Golding presents his characters as finding the wonder[14] of this ultimate ground or turning from it. He is, it seems, content to name it as God,[15] though he speaks only of our *experience* of this ultimate reality through becoming aware of our own selves (what Golding has called the 'My Godness of the self')[16] and is silent about the being of God *in himself*.[17]

Thus Chris ('Pincher') Martin, locked in upon his own centre and stranded upon the rock which is both a symbol of his will-power and a projection of his own darkness, descends into his cellar and turns away from the offer that is there. His descent is the closest echo of Golding's own childhood nightmare-fears of the cellar next to the graveyard which underlies all his imagery of pit and cellar: 'Past the kitchen door. . . . Down, pad, down. Coffin ends crushed in the wall. Under the churchyard back through the death door *to meet the master*' (p.178). Since we can only know God through ourselves, the 'master' to be met in the darkness will reflect one's openness or closedness to the wonder of Being beyond the self. For Martin, the thing that is encountered mirrors his own refusal of grace;

> Pattern repeated from the beginning of time, approach of the unknown thing, a dark centre that turned its back on the thing that created it and tried to escape (p.179).

Martin turns his back on his creator, and climbs up from the cellar, treading on the faces of others for steps, crying not 'help' but 'I am! I am! I am!' (p.145) This is the move from dark to dark. An attempt to cope with anxiety by turning from the source of grace leads to a deeper dark. As Golding himself expresses it, 'God is the thing we turn away from in life, and therefore we hate and fear him and make a darkness there.'[18]

THE RIDDLE OF THE FALL

If a theological perspective upon sin and fallenness alerts us to the different shades of darkness within Golding's portrayal of humanity, his landscape of dark figures should, conversely, influence the theologian towards certain conclusions upon the human predicament. Golding's fables describe the boundary between dark and deeper dark, between anxiety and evil, as a shifting one. The theologian is well aware that this is an extraordinarily difficult boundary to analyse. As we have already seen (especially in Chapter 3 above), though the anxiety arising from the tensions of human existence is unavoidable, many theologians will want to say that the fallenness which results from it is not a logical necessity of creation. Such are the pressures upon human beings, stretched between their freedom and their limitations, that it is inevitable in practice that they should fall towards inauthentic life. But this move away from the Good is still a 'leap' and not simply part of the structure of the world. We move inevitably from dark to deeper dark, and yet we know that we are responsible. As I have admitted before, this view of fallenness has an irreducible element of riddle, which other theologians may attempt to *remove* altogether.

One way of eliminating the riddle is taken by Augustine, who recognises that sin is certainly inevitable for human beings now, but traces the beginning of this predicament to one past moment of choice by Adam. Though this seems to excuse God from any responsibility, we have already noted deep problems with this view of a fall in and from a perfect world.[19] The opposite way of cutting the Gordian knot would be to suggest that the sense we have of an inclination towards sin does not reflect an objective state of affairs at all, but is a psychological mechanism. As R.S. Lee argues the case, for example, 'it is part of man's moral nature to feel that he has sinned, whether or not he has done so in actual fact'.[20] The persistent sense of 'having sinned' together with guilt is a normal factor in the growth from childhood to adult life; without this consciousness, promoted by the superego as our severe moral critic, we would not come to moral awareness. Further, we go on as adults feeling that we have a 'bias to sin' because we are continually aware of our failure to reach the potentials which our ego holds out to us as ideals. Again, as Lee puts it:

This inevitable gap between the real and ideal self explains the sense of proneness to sin which underlines the doctrine of the Fall. Nothing we can do will close the gap, for the ideal ever recedes from the real.[21]

In partial accord with this view, the symbol of fall does express our failure to fulfil our potential, pointing forward to the possibility that we can 'rise' higher. The question, however, is whether we achieve our aims only to find new ones opening beyond, so that we 'always fall short of [our] current ideal' (as Lee suggests), or whether we constantly betray *whatever* ideal aims we have. A view of the fall as 'riddle' suggests that the latter, darker view, is true. By contrast, an even more extreme way of reducing the riddle would be to suggest that sin itself (or a certain amount), and not just consciousness of it, is necessary for moral growth.[22]

Now, to the theologian faced by these issues and options in understanding human fallenness, Golding offers the experience of living on the boundaries between dark and dark, and feeling the movement from one to the other. He is, of course, not writing allegories of the fall, but deliberately setting his own stories alongside the Christian story, evoking interactions and echoes. Through his fables he explores the shadows and half-tones on the human landscape, and the theologian will gain in sharing that experience as part of his doctrinal work. My own perception is that Golding's world supports the understanding of fall as a riddle; what he portrays is an inevitable pull from dark to deeper dark, while at the same time evoking a strong sense of moral responsibility within the fall. The paradox is not intellectually stated, but is felt in experience, and this itself makes the paradox more tolerable.

When Simon confronts the 'Lord of the Flies' in the form of the head of a pig spiked on a stick, he 'saw the white teeth and dim eyes, the blood – and his gaze was held by that ancient, inescapable recognition' (p.132). The natural fear of Simon, confronted by the unknown, slides into a recognition that the darkness is both deeper and inevitable: 'You knew, didn't you? I'm part of you? Close, close, close! I'm the reason why it's no go?' (p.137) Simon realises that the beast is within him and 'inescapable'. But the scene eludes all simple reduction to this explanation. The head lectures him like a pedantic schoolmaster, warning him not to interfere with the evil fun it is planning. What is happening cannot be simply paraphrased (indeed, the author himself felt that the event was taking on a life of its own),[23] but we begin to feel that this evil is not essential after all, that it can and ought to be resisted. The scene ends with Simon 'inside the mouth. He fell down and lost consciousness'. As with other traumatic scenes when characters descend the steps into their own cellars to confront the darkness there, we feel that the dark is 'original' and inevitable, and yet it is still alien to their true being. It is their own ('close') and yet not their own.

The title of the novel *Free Fall* nicely sums up this riddle. The fall is freely chosen (as in Milton's phrase from *Paradise Lost*, 'free to fall'),[24] but it is also 'free' in the technical sense of being unrestrained movement, an inevitable pull downwards. The artist, Sammy Mountjoy, asks 'What am I looking for? I am looking for the beginning of responsibility' (p.47). He finds his own nature to be unendurable, especially his treatment of Beatrice Ifor whom he has exploited and degraded sexually, and then deserted despite all his promises to her. But he cannot see how he could have avoided betraying her, given the kind of person he had become: 'I had given away my freedom. I cannot be blamed for the mechanical and helpless reaction of my nature' (p.131). So recalling, like a series of pictures, his growth from the innocence of childhood into young manhood, he is continually asking 'where did I lose my freedom?' When did he freely fall and cease to be free? He finally believes he may have found the critical moment in a decision he made as he left school. The answer to his headmaster's question 'Isn't anything important to you?' is spoken within himself; it is 'the white, unseen body of Beatrice Ifor, her obedience, and for all time my protection of her; and for the pain she has caused me, her utter abjection this side death'. A voice within him asks 'What will you sacrifice?', and he replies 'everything' (pp.234–6).

Sammy thinks that he may have isolated the point of self-damnation in which he fell freely, never to act freely again. However, he also recognises that his being was already conditioned before this point; as soon as he became aware of his sexuality and the amoral form it took, he was saying 'musk, be thou my good' and so 'Guilty am I, therefore wicked I will be. . . . Guilt comes before the crime and can cause it' (p.232). In his moment of choice he becomes what he already is; as the critics Ian Gregor and Mark Kinkead-Weekes neatly put it, 'Here Being and Becoming meet as Sammy chooses his determinism.'[25] He has chosen his being. Here is the paradox of unnecessary inevitability. Another critic, Virginia Tiger, attempts to reduce this paradox to rational order by suggesting that there comes a crucial occasion when the being which a man carries within him 'confronts him in the lineaments of choice. And Golding seems to be saying that at this point there is evidence. . . . that freedom exists. At this point one is not determined by one's predetermined nature.'[26] This seems to be Sammy's own conclusion, but the abiding image the novel offers us is that of Sammy searching through the portrait gallery of his life, leaving us with the impression that the answer is unsatisfactory. Reducing everything to this one moment does not do justice to the complexity of his being and to the influences that brought him to that decision. In the last sentence of the novel, the verdict of the commandant upon the method of Sammy's interrogator invites us 'to see without pattern':[27] 'The Herr Doctor does not know about peoples.' Sammy himself asks whether that adolescent occasion was really the moment of loss, and while he does not say (as before) 'Not here', he leaves the question 'Here?' suspended in the air. (p.236) All we can really say about the story of Sammy's fall is that both inevitability (being) *and* responsibility (becoming) are affirmed.

A critical part of the web of influences that have made the fall inevitable is the way that two pictures of the world are presented to him as he grows into adolescence. The chemistry master, Nick Shales, presents a world of law, a 'dreary rationalistic universe' but does so with a genuine goodness and generosity that draws others to him. The scripture teacher, Rowena Pringle, presents a world of the spirit, but combines her gift of storytelling with an obsessive cruelty, inflicting her own bitter Gethsemane upon Sammy. On the one hand there is the world of finite limitations; the burning candle in Nick's experiment of the bell-jar witnesses to the truth of the conservation of energy, proving that 'matter is neither created nor destroyed'. But there is also the universe from which Miss Pringle can lift the veil and which Sammy as an artist 'inhabited by nature', a world of miraculous freedom from all limits in which a burning bush is not consumed. (p.217) In the tension between freedom and limit, made the more acute by the characters of the presenters, he chooses not so much materialism as Nick (p.226). Yet in choosing, he turns Nick's 'innocent, paper world' into amorality and hedonism, and only breaks back through its poverty into the rich world of 'Jehovah and Moses' within the dark cupboard of the prison-camp.

Could he have kept a double vision? His concluding reflections about living in one world or two are central to our theme, and curiously evade any easy reduction to a pattern. 'Her world was real, both worlds are real. There is no bridge' (p.253). At the same time, he affirms that 'the innocent and the wicked live in one world. But . . . we are the guilty. We fall down. . . . we. . . . live in two worlds at once' (p.251). Critics try, uneasily and unsuccessfully, to identify the 'one world' in which the innocents (such as Nick) and the wicked (such as Rowena Pringle) live, with each or one of the two worlds already portrayed.[28] But this is a confusion. Nick, for instance, can hardly be fitted into the world of Pentecostal fire, but neither does he merely live in the sphere of mechanical causation he believes in; his world is not actually 'a real thing' (p.212), and 'illogically' he fails to notice the spirit because 'what is nearest the eye is hardest to see' (p.214). The point is that neither Nick nor Miss Pringle feel the *tension* between the two worlds of freedom and limitation, Nick because he is innocent in spirit like a young child and Miss Pringle because she has escaped from her anxiety by denying the flesh, and so imprisoned herself in a solitary world of her own self-deception.

Sammy concludes that there is 'no bridge' in the sense of an easy synthesis. Sammy (and Golding with him)[29] knows that he can and must bear the pain of living in two different worlds at once. It is in this extremity, with the awareness that we constantly lurch from one sphere to the other and fail to hold our balance, that guilt arises: 'We are the guilty. We fall down . . . We weep and tear each other' (p.251). But only with guilt comes the possibility of forgiveness. 'The innocent cannot forgive' (pp.75, 248), as they do not understand the injury for what it is; the infant Sammy could not forgive the verger who cause his mastoid, refusing to take his outstretched hand, just as Beatrice in her second childhood cannot forgive Sammy, wetting his shoes with her urine. When Beatrice was in her adult mind, she could write a letter pleading for forgiveness and offering it. Forgiveness, reflects Sammy, is 'the sign and seal of adult stature, like that man who reached out both arms and gathered the spears into his own body' (p.74). All those who live in one world are deficient here. The wicked, like Miss Pringle, are too cocooned in the false comfort of their one world, complete with plaster rabbit beside the plaster bird-bath (p.252), to be able to receive forgiveness. But even the innocent are not living in a real world but an immature one, as Johnny Spragg exults in the speed of his motorbike and Nick delights in what he can 'touch and see and measure' with his laboratory apparatus but recoils from his own sexuality: 'If the devil had invented man he couldn't have played him a dirtier, wickeder, a more shameful trick than when he gave him sex!' (p.231)

Golding's reference to the 'one world' in which the innocent live is thus highly ambiguous. It seems admirable, until it is measured by the standards of forgiveness. As Philip Redpath suggests in his 'structural' reading of Golding's fiction, the text of *Free Fall* with its 'I' makes the reader aware of possessing an 'I' too, and makes him realise that only through forgiveness can he break out beyond the self to others.[30] If there is to be growth, we have to be exposed to the tensions of the two worlds, with inevitable guilt. We recall the portrayal by Irenaeus of Adam and Eve in Eden, as imperfect and infantile creatures, needing to learn through the experience of 'passing through all things'.[31] But Golding does not simply conclude that the fall is logically necessary for moral growth. He makes us feel the riddle of an inevitability which is unnecessary, for despite Sammy's words we know from his own experience that there *is* a bridge, a 'place' where the whole business of the universe converges (p.187). There is a way of holding the two worlds together in harmony, though we only ever begin to approach it; as Paul Tillich puts it, 'the New Being does conquer (though fragmentarily) the ambiguities of life in time and space'.[32]

Beatrice, in the glory of her young womanhood and the quiet mystery of her being, testifies to the bridge; with a few joyous strokes of the pencil, the adolescent Sammy catches her on paper and finds himself confronting an 'astonishment': 'I saw there in her face and around the openness of her brow, a metaphorical light that none the less seemed to be an objective phenomenon, a real thing' (p.222). He has seen the holy fire of the burning bush, a 'light of heaven' in a model of flesh and blood. He remembers her with a picture of a bridge in the background;[33] she is, or witnesses to the bridge between spirit and flesh – for together with the holy light she has 'knees sometimes silk and young buds that lifted her blouse'. However, unlike Dante with his heavenly guide Beatrice,[34] he reduces her to a 'shoddy temple' of the merely physical, and she ends in the 'grey house of factual succession' (p.237).

The innocent also live in one world in *The Inheritors*, secure in the embrace of earth and friendly darkness. But these Neanderthals are not going to ascend the slope of evolutionary development. They come to the waterfall at the same time as the New People, but are not going to progress beyond this Fall to the higher ground. They are swept over and down the river by the very logs that the New People are able to exploit to work their way up the river. Lok climbs the tree of knowledge to look, though without understanding, upon the stag rituals by which they claim a freedom over the world, as well as propitiate the forces they feel as limits. But he cannot use the trees as they do. In his picture-thoughts he sees them as trees themselves, upright and wielding the awesome destructive power that a *falling* tree possesses. When Lok discovers the concept 'like', he thinks 'They are like the river and the fall, they are a people of the fall; nothing stands against them' (p.195). When they port the log-boats past the fall using log-levers, it is 'as though the river itself were flowing uphill' (p.209). Yet at the same time, with this very mastery over the environment comes the sense of their limits: 'they are frightened of the air'. The Inheritors live in two worlds; even before they appear Lok knows (though without concepts) that 'only some creature' [both] more agile and frightened would dare that leap' to the high plateau of the island beyond the fall (p.41).

The central image of the book is the waterfall, a Fall by means of which some mount higher, and incur guilt as they push others down the path to death. They have experienced an upward fall ('as though the river were flowing uphill'), which contradicts the Second Law of Thermodynamics as much as the spiritual fire of *Free Fall* contradicts the Law of conservation of energy. The whole of nature, regarded as finite world, witnesses to the fact that change results in the return of a substance to its original condition; the energy of water, for example, moves back to a state of low organisation. But, as Golding himself expresses it, in the free spirit of man 'life refuses to submit to a general levelling down of energy and simply winds itself up again'.[35] The Inheritors of the human race are pushed up the river by a new intensity and a new vision. In this upward fall, there is a sense of inevitability, but Golding does not present it as a strictly necessary means of moral progress; there is also a recognition of guilt.[36] Tuami finds himself to be in a state of 'confusion . . . haunted . . . full of strange irrational grief'. The boat is like an island of darkness in a world of light; it is 'untidy, hopeless, dirty' (p.225). In his question 'What else could we have done?' (p.227) there are strains both of inevitability and responsibility. Strict necessity is further undermined as Golding hints at undeveloped options, for in exploring the intuitive minds of the Neanderthal people, we have discovered the first glimmerings of abstract and deductive thought in Fa and Lok. It seems that they might after all have the capacity to be Inheritors, and their infant does in fact survive to mingle his genes with the New

People. When Fa struggles to express her deductive concept by saying 'This is a picture of a picture' (p.62), the old woman, as keeper of the tradition, responds sharply 'that is a new thing'. This is a possibility not to be actualised, a path not in the end trodden. But it helps to assure us that though creativity and fall coincide, there is no logical necessity in it.

The theme of upward fall and reversed entropy is taken up again at the end of *The Spire*. Jocelyn has admitted his part in the ruin of four lives, recognised the dark cellarage in his personality and asked for forgiveness. If he could go back he would 'take God as lying between people and to be found there'. The spire threatens to fall, pressing down remorselessly, like a 'stone hammer' for which he had traded the lives of four people. 'He felt [its] weight' (p.220) as he had always felt it on his shattered back, but now without the will-power to hold it up. In his dying moments, however, all this transfer of energy downwards is reversed; he sees the spire which is the symbol of his fall now 'rushing upward to some point at the sky's end'. As in *The Inheritors*, there is 'an upward waterfall', and its beauty fuses together the two worlds of flesh and spirit:

> It was slim as a girl, translucent. It had grown from some seed of rosecoloured substance that glittered like a waterfall, an upward waterfall. The substance was one thing, that broke all the way to infinity in cascades of exultation that nothing could trammel (p.223).

Jocelyn lives in two worlds; there is the freedom of spiritual vision like the flashing of the kingfisher over water, and the limiting pull of the flesh. Amid this tension fall is unavoidable – 'there is no innocent work' (p.222). Yet in accepting responsibility and offering forgiveness there is the possibility for fall to become rise. In *The Inheritors*, Golding aimed to counterbalance simplistic and popular views of evolution (in which Neanderthal man was portrayed as beastlike) by making us see the presence of moral devolution. Rise is also fall. Here the check is the other way; there is the mercy that even a work which springs from an elementary mistake about the nature of prayer and from a suppressed lust can be genuinely creative after all. In his bitterness of regret Jocelyn sees the building of the spire as 'growth of a plant with strange flowers and fruit, complex, twining, engulfing, strangling' (p.194). It is a tree of evil.

But in his dying moment he can cry 'It's like the apple tree.' The apple-tree of mythical Eden (though not so named in the Genesis story) is certainly the tree at the heart of the fall. But earlier, setting out on his pilgrimage to seek forgiveness from Roger Mason, Jocelyn had seen an apple tree in blossom as a 'bursting up with cloud and scatter, laying hold of the earth and air, a *fountain*, a marvel . . .' (p.205). As in the earlier novel, the tree which falls to wreak destruction can also be the tree of ascent, in which life can make new beginnings, denying the law of entropy.

In the dense image of the spire, the tree and waterfall of *The Inheritors* have been unified. There is a riddle: fall is rise and the unavoidable still involves guilt. The spire also forms the focus of tension between freedom and limit, as both fountain of prayer and phallus. In the same spire there is, finally, the bridge between the worlds, because Jocelyn is able to offer forgiveness and accept himself. He knows now what the significance is of the 'tangle of hair blazing among the stars; and the great club of his spire lifted towards it'. (p.221) He can name the experience as Berenice, from the love-poetry of Catullus; he can also enjoy the humour and truth of his Chaplain's assuming that he is invoking *Saint* Berenice. By contrast, Colley in *Rites of Passage* cannot accept and forgive himself when he falls. He turns his face to the wall and loses all energy to live, becoming a startling witness to the law of entropy.

If the fall *were* a structural necessity of creation, entropy (both spiritual and material) would in fact be the truth about reality. There could be no salvation. Sophy in *Darkness Visible* essentially takes this view: 'Everything's running down. Unwinding . . . Everything is just a tangle and it slides out of itself bit by bit towards something simpler and simpler – and we can help it'.[37] She surrenders to the inevitability of the fall towards non-being: 'What it wants, the dark, let the weight fall.' She shows the only way to live with this fatalism, using her intuitive senses to manipulate others, and so to 'take what you can on the way'. But in protest against this reducing down to the simple, the apple-tree bursts upwards into a diversity of new creation: 'suddenly [Jocelyn] understood that there was more to the apple tree than one branch' (p.205). In the complexity of human experience, freedom in tension with limits, spirit with flesh, there is the riddle of the fall which is inevitable but not essential. Through the images of 'free fall' and 'upward fall' Golding allows the theologian to test out this idea in vicarious experience. The symbol of fall is felt as a sign of hope that we can rise higher, reversing spiritual entropy as Matty does when he walks from the fire as a young child. Like the burning bush which Moses saw, he is not consumed.

ENCOUNTER WITH NON-BEING: A THEOLOGICAL CRITIQUE

In Golding's understanding of salvation, a character takes courage to descend the steps into the cellar of his personality, there to confront the darkness, a double dark of his own basic 'isness' (his opacity) and the evil to which he has succumbed. The self has become locked into its own dark, self-enclosed, and needs to open itself to the power of Being. The openness comes simply with the cry for help, bursting through the darkness into a lighted centre. In theological terms, the self amid its tensions has turned towards God in a new attitude of trust rather than self-justification. In this light, a person knows not only *who* he is, but *what* he is, and what he is for. Sophy, in *Darkness Visible*, knows *who* she is; she fosters a dark self which emerges from the depths to sit at the mouth of the dark tunnel at the back of her head, a '*this* [which] lived and watched without any feelings at all, and brandished or manipulated the Sophy-creature like a complicated doll' (p.124). To cultivate the 'this' is 'to choose what was real and what you knew was real' (p.123), which is a 'naked and unemotional "I am" or perhaps "it is" (p.188)'. Pincher Martin too cries 'I am! I am! I am!' as he climbs out of the cellar, treading on the faces of others. But it is not so important for Matty Windrove to know who he is; in fact, a name has been invented quite arbitrarily for this anonymous child who came walking from the flames, and nobody in the story can remember it correctly until Pedigree recognises him in his moment of death. The important thing, reflects Matty, is 'What am I': 'How can I help until I know what I am?' (p.56). The question shifts again after the 'crucifarce by the black man leaping on him out of the sky', when Matty has his testicles and manhood crushed by an aborigine as he lies spreadeagled upon the ground: he now asks, 'What am I for?' (p.68)

To lose one's preoccupation with oneself (who am I? I am.) is to notice the wonder of things, to see what they are in themselves. This is the vision that Sammy has after his release from the dark cupboard. He raises his eyes, 'desiring nothing, accepting all things and giving all created things away', and he thus sees the 'crowded shapes' of the rich earth as 'aflame at the surface and daunting by right of their own natures' (p.186). He also notices that these objects that 'shone with the innocent light of their own created nature' are all related in a music of harmony. What we 'are for' is relationship, which is 'a kind of vital morality' (p.189). His own self, he now notices, is wonderfully creative, constantly denying the law of entropy or conservation of energy, but unfortunately in his case producing shapes which are, 'the most loathsome and abject creatures' (p.190). Other selves, such as Beatrice, he now credits with a natural goodness and generosity, so that what he thought was a merely empty vacuum at their centre (because they were not promoting themselves) he now realises to have been full of being (p.191).

This vision of the otherness of things we have already found to be expressed by Hopkins and Iris Murdoch, together with the need to be released from the self-absorption of the self. Golding's particular contribution is to depict the attaining of release and the noticing of all being through confrontation with darkness or non-being. It comes through descent into the cellar, burying in earth, baptism in mud. This theme is, of course, not absent in other writers. Murdoch's characters are brought to notice the details of the world as they confront death, usually through drowning.[38] Hopkins finds the fretted detail of nature etched against the encroaching shadows of the night of God's hiddenness.[39] This is the age-old pattern of resurrection through crucifixion. But, with his constant use of the image of darkness, Golding weaves the encounter with non-being into the very warp and woof of the personality.

Various currents of modern theology have also stressed the dialectical relationship between being and non-being. Theologies influenced by existentialism have stressed that the ultimate limit which confronts the free self is death, the threat of ceasing to be. In contrast to Wittgenstein, who insisted that 'death is not an event of life',[40] Heidegger defined life as a being-towards-death, a leaning towards the final boundary which affects the whole process of living.[41] In face of this possibility of nothingness, everything in life falls to nothing, and appears to lose its meaning. An inauthentic existence tries to cover up the fact of death, but the anxiety that arises from facing up to death can be a means of awakening us to the wonder of Being that we have otherwise forgotten. John Macquarrie, building upon Heidegger, points out that God as Holy

Being is incomparable, unclassifiable with beings in the world, and thus eludes attempts to talk about him directly. While he is Being who lets all beings be, we can be so distracted by the multiplicity of beings that we fail to be aware of Being as their Ground; but when beings 'fall to nothing', by contrast we suddenly notice Being, or recognise the gracious approach of Being to us.[42] Employing an illustration which Macquarrie does not, we may say that when the darkness of non-being falls, we notice the candle flame which we cannot see in the daylight. The darkness is of course compounded by the despair that arises from trying to resolve the polarity of freedom and limit in our own way; neutral non-being becomes an aggressive, destroying *nihil*. Faced with the shock of this non-being, as Paul Tillich expresses it, we are disposed to receive revelation.[43]

The parallel with Golding's thought is clear, though the non-being that he evokes is much more the despair which arises from neglect of Being and assertion of self than from death itself. Moreover, theologians such as Macquarrie suggest that the impact of non-being also prompts the self to find a unity. The wholeness of a self derives, he suggests (again following Heidegger), not from some kind of underlying substance but from an enduring through time; the identity of the self is its sameness through past, present and future.[44] Actually, however, our selves are fragmented in time; we cannot bring our past, present and future together. In particular, a sense of guilt keeps us from coming to terms with our past. Heidegger suggests that a movement of the will, fixed upon some master concern, will achieve this binding together, and he identifies this as a concentration upon the fact of death. Christian theologians, such as Macquarrie and Tillich,[45] modify this account; the 'final concern' that will unify the self is God, and an attitude of trust and acceptance is the kind of movement of will that is appropriate to this concern. Non-being, and especially the fact of death, will however awaken us to the offer of God. In the novels of Golding, we can again find a parallel; the flashback technique used in *Pincher Martin*, *Free Fall* and *The Pyramid* makes clear the need to find the self in time. It is by crying 'help', and being open beyond the self in trust that such as Sammy find some way to bring their present and future into unity with the past. This ultimate concern brings, as we have seen, an acceptance of the fact of the past and some acknowledgement of responsibility for it.

In current theology this strand of thought has been combined with an older one, from Hegel, in which the vitality of the divine Spirit consists in its going out from itself and exposing itself to non-being. Similar to Tillich's phrase 'shock of non-being' is Hegel's speaking of 'the Golgotha of the Spirit'. When we are shocked into realising, from the revelation of the cross of Jesus, that Absolute Spirit has entered the realm of death and nothingness and become alienated from itself, then we recognise both that we are ourselves estranged from Spirit and that we really belong to it all the time.[46] Thus, in the thought of Tillich, it is because Being-Itself, God beyond all concepts of God, eternally confronts non-being and is victorious over it that we can have 'the courage to be' in the face of non-being. This empowers us to refuse the temptation to quieten our anxiety by creating idols. The cross discloses, according to Tillich, that Being-Itself participates in our existence, taking the consequences of our existential estrangement (non-being) upon itself.[47] This deals with our sense of guilt, assuring us that we are accepted, and giving us the courage to accept our acceptance. In traditional Christian language, this is atonement in which God-in-Christ suffers our predicament in order to turn us back to himself. We might ask of Tillich's scheme, how a God who is 'beyond essence and existence' can really participate in the estrangement we experience.[48] In the utterly personal concept of God held by Karl Barth, however, God chooses to limit himself by entering the realm of nothingness and enduring its consequences, in order to overcome it. God is simply free to do this as the Lord, and we impose pagan metaphysics upon him if we protest that his glory cannot allow it.[49]

From this latter perspective, we are alerted to an aspect of Golding's fable-making that we might otherwise miss. The last paragraph of theological exposition hardly seems to connect with Golding's novels at all. The transcendent reality from which his characters constantly 'turn away. . . . and make a darkness there', and to which some of them finally open themselves, does not appear to be an objectively existing reality of which we could say that 'it risks exposing itself to non-being'. It is closer to Tillich's concept of the 'God beyond God' who is Being-Itself than to Barth's concept of the personal God, but nearer still to Iris Murdoch's unknowable God. Sammy's plea for help is directed at 'a place where help may be found', and his cry of joy at the marvel of things travels 'to a place. . . . I had forgotten merely; and once found the place was always there, sometimes open and sometimes shut, the business of the universe proceeding there in its own mode, different, indescribable' (p.187).

What Golding believes we *can* know is the 'My Godness' of the self, the image of the Creator God (or love) in the mysterious depth of the self that challenges self-centredness, and which reverses all the values that we produce as we try to cope with our tensions by manipulating others.[50] Thus, when Golding visualises the presence of God or the divine realm, it is in terms of a dimension of the self. The God who confronts Pincher Martin on the sixth day of his creation, asking 'Have you had enough Christopher?' and inviting him to let go the hard protection of his greedy centre, is Christopher (literally 'Christ-bearing') Martin as the true self that he could be. He wears shiny seaboots, belted oilskin and his skin is unshaven, leathery brown from exposure to the sun. But while Martin asserts that he is a projection of his own mind, made in his own image, the figure refuses to keep to the script Martin writes; his face, moreover, 'had [the] quality of refusing overall inspection', and the eye and the sunset could not be seen at the same time (p.195). As Golding has commented, the elusiveness of the face recalls the saying of Pseudo-Dionysius that 'there remains that secret part of God that cannot be known'.[51]

Similarly, in *Darkness Visible*, the spirits that appear to Matty bear an uncanny resemblance to himself. Critics have remarked on the incongruous feature that they wear hats of office, 'the red spirit with the expensive hat and the blue spirit with a hat but not so expensive', but Matty is of course inseparable from his hat, covering the wreck of one side of his head and his badly-mended ear. Matty finds speech difficult, mouthing words like golfballs, and the spirits 'show' messages written in a Book rather than speak; what they show is in literalistic cadences characteristic of Matty himself. Though they supposedly show him his vocation, which will be to protect a child, they only confirm what he has felt intuitively from the 'wonderful' experience of being accepted by children at the school despite his mutilated appearance. Significantly they explain that 'we do not come to you. We bring you before us' (p.90). Matty has the gift of making 'darkness visible', externalising not a dark self of sin but the dark mystery of the true self of love. The phrase 'darkness visible' is (like 'free fall') a quotation from Milton, referring there to the flames of hell.[52] Here the phrase is ambivalent, referring both to Sophy's ability to 'see' her inner dark self, the 'thing' sitting at the mouth of the tunnel, and Matty's ability to see the spirits. In his case the fire is not hellish but the holy fire of Pentecost which fell upon the disciples like flaming tongues, inspiring speech without words (as Edwin utters it in the silence of their gathering).[53] Earlier, we recall, Sammy in his moment of ecstatic joy that changed him for ever had been 'visited by a flake of fire, miraculous and Pentecostal' which 'flicked out of the hidden invisible'. Matty has come from the fire, and will return to the fire as a 'burnt offering' when he staggers, alight with petrol, to prevent the kidnapper from taking the child as Sophy had planned.

As with the vision of Pincher Martin (and indeed the vision of Moses which so impresses Sammy), there is something of the face of divinity which Matty cannot see. A third figure joins the other two spirits, and as Pincher Martin could not clearly see the face in front of the sunset, Matty is prevented from seeing the face of the spiritual being dressed in white with the circle of the sun round his head: 'the sword proceeded out of his mouth and struck me with a terrible pain' (p.239). Though the scene is explicitly compared to the visit of the three angels of Abraham, celebrated in church tradition as an appearing of the Holy Trinity, we must not find exact allegorical correspondences. The appearance of the figure in white recalls the text of Revelation 1:13–16 about the Son of God, but the other two can hardly be identified with Father and Spirit. The point is that the reality of God cannot be exhausted by the image of love in the self; there is a 'hidden place' at the intersections of the universe. However, the spirits do make the hidden self visible, and we are surely to find the same kind of scene at the end of the book. As Sebastian Pedigree dies, the vision of Matty before him merges into another figure, 'and the face was no longer two-tone but gold as the fire and stern and everywhere there was a sense of the peacock eyes of great feathers. . . .' Who is a peacock but Sebastian, strutting and preening himself, and lamenting 'a life wasted, a life that might have been so, so beautiful . . .'? (p.212) His real sense of beauty that has been so terribly distorted into pederasty is here transfigured; the awesome being who tears the ball of temptation and desire from him is no less than the image of God *in himself*. We are prepared for this shattering shift of perspective, akin to the shifts at the end of other novels, as the dying Pedigree muses about the Matty who has just appeared before him, 'is he all connected with everything else?' (p.264) So deep is his love for Pedigree, he forms a relationship in which the divine image in himself and Pedigree merges into the one My-Godness of Matty-Sebastian. This is 'what Matty is for'.

Before coming finally to the visualisation of the divine offered in a third novel, *The Paper Men*, we must pause to let a critique emerge from our theological perspective. Golding's characters find God in the heart of darkness, noticing Being against the foil of non-being. They have descended the steps, going 'through the death door to meet the master'. Pincher Martin on his rock feels the centre coming apart, 'a gap of not-being, a well opening out of the world' (p.168); Matty has gone down into the depths of his being through an outer symbolic act of immersion into muddy and filthy water (suitable for his literalist mind); Pedigree has faced the darkest truth of all about himself, that one day he will be brought to the hell of killing a child to keep it quiet. But the theologian notices that the God they meet is the deepest and truest dimension of themselves. Whether or not Golding himself believes that God has a more independent existence, the divinity of the novels is not alluded to objectively. He is not, above all, one who has himself encountered non-being on behalf of his creation. The nature of this God means that, in aesthetic terms, they enounter only a Judge. Though he is love, he cannot offer forgiveness, but only clarity, throwing light on the possibilities within themselves.

It is not that this divinity refuses forgiveness; it is simply irrelevant. As the dimension of their own self which challenges their idols, offering what Nietzsche called a 'revaluation of all values', he can only be experienced as a Critic, saying as to Martin, 'Consider now'. The sunset face 'did not move' (p.195). The black lightning that seeks for eternity to pry open the lobster-claws that clamp over the dark centre of Pincher's being is 'a compassion that was timeless and without mercy'. The golden figure who tears the ball from Pedigree, promising freedom, is 'stern . . . and the smile round the lips was loving and terrible'. Even the spirits who appear to Matty 'seemed a bit severe with me, I thought' (p.102) Sammy reflects that 'the innocent cannot forgive', as they have never lived in the two worlds of freedom and limit at the same time and known guilt; even more is the My-Godness of the self the dimension of absolute innocence. At the end of *The Spire* Jocelyn begs forgiveness from his fellow-sinners, especially Anselm and Roger Mason; what he receives from God, as he faces the nothingness of his own pit, is not forgiveness but the gift of awareness of a beauty in the world that he thought had been lost for ever. Even the crooked spire is like the apple tree.

The theological observation that the God whom Golding's characters confront is not one who has himself experienced non-being, and that he is not one who has identified himself with the human consciousness of guilt in incarnation, does not of course devalue Golding's achievement. One story is not obviously right and the other wrong. It requires a particular perspective of faith to prefer the version in which God pours out his being into non-being for our sake. However, it *is* legitimate to make a critical point. Golding's vision of God as Judge, Clarifier and terrible Liberator can accentuate a confusion between different levels of darkness. On the whole Golding avoids simply equating the neutral darkness of life, the 'fear of the dark' or basic anxiety, with the deeper dark of sin. He wants his readers to face up to the mixture between good and evil in their natures, to recognise that 'we are neither the innocent nor the wicked. We are the guilty. We fall down.' (*Free Fall*, p.251). But, as with his predecessor Jonathan Swift, it is a dangerous business to be the scourge of human folly and wickedness; savage indignation can slide into disgust at the human condition itself. In facing up to judgement upon life, we may lose the hope that moral entropy can be reversed.

The more recent novel *The Paper Men* betrays this note of disgust. A successful novelist, Wilfred Barclay, is plagued by the attentions of one Rick Tucker, an assistant Professor of English at a minor American University, who wants Barclay to appoint him his official biographer. They are both paper men, recalling the globe of rock, sea and sky created by Pincher Martin which was finally torn apart, revealing itself to have no reality but 'painted paper'. In running from the remorseless Tucker, Barclay is in flight from the facing up to the hollowness of his spiritual life. At the beginning of the story, Tucker rummages in Barclay's dustbin, and the letter he uncovers from a past mistress is the final blow which destroys his tottering marriage. Barclay is constantly escaping from whatever else might lie in his dustbin, as Jocelyn tries to ignore the pit. Tucker is himself driven by his rich sponsor, the mysterious and godlike Halliday, who was attracted to Barclay's work by one sentence: 'it was where you admit to liking sex but having no capacity for love' (p.65). Things come to a climax for Barclay on a Greek island, in a decaying cathedral whose interior was 'darker than it had any right to be'. He finally has to confront the terror in the cellar, as a statue of Christ triggers off a vision;

> Perhaps it was Christ. Perhaps they had inherited it in these parts and just changed the name and it was Pluto, the god of the Underworld, Hades, striding forward. I stood there with my mouth open and the flesh crawling over my body. I knew in one destroying instant that all my adult life I had believed in God and this knowledge was a vision of God. Fright entered the very marrow of my bones. Surrounded, swamped, confounded, all but destroyed, adrift in the universal intolerance, mouth open, screaming, bepissed and beshitten, I knew my maker and I fell down (p.123).

In the dark place Barclay is confronting a Judge, who rips his paper life wide open. He feels the judgement as having the same edge of intolerance he wields to others, and in this sense the image of this God is an aspect of himself. But the confession 'I knew my maker' is ambiguous, as are the broken words Barclay mumbles in the stroke that ensues: 'Not. Sin. I am. Sin' (p.127). Is this really an encounter with God, or with the Lord of the Flies? Is he meeting the My Godness of his self, or a projection of the sinful darkness of his heart? What he learns from it is simply 'the natural blasphemy of our condition, why this is hell nor am I out of it' (pp.125–6). Like Sophy, believing the world to be in the grip of entropy and identifying himself as 'one of the predestinate damned' the only course is to affirm himself by committing some outrage. The most 'theologically witty' act that occurs to him is to make Rick debase himself ritually by pretending to be a servile dog: 'You get a permit. I get a commit' (145).

Later Barclay has another vision, more like that of Sammy, in which he rejoices in the sheer 'is-ness' of things, hearing a song for which he has no words at all (p.161). Yet the effect of going down within himself to a 'dark calm sea', deep as it is, is not deep enough. When he tries to explain to his dying wife his experience that 'I found myself part of the universe' she sees the truth of his still-existing egocentricity: 'You're the whole bloody lot!' (p.173). In reaction to his vision of the wonder of things as they are, he resolves to write his own biography and thereby breaks his word to Rick, sealing his own death. The question the reader is left with is what *could* bring Barclay the sense of mercy and acceptance that would enable him to move out properly beyond himself and reverse the entropy of existence. A theologian may suggest that it is a personal God who himself has shared 'the natural blasphemy of our condition'. But this is an answer of faith.

IN CONCLUSION

It is apt that this whole study should have ended with commentary on a novel which is self-consciously about the construction of a literary text. I observed at the beginning that creative writing is open beyond itself to a mystery that it can only hint at, and that this is grounds for a dialogue between literature and theology. I also suggested that the best writing imitates the Creator himself in being incarnational.[54] Golding's *The Paper Men* embodies both these aspects by deconstructing (one might almost say 'debunking') itself, and thereby pointing to the unspoken story or the song for which there are no words, precisely by its reference to the experience of incarnation.

For Wilfred Barclay is a poor writer (unlike his inventor, for whom he must not simply be mistaken), but he knows that his earlier and better work contained 'episodes that had blazed, hurt, been suffered for'. Discouraged by lack of response, he had gone on to write material which simply rearrranged his surface experiences, for which there was no need to 'dive, suffer, endure that obscurely necessary anguish. . . .' He knows that the best novelwriting is like incarnation and passion, and he seems to be set back on this path after his second vision, when he suffers something like stigmata.[55] The pain in his hands, he notices, was sharpened by writing (pp.158-9, 163). Yet Golding undercuts this view of the novelist as Christ or saint when a vicar remarks that there were *three* crosses, and Barclay readily recognises himself as one of the crucified thieves. As the critic Julia Briggs suggests, there is some irony here at the expense of a literary religion, where 'certain writers are elected to the status of secular saints. . . . The more they sin . . . the closer they come to the ideal of the artist as martyr, suffering an artificial passion for the sake of their art'.[56] She concludes that Golding is writing a novel which protests against the elevation of writers to a priesthood, and the attempt to find 'in their flawed gospels . . . keys to the universe'.

While it surely remains true that the artist creates only through incarnation and vicarious suffering, nevertheless the ambiguities of the writer's stigmata tell us that there is a story and a truth which he cannot himself capture. The theologian does not claim to supply the whole story either, but takes the opportunity to place alongside the writer's work his own sense of the oneness of the Story, together with the concepts by which he interprets it. As doctrine and novel or poem shape each other and offer mutual criticism within the dialogue, the mystery appears more clearly in the midst.

Exploring the theme of a tension between human freedom and limit, with the consequent predicament of fallenness in existence, has provided us with one example of the process of dialogue. At the same time, this very tension is embodied in the actual relationship between literature and doctrinal theology. Doctrine tends to hedge meaning around with more limits than creative literature does, unifying the Story and reducing it to a set of concepts. But, regarded from a Christian perspective, when the exponents of either art ignore the other and pretend to self-sufficiency, they exalt their freedom above their finitude. It is only by recognising their boundaries through each other that they can approach that freedom which is the image of God.

Notes

1 Imagination and Revelation

1. Koheleth (Ecclesiastes) 12:12. On the following comments, cf.G. Von Rad, *Wisdom in Israel*, trans. J.D. Martin (London, 1972), pp.97–110, 226–36. For greater detail, see my unpublished D.Phil. thesis, *The Hiddenness of Wisdom in the Old Testament and Later Judaism* (University of Oxford, 1976).
2. For an account of this development, see J.C. Rylaarsdam, *Revelation in Jewish Wisdom Literature* (Chicago, 1946), Ch.4.
3. Marcel Proust, *Remembrance of Things Past*, Vol.III, trans. C.K. Scott-Moncrieff (London, 1981), p.308.
4. Frank Kermode, *The Sense of an Ending* (New York, 1967), pp.45–50, 55–8.
5. Shakespeare, *Hamlet*, V.2.348.
6. Shakespeare, *Othello*, V.2.342–45.
7. Virginia Woolf, *Between the Acts* (repr., Harmondsworth, 1953), p.107.
8. For further examples and comment, see G.B. Caird, *The Language and Imagery of the Bible* (London, 1980), pp.154ff.
9. The phrase was coined by H. Wells, and is discussed by René Wellek and Austin Warren, *Theory of Literature* (3rd ed., Harmondsworth, 1963), p.202.
10. See Donne's poems, 'A Valediction: forbidding mourning', 'A Nocturnall upon S. Lucies Day', and 'Hymne to God my God, in my sicknesse'.
11. C.S. Lewis, 'A Confession' in id., *Poems*, ed. W. Hooper (London, 1964), p.1.
12. S.T. Coleridge, *Biographia Literaria*, Vol.I, ed. J. Shawcross (London, 1907), p.102.
13. Patrick White, *Voss* (London, 1957), pp.414–15.
14. Shakespeare, *Midsummer Night's Dream*, IV.1.193.
15. Shakespeare, *The Tempest*, IV.1.147–58.
16. See below, pp.188–9, cf. 69–70.
17. Following I.A. Richards, in *The Philosophy of Rhetoric* (Oxford, 1936), p.93.
18. 'Interaction theory' of metaphor was developed by Max Black, *Models and Metaphors: Studies in Language and Philosophy* (Ithaca, 1962), pp.35–47, 236–7.
19. Paul Ricoeur, *The Rule of Metaphor*, transl. R. Czerny et al. (London, 1978), pp.221–4, 255–7.
20. I. Kant, *The Critique of Judgement*, trans. J.C. Meredith (Oxford, repr.1952), 'Analytic of the Beautiful', para 9 (p.58). Cf. Kant, *Critique of Pure Reason*, trans. N. Kemp Smith (London, 2nd ed. 1933), 'Transcendental Analytic' A100–2 (pp.132–3), A115–19 (pp.141–3). The

imagination brings the particular perceptions of the senses into contact with the general concepts of the understanding.

21. Kant, *The Critique of Judgement*, 'Analytic of the Beautiful', para. 22 (pp.86–9).
22. Ibid., 'Analytic of the Sublime', para. 23 (pp.90–3); cf.Introduction VII (pp.32–3).
23. This terminology is adopted by John Macquarrie in his system of theology; see his *Principles of Christian Theology*, Revised Edition (London, 1977), pp.94–5.
24. 'The Wreck of the Deutschland', stanza 32; further on this poem, see below pp.120–3.
25. Karl Barth, *Church Dogmatics*, English Translation, ed. G.W. Bromiley and T.F. Torrance (Edinburgh, 1936–77), I/1 (2nd ed. 1975), p.430.
26. Mark 4:11–12. Frank Kermode argues that the motif of secrecy not only perpetually provokes the reader to provide interpretations, but also to attribute further mystery to the text: *The Genesis of Secrecy: On the Interpretation of Narrative* (Cambridge, Mass., 1979), pp.71–3, 143–5.
27. Eberhard Jüngel, *God as the Mystery of the World: On the Foundation of the Theology of the Crucified One in the Dispute between Theism and Atheism*, trans. D.L. Guder (Edinburgh, 1983), p.295. Jüngel stresses that the coming of God makes human stories correspond to him: pp.300–4.
28. John Henry Newman, *An Essay on the Development of Christian Doctrine*, ed. C.F. Harrold (New York, 1949), p.49.
29. John Coulson, *Religion and Imagination* (Oxford, 1981), pp.61–2, 72–8.
30. Coleridge, *Shakespearean Criticism*, Vol.II, ed. T. Raysor (repr. London, 1960), p.103.
31. For example, David Jasper, *The New Testament and the Literary Imagination* (London, 1987), pp.89–99; T.R. Wright, *Theology and Literature* (Oxford, 1988), pp.2–3, 12–13.
32. See Gabriel Josipovici, *The Book of God: A Response to the Bible* (New Haven and London, 1988), pp.87–9, 307.
33. Langland, *The Vision of William Concerning Piers the Plowman*, ed. W.W. Skeat, Text B (Early English Text Society, London, 1869), 15.190, 15.206.
34. Ibid., 19.6–8, cf.18.21–7.
35. Ibid., 8.58.
36. Ibid., 20.378–80.
37. Dante, *Paradiso*, Canto 30.14–15.
38. Charles Williams, *The Figure of Beatrice: A Study in Dante* (London, 1943), pp.230–31, cf.pp.218ff, 101–2.
39. Ibid., p.231.
40. Gabriel Josipovici, *The World and The Book: A Study of Modern Fiction*, 2nd ed. (London, 1979), pp.47–51, 194.
41. W.B. Yeats, 'William Blake and his Illustrations', in *Essays and Introductions* (repr. London, 1961), p.116.
42. Yeats, 'Byzantium'. In my comment I pass over the more esoteric levels of meaning concerning Neo-Platonist concepts of generation and pre-existence; see the exegesis in F.A.C. Wilson, *W.B. Yeats and Tradition* (London, 1958), pp.231–43.

43. T.S. Eliot, 'Burnt Norton', I, from *Four Quartets* in *The Complete Poems and Plays of T.S. Eliot* (London, 1969), p.171.
44. Josipovici, *The World and the Book*, p.298.
45. Ibid., pp.306–7.
46. The phrase is by Ferdinand de Saussure, from his *Course in General Linguistics* (1916), ed. C. Bally and A. Sechehaye, trans. W. Baskin (London, 1978); for discussion see David Robey, 'Modern linguistics and the language of literature' in A. Jefferson and D. Robey (ed.), *Modern Literary Theory* (London, 1982), pp.38ff.
47. The word is used by Roland Barthes, *Critique et vérité* (Paris, 1966), p.52.
48. Tzvetan Todorov, *The Poetics of Prose*, trans. R. Howard (Oxford, 1977), pp.149–50, 243–4.
49. See J. Derrida, *Writing and Difference*, trans. A. Bass (London, 1978), pp.155–9.
50. Umberto Eco, *The Name of the Rose*, trans. W. Weaver (London, 1984), p.502.
51. In his book *Towards a Christian Poetics* (London, 1984), M. Edwards greets the attack of Derrida on 'Logocentrism' (confidence in the reference of words to external truth) as a prologue to Christian thinking (pp.220ff). He understands it as a realistic description of man's fallen state where words are no longer united with reality. We have lost Adam's ability in Eden to name the animals. In Chapter 3 I am going to question whether this theme of the 'loss of a past paradise' is in fact as central to the Christian story as is often supposed.
52. Eco, op.cit., p.492.
53. Tzvetan Todorov, 'The Typology of Detection Fiction' in *The Poetics of Prose*, p.46.
54. Paul Ricoeur, *The Rule of Metaphor*, p.255.
55. See *The Notebooks of Samuel Taylor Coleridge*, ed. Kathleen Coburn (London, 1957–73), Ill. 3632, cf.Ill. 3268.
56. John McIntyre, *Faith, Theology and Imagination* (Edinburgh, 1987), pp.80–3, 55.
57. Doris Lessing, *Canopus in Argos: Archives. The Marriages Between Zones Three, Four and Five* (1980; repr. pb. London, 1981), pp.242–4.
58. Auden, 'The Novelist', in *Collected Shorter Poems 1927–1957* (London, 1966), pp.124–5.
59. McIntyre, op.cit., p.74.
60. Barth, *Church Dogmatics* I/1, p.304, cf.pp.137–9.
61. See for example, J. Macquarrie, *Principles of Christian Theology*, pp.143–4; Paul Tillich, *Systematic Theology*, Combined Volume (Welwyn, 1968), Vol.I, p.271.
62. This is Barth's expression; see his *Church Dogmatics* I/1, pp.109–10.
63. Tillich, *Systematic Theology* I, pp.265ff.
64. Stephen Sykes, *The Identity of Christianity* (London, 1984), p.247.
65. George Lindbeck, *The Nature of Doctrine: Religion and Theology in a Postliberal Age* (London, 1984), pp.32ff, 83–4.
66. Sykes, op.cit., pp.251–4.
67. Ibid., p.259.

68. Lindbeck, op.cit., pp.80–84.
69. Lindbeck, op.cit., p.96 expands the principle of 'historical specificity' into 'Christological maximalism'. Cf.Sykes, op.cit., pp.257–8.
70. Lindbeck, op.cit., pp.80, 94.

2 The Creative Dialogue

1. Samuel Johnson, *Lives of the English Poets*, Vol.I, (London, 1952), p.204.
2. Alexander Pope, *An Essay on Criticism*, 1.297.
3. C.S. Lewis, 'Christianity and Literature' in *Christian Reflections*, ed. W. Hooper (London, 1962), pp.3–4; Helen Gardner, *Religion and Literature* (London, 1971), pp.134–8.
4. See *Biographia Literaria*, Vol.I, Ch.XIII, p.202, cf. Ch.XII, pp.185–6.
5. Coleridge, *Aids to Reflection* (London, 1904), p.349: 'the power of Universal and necessary Convictions, the Source and Substance of Truths above Sense, and having their evidence in themselves'; cf. pp.143, 155: 'an intuition or immediate Beholding'.
6. See e.g. Kant, *Critique of Pure Reason* (ed. N. Kemp Smith), pp.450ff., 464ff., 514–18. However, in the realm of the moral life, or Practical Reason, these transcendent ideas are 'inseparable corollaries' of moral laws; see *Critique of Practical Reason*, trans. L.W. Beck (Indianapolis, 1956), p.127.
7. Paul Hamilton, *Coleridge's Poetics* (Oxford, 1983), pp.198–200, finds that Coleridge's theory of direct religious intuition is 'irreconcilable' with his poetics. David Jasper, *Coleridge as Poet and Religious Thinker: Inspiration and Revelation* (London, 1985) argues for harmony of poetic imagination and revelation in Coleridge's thought.
8. See *Aids to Reflection*, p.143, 'This universal light'. Cf. 'a light from God directly and immediately such'; unpublished *Notebook 26*, cit. James D. Boulger, *Coleridge as Religious Thinker* (New Haven, 1961), p.226.
9. *Biographia Literaria*, Vol.I, Ch.XII, pp.185–6. Cf. 'eternally self-personal, the I AM'; unpublished *Notebook 55*, f.25, cit. Jasper, *Coleridge*, p.130.
10. See Tillich, *Systematic Theology*, Vol.I, pp.88–93, 181–4; Vol.II, pp.203–4; Vol.III, pp.235–7.
11. Paul Tillich, *Theology of Culture*, ed. R.C. Kimball (New York, 1959), pp.54, 72–3.
12. Karl Rahner, *Foundations of Christian Faith: An Introduction to the Idea of Christianity*, trans. W.V. Dych (London, 1978), p.32.
13. Ibid., p.127.
14. See further below for necessary qualifications of the description 'general'. While Tillich, *Systematic Theology* I, p.154, rejects the term, he uses the phrase 'universal revelation' in the same sense as I am using 'general revelation'. An influential advocate of the concept has been John Baillie, in e.g. *Our Knowledge of God* (London, 1939), pp.35–43.
15. Samuel Beckett, *Waiting for Godot* (London, 2nd ed. 1965, repr. 1972), p.52.
16. The phrase has been much used by Hans-Georg Gadamer in his hermeneutics: see *Truth and Method* (London, 1975), pp.269ff.

17. T.S. Eliot, 'Imperfect Critics', in *The Sacred Wood* (1920, 7th ed. London, 1950), p.38.
18. Helen Gardner, op.cit., p.135.
19. Ibid., p.136.
20. *The Table Talk and Omniana of Samuel Taylor Coleridge*, ed. T. Ashe (London, 1917), pp.416–17.
21. C.S. Lewis, in *Review of English Studies* XVII (1941), p.101.
22. T.S. Eliot, *The Complete Poems and Plays*, p.109.
23. Ibid., pp.192, 195, 181.
24. Coulson, op.cit., p.52.
25. Josipovici, *The Book of God*, p.274.
26. See above, pp.13–14.
27. Walther Zimmerli, 'Promise and Fulfilment' in C. Westermann (ed.), *Essays on Old Testament Interpretation*, trans. J.L. Mays (London, 1963), p.107.
28. See above, pp.14–15.
29. Caird, *The Language and Imagery of the Bible*, pp.256–60.
30. S. Kierkegaard, *Fear and Trembling: A Dialectical Lyric*, trans. R. Payne (London, 1939), p.11.
31. Robert Alter, *The Art of Biblical Narrative* (London, 1981), p.157.
32. Op.cit., p.164.
33. Jasper, *The New Testament and the Literary Imagination*, p.47.
34. Coulson, op.cit., p.28.
35. Matt. 27:14, Mark 15:5, Luke 23:9.
36. John 14:9–11, cf.17:1–11, 10:37–8.
37. John 6:35, 8:12, 10:11, 15:1.
38. Isa. 43:10–13.
39. Josipovici, *The Book of God*, p.225.
40. 1 Cor. 15:20–1, 24–8; Rom. 8:18–22.
41. Jürgen Moltmann, *Theology of Hope: on the Ground and Implications of a Christian Eschatology*, trans. J.W. Leitch (London, 1967), pp.201–2, cf. p.229.
42. Wolfhart Pannenberg, *Jesus – God and Man*, trans. L.L. Wilkins and D.A. Priebe (London, 1978), pp.74, 187.
43. Moltmann, *Theology of Hope*, p.202.
44. Barth, *Church Dogmatics* I/1, pp.320–1.
45. Hilary, *de Trin.* VI, 16, commenting on Psalm 110:3.
46. See above, p.20.
47. For instance, Maurice Wiles, *God's Action in the World* (London, 1986), pp.21–6.
48. George MacDonald, 'The Imagination: Its Function and Its Culture', in *A Dish of Orts* (London, 1907).

3 The Shape of the Story

1. Lessing, op.cit., p.243. See above, p.20.
2. V.A. Kolve, *The Play Called Corpus Christi* (London, 1966), p.119.
3. John Donne, *The Divine Poems*, ed. Helen Gardner (Oxford, 1952), p.50.

4. Northrop Frye, *The Great Code: The Bible and Literature* (London, 1983), p.169.
5. Edwards, op.cit., p.6.
6. Ibid., pp.72–3.
7. Josipovici, *The Book of God*, p.12.
8. For example, Herbert Schneidau, *Sacred Discontent. The Bible and Western Tradition* (Berkeley, California, 1977); John Dominic Crossan, *The Dark Interval: Towards a Theology of Story* (Niles, Illinois, 1975). Also see above, pp.23–4, 41–5.
9. The taunt-song over the king of Tyre in Ezekiel 28:12–19, and the reference to a 'first man' in Job 15:7–8, employ different traditions about a primal man on a paradisial mountain, though they are no doubt related to the Adam story. See Walter Eichrodt, *Ezekiel: A Commentary*, trans. C. Quin (London, 1970), pp.392–5.
10. For references to the angel story, see 1 Enoch 10:7–8, 1 Enoch 86, Testament of Reuben 5:5–7, Testament of Napthali 3:5. For references to the fall of Adam, see Jubilees 3:17–35, Testament of Levi 18:10–11, 2 Esdras 7:11–14, Wisdom of Solomon 2:23. There are useful discussions in N.P. Williams, *The Idea of the Fall and of Original Sin* (London, 1927) pp.20–35, and W.D. Davies, *Paul and Rabbinic Judaism: Some Rabbinic Elements in Pauline Theology* (London, 1955), pp.38ff, 120ff.
11. Col. 1:16, 2:15; 1 Cor. 15:24; Eph. 3:10, 6:12; cf. 1 Cor. 2:16, Gal. 4:3. See G.B. Caird, *Principalities and Powers: A Study in Pauline Theology* (Oxford, 1956).
12. Job 1:6–7, Zech. 3:1–2.
13. Josipovici, *The Book of God*, p.275.
14. The theme perhaps continues in Rom.8:20. References to the Adam–Christ typology in general include 1 Cor.15:45–9 explicitly, and implicitly the contrast between 'old man' and 'new man' in Col.3:5ff and Eph.4:27; cf. Eph.5:31, Gal.5:24.
15. See C.K. Barrett, *A Commentary on the Second Epistle to the Corinthians* (London, 1973), p.272–3.
16. On Mark 1:13, see Ernest Best, *The Temptation and the Passion: The Markan Soteriology* (Cambridge, 1965), pp.6, 8–10.
17. Jasper, *The New Testament and the Literary Imagination*, p.46.
18. Davies, *Paul and Rabbinic Judaism*, p.32.
19. Ernst Käsemann, *Commentary on Romans*, trans. G.W. Bromiley (London, 1980), p.142.
20. Wolfhart Pannenberg, *Anthropology in Theological Perspective*, trans. M.J. O'Connell (Edinburgh, 1985), pp.71–4; *What is Man?*, trans. D.A. Priebe (Philadelphia, 1972), pp.3–12.
21. Reinhold Niebuhr, *The Nature and Destiny of Man: A Christian Interpretation. Volume I: Human Nature* (London, 1941) pp.179–83, 194–6; Tillich, *Systematic Theology* II, pp.36–41; Macquarrie, *Principles*, pp.62–6, 71–3; Pannenberg, *Anthropology*, pp.104–6, cf. *What is Man?*, pp.56–8.
22. Macquarrie, *Principles*, pp.71–2, 259–61.
23. Claus Westermann, *Genesis 1–11. A Commentary*, trans. J.J. Scullion, SJ (London, 1984), p.224.

24. Søren Kierkegaard, *The Concept of Dread*, trans. and ed. Walter Lowrie (London, 1944), pp.40–6.
25. Tillich, *Systematic Theology* II, p.39.
26. Schneidau, *Sacred Discontent*, pp.4–12.
27. Josipovici, *The Book of God*, p.306, cf. p.230.
28. See Gerhard Von Rad, *Old Testament Theology. Volume I: The Theology of Israel's Historical Traditions*, trans. D.M.G. Stalker (Edinburgh, 1962) pp.334–41.
29. See Brevard S. Childs, *Isaiah and the Assyrian Crisis* (London, 1967), pp.31–8.
30. Frye, *The Great Code*, p.128.
31. See, for example, the argument of James L. Crenshaw, *Prophetic Conflict* (Berlin, 1971), pp.106ff.
32. I argue this point extensively in my thesis, *The Hiddenness of Wisdom*; see above p.3–4.
33. Also see Isa.43:16ff, Ezekiel 34:25–7.
34. See Heb.1:1–3, 2:6–9, Col.1:15–17, 2 Cor.4:4 and references in note 14 above. Further, N.A. Dahl, 'Christ, Creation and the Church' in *The Background of the New Testament and Its Eschatology*, ed. W.D. Davies and D. Daube (Cambridge, 1956) pp.422–43.
35. Frye, op.cit., pp.128–9.
36. Macquarrie, *Principles*, pp.356–7.
37. Gen.Rabbah iii.6, 2 Esdras 6:49–52, 2 Baruch 29:4. On the theme of the 'reserved things', see Dahl, op.cit., pp.426–9.
38. For instance, John 3:13, 6:33–40, 8:21–4.
39. *The Gospel of Nicodemus*, XX–XXII, in *New Testament Apocrypha*, Vol.I, ed. E. Hennecke and W. Schneemelcher, trans. R. McL. Wilson (London, 1963), pp.472–4. There are admittedly foreshadowings of this idea in New Testament passages such as 1 Pet.3:18–22, Romans 10:7, Colossians 1:18. Of course, the more general theme of 'Christus Victor' is widely present in the New Testament; see the study by G. Aulen, *Christus Victor*, trans. A.G. Hebert (London, 1931) pp.81–96.
40. Frye, *The Great Code*, p.176.
41. For example, Rom.8:1–4, Phil.2:7, 2 Cor.5:21, Gal.4:4, Col.2:15. See John A.T. Robinson, *The Body. A Study in Pauline Theology* (London, 1952), p.37: 'The first act in the drama of redemption is the self-identification of the Son of God to the limit, yet without sin, with the body of the flesh in its fallen state.'
42. Tillich, *Systematic Theology* II, p.50.
43. Romans 7:15–20.
44. Hopkins, 'The Wreck of the Deutschland', stanza 18.
45. Tillich, *Systematic Theology* II, p.33.
46. Niebuhr, *The Nature and Destiny of Man* I, pp.279, 257.
47. Macquarrie, *Principles*, p.256.
48. So Hick, *Evil and the God of Love* (London, 1968), pp.361–2.
49. Augustine, *De Civitate Dei* 14: 11–17.
50. Augustine, *de Nuptiis et Concupiscientia* 2: 57.
51. Ibid, 1: 20; 2: 25, 36.

52. Josipovici, *The Book of God*, pp.68–9.
53. Albert Camus, *The Myth of Sisyphus*, trans. J. O'Brien (New York, 1955).
54. Jean-Paul Sartre, *Nausea*, trans. R. Baldick (Harmondsworth, 1963), p.185.

4 Comedy and Tragedy: the Shakespearian Boundary

1. *A Midsummer Night's Dream* V.1.57–60. All quotations from the plays of Shakespeare are from The Arden Shakespeare series, General Editors: Harold F. Brooks and Harold Jenkins (London, 1959–).
2. This phrase is used by S.L. Bethel in his assessment of Elizabethan audiences, in his *Shakespeare and the Popular Dramatic Tradition* (London, 1944), p.108.
3. The device of 'gaps of awareness' is analysed at length by Bertrand Evans, though more in terms of stagecraft than ideas; see his *Shakespeare's Comedies* (Oxford, 1960).
4. This theme is well explored by John Russell Brown, *Shakespeare and his Comedies* (London, 2nd ed. 1962), pp.82–103.
5. Gregory of Nyssa, *Oratio Catachetica Magna* 24.26; Augustine, *Sermones* 263.1.
6. The image is used effectively by B. Evans, op.cit., p.127.
7. Theodore Weiss detects a hint of the later tragedies when 'worlds indeed become hospital-like'; see his *The Breath of Clowns and Kings. Shakespeare's Early Comedies and Histories* (London, 1971), pp.40ff.
8. (Genesis 18:9–15, 21:1–7; Luke 1:18–25, 57–79; cf. Rom. 4:17–22.) With regard to the story of Sarah, see Edwin M. Good, *Irony in the Old Testament* (London, 1965), pp.93–5. Good suggests that 'God will have the last laugh', as the narrator shortly tells the story of the 'sacrifice' of Isaac (Gen.22:2, following 21:5–6).
9. Edwards, op.cit., p.70.
10. Ibid.
11. Alfred North Whitehead, *Adventures of Ideas* (Cambridge, 1933), p.381, cf. p.356f.
12. This theological sketch raises large questions about the omniscience of God, which I attempt to work out in *The Creative Suffering of God* (Oxford, 1988), pp.91–109.
13. Edwards, op.cit., pp.16–18.
14. Frye, *The Great Code*, p.176.
15. J.L. Styan, *The Dark Comedy. The Development of Modern Comic Tragedy*, 2nd ed. (Cambridge, 1968), pp.6ff.
16. Frye, op.cit., pp.176, 181.
17. Nicholas Brooke judges that this is the pivotal point where the play moves from comedy to tragedy: see his *Shakespeare's Early Tragedies* (London, 1968), p.83f.
18. G. Wilson Knight, *The Imperial Theme* (London, 3rd ed., 1951), p.265.
19. *Antony and Cleopatra* I.4.47. (The phrase is used here of the common body of the people.)
20. T.R. Henn, *The Harvest of Tragedy*, 2nd ed. (London, 1966), also finds

the centre of tragedy to lie in the tension between human freedom and the limits of environment, but locates the failure of the tragic hero simply in his proud disregard of creaturely limits; from a Christian perspective he identifies this as sin, and finds its typical Shakespearian form in the failure to observe the due time for things ('unripeness'); pp.288–90, cf. pp.162, 251–6.

21. See Helen Gardner, 'The Noble Moor', *Proceedings of the British Academy*, Volume XLI (London, 1955), p.203: 'But the end does not merely by its darkness throw up into relief the brightness that was. On the contrary, beginning and end chime against each other. In both the value of life and love is affirmed.'

22. Edwards, op.cit., pp.27, 32.

5 William Blake and the Image of the City

1. See above, pp.35–6.
2. Quotations from Blake's work are from *Blake: Complete Writings With Variant Readings* edited by Geoffrey Keynes (London, 1957, 1966). This edition is abbreviated as 'K' in the references.
3. Conversely, Northrop Frye draws attention to the biblical image of the fallen city as a harlot; *Fearful Symmetry. A Study of William Blake* (Princeton, 1969), pp.392–3.
4. On Jacob Boehme's concept of the 'Grand Man' and Swedenborg's 'Divine Man' see Désirée Hirst, *Hidden Riches. Traditional Symbolism from the Renaissance to Blake* (London, 1964), pp.95ff, 205ff. On the New Testament concept of Christ as the new Adam, see above, pp.50–2.
5. H.M. Margoliouth, *William Blake* (London, 1951), p.129.
6. *Jerusalem*, 13.66–14.1: K.634. Modern Christian theological thought has also taken a more corporate view of the afterlife; see John Hick, *Death and Eternal Life* (London, 1976), pp.458ff.
7. See David V. Erdman, *Blake: Prophet Against Empire. A Poet's Interpretation of the History of his Own Times* 3rd ed. (Princeton, New Jersey, 1977), pp.338f, 270ff.
8. See e.g. 'A Descriptive Catalogue' V: K.579, 'the religion of Jesus, the everlasting Gospel'; *Jerusalem* 3: K.621, 'the Spirit of Jesus is continual Forgiveness of sin'; 38.16: K.664, 'As one man all the Universal Family, and that One Man/ We call Jesus the Christ; 43.19: K.672, 'the Divine –/Humanity who is the only general and universal form'. Cf. 'The Divine Image': K.11, 'love, the human form divine' and *Additions to Swedenborg's Divine Love*, 11, 'God is a man.' See Kathleen Raine, *The Human Face of God. William Blake and the Book of Job* (London, 1982), pp.47–8, 216, 310–11.
9. See the discussion in Frye, op.cit., pp.33ff and Kathleen Raine, *William Blake* (London, 1967), pp.17ff.
10. Subscript to the drawing, 'Joseph of Arimathea among the rocks of Albion' (1733), cit. Raine, *William Blake*, p.18.
11. 'To Noboddady': K.171. Cf. Poems from the Notebook (1793) 60.9, 'old Nobodaddy aloft': K.185.
12. 'The Marriage of Heaven and Hell', 9.5: K.152.

13. 'Earth's Answer', verse 2: K.211.
14. *The Book of Urizen* 20.8: K.234; *Milton* 4.11: K.483.
15. 'Milton' 11.10–14: K.491. The exact relationship between Urizen and 'Satan' is discussed below. For Blake, the opposition of Caiaphas to Jesus typifies the conflict between law and forgiveness: see 'The Everlasting Gospel' fragment d, 32–5, 58–64: K.752.
16. For example, Peter R. Ackroyd argues that the priestly institutions expressed 'the reality of the divine grace and the reality of the divine indwelling'; *Exile and Restoration* (London, 1968), p.100.
17. See 'The Everlasting Gospel', fragment i: K.756; also 'The Marriage of Heaven and Hell', 22–4: K.158 – 'Did he not mock at the Sabbath and so mock the Sabbath's God?'
18. Jürgen Moltmann, *The Trinity and the Kingdom of God. The Doctrine of God*, trans. M. Kohl (London, 1981), pp.57–60.
19. Alfred North Whitehead, *Process and Reality* (New York, 1929), p.532.
20. Karl Barth, *Church Dogmatics*, Vol.IV, Part 1, p.186.
21. See e.g. T.J. Altizer and W. Hamilton, *Radical Theology and the Death of God* (Harmondsworth, 1968), pp.58ff.
22. 'The Laocoön', K.777; cf. *Jerusalem* 4.18–21: K.622, 'I am not a God afar off'.
23. Thomas J.J. Altizer, *The Gospel of Christian Atheism* (London, 1967), pp.91, 113f; also Altizer, *The New Apocalypse. The Radical Christian Vision of William Blake* (Michigan, 1967), pp.71ff, 143ff.
24. *Milton* 38.29: K.529. Cf. Altizer, *The New Apocalypse*, pp.197ff.
25. Altizer, *The Gospel of Christian Atheism*, pp.145–7; *The New Apocalypse*, pp.212–15.
26. This is a strongly debated issue, of course. In support of my view, see J.G. Davies, *The Theology of William Blake* (Oxford, 1948), pp.87–90: he argues Blake's point to be that God apart from man is an abstraction. Also see Kathleen Raine, *The Human Face of God*, pp.10–11. Frye, however, *Fearful Symmetry*, pp.30–32, 52–53, argues that Blake identifies God totally with the human imagination.
27. See Hirst, op.cit., pp.90–92.
28. Frye, *Fearful Symmetry*, p.153.
29. See Aulen, op.cit., pp.84, 127–130. Also see Caird, *Principalities and Powers*, pp.32ff.
30. For instance, Jim Garrison, *The Darkness of God* (London, 1982).
31. The main channels of transmission here were Boehme, William Law and Richard Clarke; see Hirst, op.cit., pp.93–8, 159f., 255f.
32. Blake seems to have got his Neo-Platonism from Thomas Taylor; see George Mills Harper, *The Neoplatonism of William Blake* (Chapel Hill, 1961).
33. J.G. Davies, op.cit., p.97 rightly judges that Blake 'did not deal directly with the doctrine of the Fall as such, but only used it as a framework around which to build his interpretations of man's psychology'.
34. John Macquarrie, *The Scope of Demythologizing* (London, 1960), pp.198ff.
35. *Contra* Rudolph Bultmann, 'New Testament and Mythology', in

Keryma and Myth, Vol.I, ed. H.W. Bartsch, trans. R.H. Fuller (London, 1964). However, all talk about God certainly involves *metaphor*, as I have made clear.

36. See above, ch.3, esp. pp.59–62, 53–4.
37. *Jerusalem* 38.17–21: K.664. Cf. *The Four Zoas*, 1.469–74: K.227.
38. See above, pp.61–2.
39. Frye, *Fearful Symmetry*, pp.262–3, discusses the 'female will' that 'blocks vision'. Cf. 'Milton' 40.32: K.533.
40. Margoliouth, op.cit., p.91 observes that the political myths do not make clear how or why 'revolution will bring resurrection'.
41. *Europe* 12.14–20: K.242. Erdman, op.cit., pp.216–17, demonstrates that this scene is based on an actual political event, the dismissal of the Lord High Chancellor by Pitt in 1792.
42. 'Auguries of Innocence', 1–4: K.431.
43. *The Four Zoas* 1.9: K.264.
44. John Beer, *Blake's Visionary Universe* (Manchester, 1969), pp.103–4, finds these compass points as typical of disturbed and not ideal Man; this is odd in view of *Jerusalem* 97–8: K.744–5.
45. *Jerusalem* 74.2–4: K.714.
46. *Jerusalem* 96.7: K.743.
47. Margoliouth, op.cit., p.143.
48. Cf. *Milton* 40.33: K.533.
49. *Milton* 38.29–49: K.529–30.
50. Raine, *The Human Face of God*, p.236.
51. Blake's phrase, according to Crabbe Robinson; cited in Raine, op.cit., p.237. Raine has a useful discussion of the identity of Satan in general; see pp.193–201, 303–5.
52. John Beer, op.cit., p.158; he suggests that Blake introduced the Council of God and the sending of Jesus at a late stage precisely to answer that question.
53. *The Four Zoas* 1.290–1: K.272; 9.205–8: K.362; 4.255–7: K.304. My italics.
54. *The Four Zoas* 8.241: K.347; 8.286: K.348.
55. Macquarrie, *Principles*, p.319.
56. So e.g. Margaret Bottrall, *The Divine Image. A Study of Blake's Interpretation of Christianity* (Rome, 1950), p.52.
57. *Europe* iii.1: K.237. On the image of Porphyry's cave see Kathleen Raine, *Blake and Antiquity* (London, 1979), pp.3–16.
58. Thomas R. Frorsch, *The Awakening of Albion. The Renovation of the Body in the Poetry of William Blake* (Ithaca, 1974).
59. Ibid., p.26.
60. *Jerusalem* 77: K.716.
61. *Jerusalem* 69:42: K.708.
62. *The Four Zoas* 1.470–3: K.277.
63. For example, Gen. 2:10, Ezekiel 1:4–21, Rev. 6:1–8.
64. Erdman, op.cit., p.395, rightly finds Blake's move back to London to be a critical component of the poem.

6 Gerard Manley Hopkins and Mortal Beauty

1. 'The Sea and the Skylark'. Citations from Hopkins' poetry are from *The Poems of Gerard Manley Hopkins*, 4th ed., revised and enlarged, ed. W.H. Gardner and N.H. Mackenzie (London, 1967).
2. 'Pied Beauty'.
3. 'As Kingfishers catch fire'.
4. 'Parmenides', in *The Journals and Papers of Gerard Manley Hopkins*, 2nd ed., edited by Humphrey House, completed by Graham Storey (London, 1959), p.127.
5. So David A. Downes, *Hopkins' Sanctifying Imagination* (New York, London, 1985), p.21; Walter J. Ong, SJ, *Hopkins, the Self and God* (Toronto, London, 1986), p.17.
6. *The Sermons and Devotional Writings of Gerard Manley Hopkins*, ed. Christopher Devlin, SJ, (London, 1959), p.125.
7. 'As Kingfishers catch fire'.
8. This is particularly remarked upon by W.A.M. Peters, SJ, *Gerard Manley Hopkins. A Critical Essay towards the Understanding of his Poetry* (Oxford, 1948), pp.110–15.
9. *The Letters of Gerard Manley Hopkins to Robert Bridges*, ed. C.C. Abbott (London, 1955), p.89.
10. 'The Candle Indoors', 'Hurrahing in Harvest', 'Inversnaid'.
11. *Sermons*, p.197.
12. Ibid., 'the blisful agony or stress of selving in God . . .'
13. 'Pied Beauty'.
14. *Sermons*, p.193.
15. 'As Kingfishers catch fire'.
16. 'The Wreck of the Deutschland', stanza 5.
17. 'God's Grandeur'.
18. *Sermons*, p.147.
19. See David A. Downes, *Gerard Manley Hopkins: A Study of His Ignatian Spirit* (New York, 1959), especially pp.53–4, 74–5.
20. 'The Wreck of the Deutschland', stanza 2.
21. 'Hurrahing in Harvest', 'The Candle Indoors', 'As Kingfishers catch fire', 'The Windhover'.
22. Downes acutely suggests that a poem is an inscape of imagination: *Hopkins' Sanctifying Imagination*, p.23.
23. 'Deutschland', stanza 32. See Tillich, *Systematic Theology* I, pp.173, 263, 270. Boehme had described God as 'ground of all beings.'
24. 'To what serves Mortal Beauty?'.
25. 'Ribblesdale'.
26. 'Bisney Poplars.'
27. 'Duns Scotus's Oxford'.
28. 'Spelt from Sibyl's Leaves'.
29. *Sermons*, p.138.
30. 'Hurrahing in Harvest', 'The Starlight Night'.
31. *Journals*, p.199 (18 May 1870)
32. 'The Wreck of the Deutschland', stanza 23.
33. Proverbs 8:22–31, Job 28:20–28.

34. Col. 1:15–20 (probably an early Christian hymn); cf. Col. 2:2–3, 1 Cor. 2:6–8.
35. It was believed that Scotus had taught in Oxford about 1300.
36. *Journals*, p.221 (19 July 1872); cf. pp.236, 239.
37. *Sermons*, p.197.
38. For useful accounts of Hopkins' debt to Scotus here, see *Sermons*, Appendix II, and Downes, op.cit., pp.36–8.
39. Walter Ong's phrase, op.cit., p.110. Ong (pp.17–18) draws attention to the fascination of the Victorians with energy.
40. 'The Windhover', 'Hurrahing in Harvest'.
41. 'As Kingfishers catch fire'.
42. 'The Blessed Virgin compared to the Air we Breathe'. 63.
43. Daniel A. Harris, *Inspirations Unbidden. The 'Terrible Sonnets' of Gerard Manley Hopkins* (Berkeley, California, 1982), p.46.
44. See 2 Cor. 3:17–18, cf.1 Cor. 3:10–16, Rom. 8:9–11.
45. See e.g. G.W.H. Lampe, *God as Spirit* (Oxford, 1977), pp.32–33, 153–8.
46. For example, Maurice Wiles, *The Remaking of Christian Doctrine* (London, 1974), pp.54–60, 119–23.
47. For instance, John A.T. Robinson, *The Human Face of God* (London, 1973), pp.229–44; John Hick, 'Incarnation and Mythology' in *God and the Universe of Faiths* (London, 1977) pp.172–9.
48. So Karl Barth, *Church Dogmatics* I/1, pp.402–6.
49. So Wolfhart Pannenberg, *Jesus – God and Man*, pp.334–7.
50. See Jüngel, *God as the Mystery of the World*, pp.367–73.
51. H. Wheeler Robinson, *The Christian Experience of the Holy Spirit* (London, 1928), pp.136–9. On Paul's thought here, see J.D.G. Dunn, *Jesus and the Spirit* (London, 1975), pp.322–6: 'Jesus became the personality of the Spirit.'
52. Barth, *Church Dogmatics* I/1, pp.320–4; II/1, pp.183–204.
53. Ibid., II/2, pp.7–14, 115–27; III/1, pp.96–7.
54. Ibid., I/1, pp.165–9; II/1, pp.53–60.
55. Both in his early and later work (I/1, pp.55–6; IV/3, 1, pp.97–99) Barth concedes other forms of the Word. There is, of course, no question in all this of an autonomous route of the human mind towards knowing God (I/1, pp.346–7).
56. For the following, see *Church Dogmatics* I/1, pp.165–80, II/1, pp.55–6, 188–98.
57. Bonhoeffer, *Letters and Papers from Prison: The Enlarged Edition*, ed. E. Bethge, trans. R. Fuller et al. (London, 1967), p.360.
58. Downes, *Hopkins' Sanctifying Imagination*, p.22.
59. John Robinson, *In Extremity. A Study of Gerard Manley Hopkins* (Cambridge, 1978), p.95.
60. 'The Wreck of the Deutschland', stanzas 25, 21, 31.
61. 'The Bugler's First Communion'.
62. *Letters of GMH to Robert Bridges*, op.cit., p.95.
63. 'God's Grandeur'.
64. 'Spring'.
65. 'The Bugler's First Communion'.

66. 'To what serves Mortal Beauty?'.
67. 'The Bugler's First Communion'.
68. 'Spring'.
69. *Poems*, 157.
70. See Caird, *Principalities and Powers*, pp.63–9.
71. Tillich, *Systematic Theology* I, pp.43–6. See above, pp.59–60.
72. 'I wake and feel the fell of dark'.
73. Harris, op.cit., p.35.
74. Even in his early journal entries, Hopkins reports feelings of desolation: see *Journals*, op.cit., pp.236, 238.
75. *Further Letters of Gerard Manley Hopkins*, ed. C.C. Abbott, 2nd ed. (London, 1956), p.170 (2 March 1885).
76. *The Correspondence of Gerard Manley Hopkins and R.W. Dixon*, ed. C.C. Abbott (London 1935), p.154 (29 July 1888).
77. This is the convincing exegesis of Paul L. Mariani, *A Commentary on the Complete Poems of Gerard Manley Hopkins* (Ithaca, 1970), p.209. Downes finds the pattern of Ignatian exercise on hell throughout the terrible sonnets; see his *Hopkins' Sanctifying Imagination*, p.99 and his *Gerard Manley Hopkins*, p.154.
78. *Sermons*, p.199.
79. *Poems* 57 and 67.
80. *Poems* 38 and 67.
81. 'The Wreck of the Deutschland', stanza 34 and *Poems* 67.
82. 'Deutschland', stanza 4 and 'No worst, there is none'.
83. Harris, op.cit., pp.19–21, 47–53.
84. See the analysis of 'encagement' in Donald Walhout, *Send My Roots Rain: A Study of Religious Experience in the Poetry of Gerard Manley Hopkins* (Athens, Ohio, 1981), especially pp.7ff.
85. So J. Hillis Miller, *The Disappearance of God: Five Nineteenth Century Writers* (Cambridge, Mass. 1963); similarly Harris, op.cit., pp.10–14. Though Miller stresses (p.352) that 'the disappearance of God' is not incompatible with Catholicism, he confuses hiddenness with absence.
86. So Mariani, op.cit., p.212, and Downes, *Hopkins' Sanctifying Imagination*, pp.99–101. Ong, op.cit., pp.51–4 detects an 'upbeat' at the end of each sonnet.
87. Bonhoeffer, *Letters and Papers*, p.360.
88. For example, Dorothee Sölle, *Christ the Representative. An Essay in Theology after the 'Death of God'*, trans. D. Lewis (London, 1971), pp.137–8, 150.
89. Mariani, op.cit., p.228.
90. 'Hope holds to Christ the mind's own mirror out'.
91. Harris, op.cit., pp.34–7, 92–3.
92. Dietrich Bonhoeffer, *Ethics*, ed. E. Bethge, trans. N.H. Smith (London, 1971), p.113; Bonhoeffer, *Lectures on Christology*, trans. E. Robertson (London, 1978), p.107.
93. See e.g. Mark 13:32–7, cf. Rom. 13:11–14. G.B. Caird, *The Language and Imagery of the Bible*, pp.255–71, argues convincingly that biblical

writers regularly use end-of-the-world language as metaphor for decisive events within history.

94. 'The Wreck of the Deutschland', stanza 10.
95. For instance, Robinson, op.cit., pp.125–6; Harris, op.cit., p.38; Howard W. Fulweiler, *Letters from the Darkling Plain* (Columbia, Missouri, 1972), p.161.
96. 'The Wreck of the Deutschland', stanza 7.
97. 'Tom's Garland'.
98. 'The shepherd's brow'.
99. Mariani, op.cit., p.317; Downes, *Hopkins' Sanctifying Imagination*, p.105.
100. 'Thou art indeed just, Lord'; Jer. 12:1.
101. Jürgen Moltmann, *The Crucified God: The Cross of Christ as the Foundation and Criticism of Christian Theology*, trans. R.A. Wilson and J. Bowden (London, 1974), p.226.

7 D.H. Lawrence: *Agape* and *Eros*

1. F.R. Leavis, *D.H. Lawrence: Novelist* (1955; Harmondsworth, 1973), p.13, draws attention to the affinity with Blake.
2. 'Democracy', *Phoenix. The Posthumous Papers of D.H. Lawrence*, ed. E.D. McDonald (London, 1936, repr. 1970), p.713.
3. 'Education of the People', *Phoenix*, p.628.
4. D.H. Lawrence, *Women in Love* (1921; pb. Harmondsworth, 1961), p.45.
5. *Psychoanalysis and the Unconscious* (1923; repr. London, 1931), p.119.
6. Ibid., p.107.
7. Ibid., p.100.
8. 'Preface to "The Grand Inquisitor"', *Phoenix*, p.285.
9. D.H. Lawrence, *Sons and Lovers* (1913; Harmondsworth, 1948), p.307.
10. 'Love', *Phoenix*, p.151.
11. 'Love', *Phoenix*, p.155.
12. *Psychoanalysis and the Unconscious*, p.124.
13. *Psychoanalysis and the Unconscious*, p.104.
14. 'Love', *Phoenix*, p.154.
15. This bias is particularly strongly marked in *Lady Chatterley's Lover* (1928; Harmondsworth, 1960); see e.g. pp.210–11, cf. pp.90, 120–1. This results in the theory, potentially damaging psychologically, that 'coming off together' in intercourse is the norm (e.g. p.124).
16. See, for example, *The Rainbow* (1915; Harmondsworth, 1949), p.148.
17. See *The Rainbow*, p.276; *Lady Chatterley's Lover*, p.182.
18. *Women in Love*, p.225.
19. Plato, *The Symposium*, trans. W. Hamilton (Harmondsworth, 1951), p.62: 'Each of us then is the mere broken tally of a man.'
20. *Women in Love*, p.225.
21. Ibid.
22. Eugene Goodheart, *The Utopian Vision of D.H. Lawrence* (Chicago, 1963), p.35.

23. *The Virgin and the Gipsy*, in *The Short Novels of D.H. Lawrence*, Vol.II (London, 1956), p.23.
24. 'Pan in America', *Phoenix*, p.29.
25. *The Rainbow*, pp.8–9.
26. *Women in Love*, p.142.
27. Raymond Williams, *Culture and Society* (Harmondsworth, 1963), p.204.
28. *The Rainbow*, p.278.
29. The phrase is from Aidan Burns, *Nature and Culture in D.H. Lawrence* (London, 1980), p.59. See 'The Novel and the Feelings', *Phoenix*, p.757: 'the original dark forest within us'.
30. *Sons and Lovers*, p.176. Cf. p.191: 'She might have been one of the women who went with Mary when Jesus was dead.' This draws the parallel between Miriam and 'Madeleine' in *The Man Who Died*; see below.
31. Cf. Miriam's protest later, '. . it has always been so . . . you fighting away from me'. (p.362)
32. 'Love', *Phoenix*, p.154.
33. 'Love', *Phoenix*, p.155.
34. *Fantasia of the Unconscious* (1923; repr. London, 1930), p.14.
35. See, for example, Anders Nygren, *Agape and Eros*, trans. P.S. Watson (London, 1953). Useful criticisms of this approach were made by M.C. D'Arcy, *The Mind and Heart of Love* (London, 1945), pp.56–60.
36. This is the only way that Graham Hough envisages Lawrence's quarrel with Christianity as running; see Graham Hough, *The Dark Sun. A Study of D.H. Lawrence* (London, 1970), pp.241ff.
37. D.H. Lawrence, *Apocalypse*, Phoenix edition (London, 1972), p.101.
38. *The Man Who Died*, *The Short Novels of D.H. Lawrence*, Vol. Two, p.13.
39. See *Sons and Lovers*, p.183.
40. *The Man Who Died*, pp.12, 14.
41. Ibid., p.16.
42. Ibid., p.14.
43. Ibid., pp.12, 14.
44. E.L. Mascall, *He Who Is. A Study in Traditional Theism* (London, 1943), pp.66–8.
45. Mascall, op.cit., pp.108–9.
46. There is a strong defence of this position in Richard E. Creel, *Divine Impassibility. An Essay in Philosophical Theology* (Cambridge, 1986), pp.116–26.
47. For love as mutuality, see D'Arcy, op.cit., pp.112ff; Daniel Day Williams, *The Spirit and the Forms of Love* (Welwyn, 1968), pp.114–15. Some criticisms have, however, been raised by Gene Outka, *Agape, An Ethical Analysis* (Yale, 1962), pp.36–42.
48. This is the basic thesis of the study by W.H. Vanstone, *Love's Endeavour, Love's Expense* (London, 1977). Also see Keith Ward, *Rational Theology and the Creativity of God* (Oxford, 1982), pp.142ff.
49. See Charles Hartshorne, *A Natural Theology for Our Time* (La Salle, Illinois, 1967), p.105f; Jürgen Moltmann, *Trinity and the Kingdom of God*, pp.57ff.
50. See D.D. Williams, op.cit., pp.183–7.

51. Eberhard Jüngel, *God as the Mystery of the World*, pp.317–18, 338.
52. See Whitehead, *Process and Reality*, pp.528–9; both God and the world 'are in the grip of the ultimate metaphysical ground, the creative advance into novelty'; John B. Cobb, *A Christian Natural Theology. Based on the Thought of Alfred North Whitehead* (London, 1965), pp.205ff.
53. E.g. Jürgen Moltmann, *God in Creation* (London, 1985), pp.79–86; Moltmann, *Trinity and the Kingdom of God*, p.58.
54. Karl Barth, *Church Dogmatics*, II/1, p.303.
55. Ward, op.cit., pp.81f., 138f.
56. *Sons and Lovers*, p.506.
57. D.H. Lawrence, *Aaron's Rod*, Phoenix edition (1922; London, 1954), p.294.
58. Heribert Mühlen, *Die Veränderlichkeit Gottes als Horizont einer zukünftigen Christologie* (Münster, 1969), p.26. My translation.
59. 'Love', *Phoenix*, p.153.
60. Eliseo Vivas, *D.H. Lawrence: The Failure and the Triumph of Art* (Evanston, Illinois, 1960), pp.125–36.
61. 'Love', *Phoenix*, p.153.
62. Ibid., p.154.
63. *Mornings in Mexico* (London, 1956), p.46.
64. 'The Woman Who Rode Away' in *The Complete Short Stories*, II (London, 1957), pp.569–72.
65. Williams, op.cit., p.212.
66. Mark Spilka, *The Love Ethic of D.H. Lawrence* (Bloomington, Indiana, 1957), p.217.
67. T.S. Eliot, *After Strange Gods* (London, 1934).
68. *Studies in Classic American Literature*, Phoenix edition (1924; London, 1964), p.165.
69. So Moltmann, *The Trinity and the Kingdom of God*, pp.124–8.
70. H.P. Owen, *Concepts of Deity* (London, 1971), pp.31–3; K. Ward, op.cit., p.165; Hartshorne, op.cit., pp.73–5.
71. *Women in Love*, pp.87–8.
72. Ibid., p.45.
73. Ibid., p.48.
74. J. Macquarrie, *Principles*, pp.259–61; P. Tillich, *Systematic Theology* I, pp.239–40. See above, Chapter 3, pp.53–4.
75. *The Man Who Died*, p.37.
76. *Lady Chatterley's Lover*, p.315.
77. Ibid.
78. E.M. Forster, *Passage to India* (1924; repr. London, 1971), p.293.
79. Similarly, Lawrence thought he could detect an original myth underlying the Apocalypse of St John, in which a descent into hell was followed by rebirth through sexual love. In his view, the Christian adaptation of the myth had removed the sexual element from 'the woman clothed with the sun' and dismissed it in the form of 'the scarlet woman'. See *Apocalypse*, pp.71–4.
80. Hough, op.cit., p.251.

8 Iris Murdoch and Love of the Truth

1. Iris Murdoch, *The Fire and the Sun. Why Plato Banished the Artists* (Oxford, 1977, repr. 1988), p.79.
2. *The Good Apprentice* (London, 1985), p.488.
3. In *The Book and the Brotherhood* (London, 1987), p.131.
4. The word is used in *The Fire and the Sun*, p.80.
5. *The Book and the Brotherhood*, p.241.
6. *Nuns and Soldiers* (1980, pb. Harmondsworth, 1981), pp.294–9. Cf. Julian of Norwich, *Revelations of Divine Love*, trans. C. Wolters (Harmondsworth, 1966), 5 (p.68).
7. *The Fire and the Sun*, p.52. The 'good' character Tallis is always to be found 'Wherever there is a muddle': *A Fairly Honourable Defeat* (1970, repr. Harmondsworth, 1972), p.178.
8. *The Sovereignty of Good* (London, 1970), p.75. Murdoch calls for 'a vocabulary of attention' in 'Against Dryness', *Encounter* 16 (January 1961), pp.16–20.
9. *The Nice and the Good* (London, 1968), p.309.
10. *The Bell* (1958, repr. Harmondsworth, 1972), p.299.
11. Characters drown in a swimming pool (*A Fairly Honourable Defeat*), a bath (*An Accidental Man*), the sea (*The Sea, the Sea*), a flash-flood (*The Unicorn*), the Thames (*A Word Child*) and public baths (*The Philosopher's Pupil*).
12. *The Sovereignty of Good*, p.84.
13. *The Unicorn* (1963, repr. Harmondsworth, 1966), p.167.
14. The phrase is by Brendan in *Henry and Cato* (London, 1976), p.174.
15. *Under the Net* (London, 1954), pp.24, 9.
16. *The Sacred and Profane Love Machine* (1974, repr. Harmondsworth, 1976). For the same image, see also *A Fairly Honourable Defeat*, pp.112, 193, 284, 378. In *The Sovereignty of Good*, p.78 the psyche is described as a 'machine', manufacturing dreams to escape reality.
17. For the image of boxes, see e.g. *The Book and the Brotherhood*, pp.377, 595; cupboard, *The Time of the Angels* (London, 1966), p.163; cage, *The Sea, The Sea* (London, 1978), p.442; egg, *The Sacred and Profane Love Machine*, p.107 and *The Time of the Angels*, p.223.
18. On 'courts' and social identity, see Richard Todd, *Iris Murdoch: The Shakespearian Interest* (London, 1979), pp.72–4, 85–8.
19. Hartley, in *The Sea, The Sea* (p.159). Similarly, Hannah is imprisoned in *The Unicorn* (p.233 'sequestered, immaculate').
20. For example, the fantasies of Leo in *The Time of the Angels* (p.64), and the obsessions of Austin in *An Accidental Man* (London, 1971), p.291.
21. *The Fire and the Sun*, p.43.
22. *The Sovereignty of Good*, p.47.
23. *The Book and the Brotherhood*, p.85. Marcus, in *The Time of the Angels*, similarly falls into a coal cellar.
24. *The Good Apprentice* (London, 1985), p.12.
25. *The Book and the Brotherhood*, p.186. In her study of Sartre, Murdoch sets out to explain why he finds 'the contingent over-abundance of

the world nauseating': *Sartre, Romantic Rationalist* (1953, repr. London, 1967), pp.21ff.

26. *A Fairly Honourable Defeat*, pp.331–2. Tamar in *The Book and the Brotherhood* has a similar descent into hell, for similar reasons.
27. *The Nice and the Good*, pp.153–4.
28. *Nuns and Soldiers*, pp.112–13.
29. *The Good Apprentice*, p. 248.
30. *The Sovereignty of Good*, p. 54.
31. 'Shock tactics do things, they break barriers, they open vistas.' *The Book and the Brotherhood*, p.362.
32. *The Sacred and Profane Love Machine*, p.62.
33. Ibid., p.342. As Luca joins Blaise's two worlds, so Cupid unites the two Venuses in Titian's painting of 'Sacred and Profane Love'. Tamar, in *The Book and the Brotherhood*, unites Jean's two worlds of Crimond and Gerard's circle (p.168).
34. *The Sacred and Profane Love Machine*, p.74.
35. *The Sovereignty of Good*, p.84.
36. Verbally, in interview with Bryan Magee, in the series Men of Ideas, BBC TV April 1978. The phrase is slightly revised in the published version, Bryan Magee, *Men of Ideas. Some Creators of Contemporary Philosophy* (Oxford, 1982), p.230.
37. 'Salvation by Words' in *New York Review of Books*, 15 June 1972, p.4.; my italics. Cf. 'The Sublime and the Beautiful Revisited, *Yale Review* 49 (1960), p.249: 'The artist is creating a quasi-sensuous thing. He is more like God than the moral agent.'
38. 'Salvation by Words', p.5; Magee, op.cit., p.231.
39. *The Bell*, p.190. Cf. 'Christ and Myth', Murdoch in interview with F.W. Dillistone, *Frontier*, Autumn 1965, pp.219–21: 'Great art destroys the cloud of comfortable images with which each one of us surrounds himself in his daily living.'
40. *The Book and the Brotherhood*, pp.292, 307; it is also a 'magic book', p.140.
41. Ibid., p.565.
42. See Murdoch, 'The Sublime and the Good', *Chicago Review* 13 (1959), p.55.
43. *The Fire and the Sun*, pp.75–6.
44. *The Bell*, pp.220, 266.
45. *The Fire and the Sun*, p.36.
46. *The Book and the Brotherhood*, p.306.
47. She comments on its iconic meaning in an interview with Eric Robson, ITV Channel 4, September 1984, printed in *Revelations*, ed. Ronald Lello (Border Television, 1985), pp.89–90.
48. *The Black Prince* (1973, repr. Harmondsworth, 1975), p.199. Thus Shakespeare is 'King of Masochists' (p.20). Axel, in *A Fairly Honourable Defeat*, p.41, interprets the image as the agony involved in love.
49. *The Black Prince*, p.415.
50. Ibid., p.331.

51. See *Revelations*, op.cit., p.86. However, she finds the experience ambiguous.
52. *The Fire and the Sun*, p.77.
53. *Henry and Cato*, p.336.
54. See Murdoch, 'Existentialists and Mystics' in W.W. Robson (ed.), *Essays and Poems Presented to Lord David Cecil* (London, 1970), p.19: the mystic has grasped the 'for-nothingness' of the Good. Cf. *The Nice and the Good*, p.350: love which is good for nothing has a blank face.
55. *The Good Apprentice*, p.245; cf. *The Sovereignty of Good*, pp.59–60.
56. Elizabeth Dipple, *Iris Murdoch: Work for the Spirit* (London, 1982), p.30.
57. *The Philosopher's Pupil* (London, 1983), p.192.
58. *The Book and the Brotherhood*, p.533. Cf. 'God is a detail', *The Unicorn*, p.45, and 'Spirit without God', *The Philosopher's Pupil*, p.187.
59. *The Time of the Angels*, p.164.
60. See above, pp.92–3, cf. 138–9.
61. *The Time of the Angels*, p.164.
62. Ibid., p.165.
63. Ibid., p.149.
64. This is argued by Dipple, op.cit., pp.71–2.
65. *The Good Apprentice*, p.1.
66. *The Time of the Angels*, pp.100–1.
67. See *The Fire and the Sun*, p.79: 'Magic in its unregenerate form as the fantastic doctoring of the real for consumption by the ego is the bane of art . . .'.
68. *The Bell*, pp.198–9.
69. Ibid., p.267.
70. 'Salvation by Words', p.3.
71. Magee (ed.), op.cit., p.230.
72. Ibid., p.231.
73. *The Philosopher's Pupil*, p.192.
74. *The Fire and the Sun*, pp.87–8.
75. *The Philosopher's Pupil*, p.186.
76. *The Time of the Angels*, p.91.
77. Ibid., p.90.
78. *The Book and the Brotherhood*, p.324.
79. Ibid., p.452.
80. Ibid., p.488. Cf. *Revelations*, ed. Lello, p.84, 'Christ whom I regard as a mystical figure . . .'.
81. Father Brendan, Stuart Cuno, Father Bernard, Ann Cavidge.
82. *The Book and the Brotherhood*, p.490.
83. *Nuns and Soldiers*, p.310.
84. *The Book and the Brotherhood*, p.516.
85. Ibid., p.488.
86. *The Good Apprentice*, p.518.
87. *Henry and Cato*, p.192.
88. *The Fire and the Sun*, p.70.
89. Ibid., p.66.
90. *The Time of the Angels*, p.55.

91. See above, p.184, and also *The Philosopher's Pupil*, p.187.
92. *The Time of the Angels*, p.167.
93. Ibid., p.11. The scene is based on Genesis 19:1–3.
94. Ibid., p.106 (my italics).
95. Ibid., p.179.
96. In addition to the examples already given, the parable of the Good Samaritan is echoed in *An Accidental Man*, and the Prodigal Son in *The Good Apprentice*.
97. See e.g. Alistair Kee, *Constantine Versus Christ* (London, 1982), pp.153–75; Moltmann, *Trinity and the Kingdom of God*, pp.191–202.
98. Dietrich Bonhoeffer echoes the image of St Paul (Gal. 4:1–7) with his phrase 'the world come of age': *Letters and Papers from Prison*, p.326.
99. Eberhard Jüngel, *God as the Mystery of the World*, pp.185ff.
100. D. Bonhoeffer, *Letters and Papers*, p.360.
101. *The Sovereignty of Good*, p.79.
102. R. Bultmann, 'The Idea of God and Modern Man', in *World Come of Age. A Symposium on Dietrich Bonhoeffer*, ed. R. Gregor Smith (London, 1967), p.271.
103. E. Jüngel, *God as the Mystery of the World*, pp.30–4, 378–9.
104. Bonhoeffer, *Letters and Papers*, p.191.
105. D. Bonhoeffer, *Ethics*, pp.17f, 23f.
106. *The Sovereignty of Good*, p.69.
107. *The Philosopher's Pupil*, p.192.
108. Barth, *Church Dogmatics*, II/1, p.52.
109. *The Sacred and Profane Love Machine*, pp.40 1.
110. *The Good Apprentice*, p.234.
111. Ibid., p.281.
112. *The Book and the Brotherhood*, pp.231–2.
113. *Henry and Cato*, p.261.
114. *The Time of the Angels*, pp.148–9.
115. Ibid., p.202; cf. p.211.
116. *An Accidental Man*, pp.105–6.
117. *A Fairly Honourable Defeat*, p.105.
118. *The Good Apprentice*, p.54.
119. *Henry and Cato*, p.337.
120. *The Unicorn*, p.66.
121. *The Book and the Brotherhood*, p.490.
122. *The Philosopher's Pupil*, p.188.
123. *Nuns and Soldiers*, pp.295–9.
124. J. Moltmann, *The Crucified God*, pp.241–5.
125. Tillich, *Systematic Theology* II, p.203.
126. Dorothee Soelle, *Suffering*, trans. E. Kalin (London, 1975), pp.22–8.
127. Leonardo Boff, *Passion of Christ, Passion of the World* (Maryknoll, New York, 1987), pp.113–14.
128. *The Time of the Angels*, p.165.
129. *Nuns and Soldiers*, pp.297, 298.
130. Jüngel, *God as the Mystery of the World*, pp.363–4.
131. Ibid., pp.165, 72.
132. See below, pp.225–6.

133. *The Good Apprentice*, p.292; *The Red and the Green*, p.189; *A Fairly Honourable Defeat*, p.145; *The Book and the Brotherhood*, p.252.
134. See Murdoch's essay, 'Existentialists and Mystics', op.cit., and Peter Conradi, *Iris Murdoch: The Saint and the Artist* (London, 1986), pp.14–20, 45, 112ff.
135. *The Book and the Brotherhood*, p.174.
136. Ibid., pp.245, 339.

9 William Golding and the Human Darkness

1. Editions of Golding's novels cited are as follows: *Lord of the Flies* (London, 1954 repr. 1958), *The Inheritors* (London, 1955 repr. 1961), *Pincher Martin* (London, 1956 repr. 1962), *Free Fall* (London, 1959 repr. 1961), *The Spire* (London, 1964 repr. 1965), *Darkness Visible* (London, 1979 repr. 1980), *Rites of Passage* (London, 1980), *The Paper Men* (London, 1984).
2. *The Spire*, pp.38–9, 95, 107. Golding in fact imagined the mason's craft out of his knowledge of boat-building: see Virginia Tiger, *William Golding: the dark fields of discovery* (London, 1974), p.174.
3. 'Fable' in *The Hot Gates*, (London, 1965), p.88.
4. 'The Ladder and the Tree' in *The Hot Gates*, op.cit., p.167.
5. *Free Fall*, p.161. Cf. Golding's own experience of 'inexplicable' and 'indescribable' darkness: 'The Ladder and the Tree', p.167.
6. Wolfhart Pannenberg, *What is Man?*, pp.3–10.
7. Frank Kermode aptly comments that Golding has 'written a book about an expressly phallic symbol to which Freudian glosses seem irrelevant'; 'The Case for William Golding' in *New York Review of Books*, 30 April 1964, p.4.
8. See *The Paper Men*, p.161.
9. *Pincher Martin*, p.158. Cf. Golding, 'Belief and Creativity' in *A Moving Target* (London, 1982), p.195: 'the little lighted awareness . . .'.
10. Niebuhr, *The Nature and Destiny of Man*, Vol.I, op.cit., p.195.
11. Pannenberg, *What is Man?*, p.37.
12. So J. Macquarrie, *Principles of Christian Theology*, pp.72–3.
13. Tillich, *Systematic Theology* II, pp.54–5.
14. See 'Belief and Creativity', p.199.
15. Ibid., p.192.
16. In conversation with V. Tiger, op.cit., p.19.
17. See Ian Gregor, 'The Religious Imagination of William Golding', in *William Golding, The Man and his Books: a tribute on his 75th birthday*, ed. J. Carey (London, 1986), p.100: 'the sense of a Creator. . . . whose presence is apprehended most surely in the detailed movement of the writing of the novel, but not circumscribed by it . . .'.
18. In John Peter, 'Postscript' in *William Golding's Lord of the Flies, a Source Book* (New York, 1963), p.34.
19. See above, pp.61.
20. R.S. Lee, 'Human Nature and the Fall – a Psychological View' in *Man: Fallen and Free*, ed. E.W. Kemp (London, 1969), p.51.
21. Ibid., p.57.

22. See Andrew Elphinstone, *Freedom, Suffering and Love* (London, 1976), pp.18–21, 54–7, 93–5. Cf. Lee, op.cit., p.58.

23. 'Fable', op.cit., p.99.

24. Milton, *Paradise Lost*, III.99.

25. Mark Kinkead-Weekes and Ian Gregor, *William Golding: a critical study*, rev. ed. (London, 1984), p.190.

26. Tiger, op.cit., pp.158–9.

27. Gregor and Kinkead-Weekes, op.cit., p.197.

28. For example, Tiger, op.cit., pp.148–9, 157–8; Gregor and Kinkead-Weekes, pp.195–6.

29. See *Conversations with William Golding*, ed. J.I. Biles (New York, 1970), p.76: 'for me and I suspect for millions of other people this experience of having two worlds to live in all the time. . . . is a vital one and is what living is like.'

30. Philip Redpath, *William Golding: a structural reading of his fiction* (London, 1986), pp.138–41.

31. Irenaeus, *Adversus Haereses* III.20.2. On this view of the Fall, see John Hick, *Evil and the God of Love*, pp.218–19.

32. Tillich, *Systematic Theology* III, p.150.

33. *Free Fall*, pp.79, 128, 221.

34. See above, pp.16–17.

35. 'Irish Poets and their Poetry', *Holiday Magazine*, April 1963, pp.16–19.

36. Don Crompton draws a parallel with the passing of Pangall and his 'kingdom' in *The Spire*: 'a state of religious innocence . . . to be regretted . . . yet as much to be accepted': *A View from the Spire: William Golding's Later Novels*, ed. and completed by Julia Briggs (Oxford, 1985), pp.29–50.

37. *Darkness Visible*, pp.166–7. The idea appears several times: pp.131, 173, 185.

38. See above, pp.174–5, 198–200.

39. See above, pp.136–7, 140–3.

40. L. Wittgenstein, *Tractatus Logico-Philosophicus*, ed. B. Russell, trans. C.K. Ogden and F.P. Ramsey (London, 1933), p.185.

41. Martin Heidegger, *Being and Time*, trans. J. Macquarrie and E. Robinson (Oxford, 1973), pp.404–11.

42. Macquarrie, *Principles*, pp.86–8, 107–15. Cf. Macquarrie, *Studies in Christian Existentialism* (Philadelphia, 1965), pp.83–96.

43. Tillich, *Systematic Theology* I, pp.122, 207–10.

44. Macquarrie, *Studies in Christian Existentialism*, pp.59–76; id., *In Search of Humanity*, (London, 1982), pp.42–3, 238–9.

45. Tillich, *Systematic Theology* I, 122–3, 186–91.

46. G.W.F. Hegel, *Phenomenology of Mind*, trans. J. Baillie (London, 1931), pp.780–5, 808; Hegel, *Lectures on the Philosophy of Religion*, Part III, ed. and trans. Peter C. Hodgson (Missoula, 1979), pp.212, 217.

47. Tillich, *Systematic Theology* II, pp.200–3.

48. See my criticisms in *The Creative Suffering of God* (Oxford, 1988), pp.251–60.

49. Barth, *Church Dogmatics* II/1, pp.314–15; IV/1, p.186.

50. See above, notes 16 and 17. Don Cupitt calls this challenge 'the

religious requirement': see *Taking Leave of God* (London, 1980), pp.85–6, 103–4.

51. Letter to Virginia Tiger, cit. Tiger op.cit., pp.133, 138.
52. Milton, *Paradise Lost*, Book 1, line 63.
53. *Darkness Visible*, pp.232–3. Cf. Barclay's experience of speaking 'my native tongue'; *The Paper Men* p.126.
54. See above, pp.5–6, 21–2.
55. The earlier reflections on the writer's wounds were prompted by the incident of Padre Pio's stigmata: Golding, *The Paper Men*, pp.24–5, cf. p.20.
56. Julia Briggs, Chapter 6 in Don Crompton, *A View from the Spire*, p.162.

Further Reading

These are suggestions to help the reader follow up some of the theological themes and issues of literary criticism which are discussed in this book.

Robert Alter, *The Art of Biblical Narrative* (London, 1981).
——, *The Art of Biblical Poetry* (New York, 1985).
Karl Barth, *Church Dogmatics*, ed. G.W. Bromiley and T.F. Torrance (English translation, Edinburgh, 1933–77), volumes I/1 (2nd ed.), II/1, IV/1.
——, *The Humanity of God*, trans. C.D. Deans (London, 1961).
Dietrich Bonhoeffer, *Letters and Papers from Prison*, The Enlarged Edition, ed. E. Bethge, trans. R. Fuller et al., (London, 1967).
G.B. Caird, *Principalities and Powers; A Study of Pauline Theology* (Oxford, 1956)
John Coulson, *Religion and Imagination* (Oxford, 1981).
John Dominic Crossan, *The Dark Interval: Towards a Theology of Story* (Niles, Illinois, 1975).
Paul S. Fiddes, *The Creative Suffering of God* (Oxford, 1988).
Northrop Frye, *The Great Code: The Bible and Literature* (London, 1982).
Helen Gardner, *Religion and Literature* (London, 1971)
T.R. Henn, *The Harvest of Tragedy*, 2nd ed. (London, 1966).
David Jasper, *The New Testament and the Literary Imagination* (London, 1987).
——, *The Study of Literature and Religion: an Introduction* (London, 1989).
Gabriel Josipovici, *The Book of God: A Response to the Bible* (New Haven and London, 1988).
——, *The World and the Book: A Study of Modern Fiction*, 2nd ed. (London, 1979).
Eberhard Jüngel, *God as the Mystery of the World: On the Foundation of the Theology of the Crucified One in the Dispute between Theism and Atheism*, trans. D.L. Guder (Edinburgh, 1983).
Frank Kermode, *The Genesis of Secrecy: On the Interpretation of Narrative* (Cambridge, Mass., 1979).
George Lindbeck, *The Nature of Doctrine: Religion and Theology in a Postliberal Age* (London, 1984).
John McIntyre, *Faith, Theology and Imagination* (Edinburgh, 1987).
John Macquarrie, *Principles of Christian Theology*, Revised Edition (London, 1977).
——, *In Search of Humanity* (London, 1984).
H.A. Mason, *The Tragic Plane* (Oxford, 1985).
Jürgen Moltmann, *The Crucified God: The Cross of Christ as the Foundation and Criticism of Christian Theology*, trans. R.A. Wilson and J. Bowden (London, 1974).

——, *The Trinity and the Kingdom of God. The Doctrine of God*, trans. M. Kohl (London, 1981).

Wolfhart Pannenberg, *Anthropology in Theological Perspective*, trans. M.J. O'Connell (Edinburgh, 1985).

——, *What is Man?* (Philadelphia, 1970).

Paul Ricoeur, *The Rule of Metaphor*, trans. R. Czerny et al. (London, 1978).

Janet Martin Soskice, *Metaphor and Religious Language* (Oxford, 1985).

J.L. Styan, *The Dark Comedy. The Development of Modern Comic Tragedy*, Second Edition (London, 1968).

Stephen Sykes, *The Identity of Christianity* (London, 1984).

Paul Tillich, *Systematic Theology*, Combined Volume (Welwyn, 1968). Volume II is of particular relevance.

Keith Ward, *Rational Theology and the Creativity of God* (Oxford, 1982).

Daniel Day Williams, *The Spirit and the Forms of Love* (Welwyn, 1968).

T.R. Wright, *Theology and Literature* (Oxford, 1988).

Index

261

Index